ART INSTITUTE OF ATLANTA
LIBRARY

ARTHURIAN LITERATURE

XV

ARTHURIAN LITERATURE

ISSN 0261–9946

The contents of previous volumes are listed at the back of this volume

Arthurian Literature XV

EDITED BY

JAMES P. CARLEY AND FELICITY RIDDY

D. S. BREWER

© Contributors 1997

All Rights Reserved. Except as permitted under current legislation no part of this work may be photocopied, stored in a retrieval system, published, performed in public, adapted, broadcast, transmitted, recorded or reproduced in any form or by any means, without the prior permission of the copyright owner

First published 1997
D. S. Brewer, Cambridge

ISBN 0 85991 518 2

D. S. Brewer is an imprint of Boydell & Brewer Ltd
PO Box 9, Woodbridge, Suffolk IP12 3DF, UK
and of Boydell & Brewer Inc.
PO Box 41026, Rochester NY 14604–4126, USA

A catalogue record for this series is available
from the British Library

Library of Congress Catalog Card Number: 83–640196

This book is printed on acid-free paper

Printed in Great Britain by
St Edmundsbury Press Ltd, Bury St Edmunds, Suffolk

CONTENTS

Editors' note   vii

I   Who was Chrétien de Troyes?   1
    Sarah Kay

II   Irony and Gender Performance in *Le Chevalier de la Charrete*   37
    Nick Corbyn

III   A New Fragment of the *First Continuation* of the *Perceval* (London, PRO, E122/100/13B)   55
    Lisa Jefferson

IV   The Glastonbury Legends   77
    Aelred Watkin

V   *Magna Tabula*: The Glastonbury Tablets (Part 1)   93
    Jeanne Krochalis

VI   '*Arthur Redivivus*': Politics and Patriotism in Reformation Scotland   185
    David Allan

NOTE

VII   'Gentyl' Audiences and 'Grete Bookes': Chivalric Manuals and the *Morte Darthur*   205
    Karen Cherewatuk

EDITORS' NOTE

Editorial Board
David Carlson, University of Ottawa
Mark Chinca, University of Cambridge
Julia Crick, University of Exeter
Tony Hunt, University of Oxford
Lesley Johnson, University of Leeds
Sarah Kay, University of Cambridge
Edward Donald Kennedy, University of North Carolina at Chapel Hill
Ceridwen Lloyd-Morgan, National Library of Wales
Colin Richmond, University of Keele
Toshiyuki Takamiya, University of Keio
Charles Wood, Dartmouth College

Arthurian Literature is an interdisciplinary publication devoted to the scholarly and critical study of all aspects of the Arthurian legend in Europe in the medieval and early modern periods. Articles on writings from later periods will be included only if they relate very directly to medieval and early modern sources, though the editors welcome bibliographical studies of all periods. *Arthurian Literature* publishes articles of up to 20,000 words. Short items, of under 5,000 words, are published as Notes. Updates on earlier articles are welcomed.

Articles for consideration should be sent to either of the editors at one of the following addresses:

Professor James P. Carley,
Department of English,
York University,
4700 Keele Street,
Toronto M3J 1P3,
Canada

Professor Felicity Riddy,
Centre for Medieval Studies,
University of York,
King's Manor,
York YO1 2EP
UK

Contributors should follow the style sheet printed at the end of volume XII.

I

WHO WAS CHRETIEN DE TROYES?

Sarah Kay

> Christiana sum, et nominis mei sequor
> auctoritatem ut sim perpetua. (I am
> Christian, and I follow the authority of
> my name, that I may be perpetual.)
> *Acta SS Perpetuae et Felicitatis*[1]

> ... l'estoire
> que toz jorz mes iert an memoire
> tant con durra crestïentez.
> De ce s'est Crestïens ventez.
> (the story which will always be
> remembered as long as Christendom
> endures: this is Christian's boast.)
> *Erec et Enide*[2]

1. Introduction

My title invites the rejoinder that if you ask a silly question, you get a silly answer. Nearly forty years ago, Frappier wrote dismissively of attempts to uncover the identity behind the signature 'Crestïen':[3] 'Des tentatives qui ont été faites pour rendre moins obscure la biographie de Chrétien, il n'y a

---

[1] *Passiones SS. Perpetuae et Felicitatis*, ed. C. I. M. I. van Beek (Nijmegen, 1936), *Acta*, V, 9; cited by Peter Dronke, *Women Writers of the Middle Ages. A Critical Study of Texts from Perpetua (+ 203) to Marguerite Porete (+ 1310)* (Cambridge, 1984), p. 5
[2] Chrétien de Troyes, *Erec et Enide*, ed. J.-M. Fritz (Paris, 1992), vv. 23–6.
[3] Principal among these are the various writings of U. T. Holmes, Jr: *A New Interpretation of Chrétien's 'Conte del Graal'* (Chapel Hill, 1948); *Chrétien de Troyes* (New York, 1970); and with Sister M. A. Klenke, O.P., *Chrétien, Troyes, and the Grail* (Chapel Hill, 1959).

guère à retenir.'[4] Severe though this judgement sounds, most scholars today would probably agree with it; and yet we find it difficult to dispense with our notion of the author 'Chrétien' which earlier studies helped to shape. Indeed, with the passage of time, conjecture seems more readily to solidify into fact.

While historical documents provide a couple of examples of figures named Christianus from the Troyes region in the later twelfth century, we cannot know whether they can be identified with the author we call Chrétien de Troyes.[5] Our ideas about a twelfth-century author and his works arise not from the historical record but from a kind of shuffle between available names and texts. As in a magnetic field, some names and texts are either attracted or repelled, whilst others remain quivering, undecided. This process is conditioned by the way we read the texts, and by the assumptions which we bring to them. In the case of 'Chrétien de Troyes' the construction of an author corpus seems to have begun early. The works now accepted as his canon (the five romances) are associated together in two manuscripts.[6] Another, now fragmentary, early manuscript (the Annonay manuscript, in Annonay, Serrières) contains remains of all except the *Lancelot*, and may originally have included that too. However, given that there are thirty-one manuscripts transmitting the works we attribute to 'Chrétien', these collections of his 'canon' are not numerous; and 'his' works form an uninterrupted sequence in only two at most.[7] *Guillaume d'Angleterre*, meanwhile, whose attribution to 'Chrétien de Troyes' is today contested, appears with *Erec* and *Cligés* in Paris, Bibliothèque National 375.[8]

In the absence of more concrete information, our conception of who Chrétien was and what he wrote is based, then, on the reception of texts from the Middle Ages onwards. From an effect derived from these texts we postulate an entity that precedes them. The biographical approach makes a backdoor return in efforts to fathom an author's literary personality, which

---

[4] J. Frappier, *Chrétien de Troyes. L'homme et l'oeuvre* (Paris, 1957), p. 9.
[5] The identification of 'Chrétien de Troyes' with a regular canon Christianus of Saint-Loup-de-Troyes and a chaplain Christianus of Saint-Maclou in Bar-sur-Aube is affirmed by Holmes and Klenke, *Chrétien, Troyes, and the Grail*, pp. 57–9 (references in note 3) and is more cautiously revived by A. Putter, 'Knights and Clerics at the Court of Champagne: Chrétien de Troyes's Romances in Context', in *The Ideals and Practices of Medieval Knighthood* V, ed. C. Harper-Bill and R. Harvey (Woodbridge, 1995), pp. 243–66 (pp. 254–5).
[6] BN fr. 794 (the Guiot manuscript) and 1450 (where the five romances are interpolated into the *Brut*). See A. Micha, *La Tradition manuscrite des romans de Chrétien de Troyes*, 2nd edn (Geneva, 1966).
[7] In the Guiot manuscript, *Perceval* is separated from the remainder of the corpus by four intervening texts.
[8] It also appears in one other manuscript, unconnected with 'Chrétien': B9 in St John's College, Cambridge.

then sets limits on the interpretation of 'his' works and conditions on admission to 'his' canon. Thus it is that a portrait of 'Chrétien de Troyes' has taken shape over the years: he is a clerk, and his position as a court poet makes him both deferential and ironic towards the aristocratic milieu he writes about, and writes for. This conception of 'Chrétien de Troyes' draws plausibility from the dichotomy of *chevalerie* and *clergie* in the prologue to *Cligés* and is supported by evidence of the narrator's skill in rhetoric and dialectic, as well as by the ease with which irony can be discerned in all of the romances canonically ascribed to him.[9] 'Chrétien de Troyes' then becomes identified as the historical personality behind the name 'Crestïen' ('Crestïen de Troie[s]' in *Erec* alone) figuring in the prologues and/or epilogues of these five romances.[10] (Henceforth in this essay I use 'Crestïen' to designate the signatures or rubrics of medieval texts and 'Chrétien de Troyes' to refer to the canonical author of modern criticism.) Other works signed by or attributed to a Crestïen are then discussed primarily in relation to the question whether they are, or are not, by this author. The criteria for deciding attributions are complex. But among them, the principles summarized by Foucault in his account of the development of the 'author function' in modern thought play a major part, namely consistency with respect to quality, subject matter, expression, and outlook.[11]

When I ask, who was Chrétien de Troyes?, I am not concerned primarily with attribution (what did he write?) but with reception (how do hypotheses about authorship affect our reading?). I aim to cast doubt on the reliability of the literary portrait of 'Chrétien de Troyes' with which we habitually work, and on which we rely to structure our understanding of the development of medieval romance and indeed of twelfth-century vernacular

---

[9] On the universal recognition of Chrétien as clerk (which she contests), see E. B. Vitz, 'Chrétien de Troyes: clerc ou ménéstrel. Problèmes des traditions orale et littéraire dans les Cours de France au xiie siècle', *Poétique* 81 (1990), 21–42, pp. 23–5. For a fine example of a 'clerical' unfolding of the prologue to *Cligés*, see M. Freeman, 'Chrétien's *Cligés*. A close reading of the Prologue', *Romanic Review* 67 (1976), 89–101. Peter Haidu and Tony Hunt have been among the most influential scholars in forging the clerical and ironic portrait of 'Chrétien de Troyes'. See in particular P. Haidu, *Aesthetic Distance in Chrétien de Troyes. Irony and Comedy in 'Cligès' and 'Perceval'* (Geneva, 1968); T. Hunt, 'Aristotle, Dialectic, and Courtly Literature', *Viator* 10 (1979), 95–129.

[10] The editions of the canonical romances cited are those in 'livre de poche': Chrétien de Troyes, *Erec et Enide*, ed. J.-M. Fritz (Paris, 1992); *Cligés*, ed. C. Méla and O. Collet (Paris, 1994); *Yvain*, ed. D. Hult (Paris, 1993); *Le Chevalier de la Charrette*, ed. C. Méla (Paris, 1992); and *Le Conte du graal*, ed. C. Méla (Paris, 1990). The rubrics of manuscripts containing these romances, where they exist, virtually always name not the author but the title of the romance. The signatures do not occur in all manuscripts since some excise the prologues and epilogues, thus rendering the romance anonymous; see A. Micha, *La Tradition manuscrite*.

[11] M. Foucault, 'What is an author?', in *Modern Criticism and Theory. A Reader*, ed. D. Lodge (London and New York, 1988), pp. 196–210 (p. 204).

literature. Returning to the available names and texts, I inquire how the signature 'Crestïen' (and its putative transforms 'Carestia', 'Paien', or 'Godefroi') is to be read. What construction might medieval audiences put upon it, as they encountered it in its various contexts?

The full set of works signed by or attributed to a Crestïen is as follows:

i *Erec*
ii *Cligés*
iii *Yvain*
iv *Lancelot*
v *Perceval*
vi *Philomena*[12]
vii *Guillaume d'Angleterre*[13]
viii an Old French translation of the *Gospel of Nicodemus*[14]

Five or six lyrics are also attributed to a 'Crestïen de Troies' by *chansonnier* rubrics but bear no internal signature.[15] The name 'Crestïen de Troies' appears in the prologue to *Le Chevalier à l'épée*, but whether as that of its author or a precursor is debated; and it has been thought to appear in inverted form as 'Paien de Maisières' in another Gawain romance, *La Mule sans frein*.[16] There are a number of references in medieval texts to an author 'Crestïen', several of which credit him with *Perceval*, and one with *Perceval* and *Cligés*, while a further two allude to his composing *Yvain*.[17] As is well known, our 'Chrétien de Troyes' is generally identified with the author of two of the lyrics, is usually accepted as the author of *Philomena*, is less widely agreed to have composed the *Guillaume d'Angleterre*, and is not generally thought to be responsible for the Gawain romances or the Gospel translation. Discussions of attribution are pursued on Foucauldian lines. Thus the belief that 'Chrétien' is a fundamentally secular writer is invoked to exclude from the canon the two overtly religious works *Guillaume*

---

[12] *Philomena*, ed. C. de Boer (Paris, 1909). I shall also refer to the text as it appears in book VI vv. 2217 ff. of the *Ovide Moralisé*, ed. C. de Boer, *Verhandelingen der Koninkliejke Akademie de wetenschappen de Amsterdam*, n.r. 21 (1922), 337–66.
[13] Chrétien, *Guillaume d'Angleterre*, ed. A. J. Holden (Geneva, 1988).
[14] *Trois Versions rimées de l'Evangile de Nicodème par Chrétien, André de Coutances et un anonyme*, ed. G. Paris and A. Bos (Paris, 1885).
[15] M.-C. Zai, *Les Chansons courtoises de Chrétien de Troyes. Edition critique avec Introduction, notes et commentaire* (Berne and Frankfurt, 1974).
[16] R. C. Johnston and D. D. R. Owen, *Two Old French Gawain Romances Edited with Introduction, Notes and Glossary* (Edinburgh and London, 1972).
[17] See C.-A. van Coolput, 'Références, adaptations et emprunts directs', 'Appendice' to *The Legacy of Chrétien de Troyes*, ed. N. J. Lacy, D. Kelly and K. Busby, 2 vols. (Amsterdam, 1987), I, 333–42. David Hult has produced a further possible example from the prologue to the prose *Vie des pères* (unpublished paper).

d'Angleterre and *Nicodemus*; the criterion of quality is used to exclude these and also the Gawain romances.[18]

It is noteworthy, however, that the set of texts signed 'Crestïen', combining as it does antique, Arthurian and religious writings, resembles the virtually contemporary oeuvre attributed to Wace:

> *Roman de Rou*
> *Roman de Brut*
> *Vie de saint Nicolas*
> *Vie de sainte Marguerite*
> *Conception Nostre Dame*

It is also not unlike that (nowadays controversially) assigned to 'Marie de France':

> *Lais*
> *Fables*
> *Espurgatoire saint Patrice*

A comparable miscellany of religious and secular works was dedicated to Marie de Champagne, and is recorded by John Benton as indicating her tastes as a patron:[19]

> *Lancelot*
> Evrat, *Genesis*
> Gace Brulé, a lyric poem
> anon., *Eructavit*

(She is also said to have encouraged Gautier d'Arras with his *Eracle*.) The topos of beginning a devotional text by repudiating a previous career as the author of secular works is one way twelfth- and thirteenth-century poets signal – as well as excuse – their heterogenous output.[20] Whatever the actual

---

[18] For a clear example of the view Foucault critiques, see H. F. Williams, 'The Authorship of Two Arthurian Romances', *The French Review* 61 no. 2 (1987), 163–9: 'Since linguistic studies or motifs rarely determine authorship, we must seek answers in literary aspects and in logic' (p. 165). This essay surveys the debate about the attribution of the Gawain romances. For an overview of discussions of the attribution of *Guillaume d'Angleterre*, see E. J. Mickel, Jr, 'Studies and reflections on Chrétien's *Guillaume d'Angleterre*', *Romance Quarterly* 33 (1986), 393–406. On the *Nicodemus*, see Paris's Introduction to his edition.

[19] J. F. Benton, 'The Court of Champagne as a Literary Center', *Speculum* 36 (1961), 551–91 (p. 587).

[20] Examples are Denis Piramus's *Vie de seint Edmund le rei* which sketches a c.v. of antecedent courtly compositions – 'chanceunettes, rimes, saluz' (v. 7) – and the prologue of the Old French *Vie de Saint Martin*. See *La Vie de Seint Edmund le rei. Poème Anglo-Normand du xiie siècle par Denis Piramus*, ed. H. Kjellman (Göteborg, 1935; repr. Geneva, 1974); *Leben und Wunderthaten des Heiligen Martin. Altfranzösisches*

authorship of the various texts signed 'Crestïen', or attributed to a 'Crestïen' by medieval sources, a late twelfth-century public would not necessarily have had difficulty in accepting them as the output of a single individual.

The name which links all these texts, diverse as they are, is not just a proper noun (like 'Wace') but also a common one, which has powerful resonance for medieval readers. Its meaning is foregrounded through the wordplay with *crestïenté* in *Erec* (quoted as epigraph), and perhaps also through jocular inversion to 'Paien' in other contexts. This capacity to signify has prompted the suggestion that it might be a pseudonym. For Roger Dragonetti, the name 'Christian of Troy' alludes, via an oxymoron, to the dilemma of twelfth-century humanism: composing works deriving from antique models in the tradition of *translatio studii* (which of course goes back to Troy) cannot be a simple act of imitation when the models are pagan and the writer and his public Christian.[21] Luciano Rossi is more interested in the links between 'Chrestïen', 'Carestia', and the *senhals* adopted by Raimbaut d'Aurenga and his circle, names which he sees as encoding playful contradictions.[22]

Clearly we cannot prove that the name Crestïen is a *senhal*,[23] but there are arguments to support the view that it is:

(i) The use of sobriquets and *senhals* is widespread among twelfth-century troubadours, with whom the 'Crestïen' of some of the canonical romances and lyrics seems to have been in contact,[24] and there is evidence too that Northern writers of romance also used *noms de plume* in names such as La Chièvre, Paien de Maisières, or later Jean Renart.[25] 'Andreas' too may be a jocular pseudonym adopted by the author of the *De Amore*.[26]

Gedicht aus dem Anfang des xiii. Jahrhunderts von Péan Gatineau, ed. W. Söderhjelm (Tübingen, 1896).

[21] R. Dragonetti, *La Vie de la lettre au moyen âge (le conte du Graal)* (Paris, 1980), pp. 20–2. The self-attribution 'de Troie(s)' occurs only in *Erec*.

[22] L. Rossi, 'Chrétien di Troyes e i trovatori: Tristan, Linhaure, Carestia', *Vox Romanica* 46 (1987), 26–62.

[23] The identification of 'Troie' with the ancient city is fostered, in Van Coolput's 'Appendice', by nos. 5 and 12 but discouraged by nos. 1 (from *Le Chevalier à l'épée*), 3, 6, 8, and 13.

[24] See L. T. Topsfield, *Chrétien de Troyes. A Study of the Arthurian Romances* (Cambridge, 1981); T. Hunt, *Chrétien de Troyes: Yvain (Le Chevalier au lion)* (London, 1986), pp. 94–5; and the now considerable literature about the significance of Raimbaut d'Aurenga's 'Carestia', on which see more below.

[25] La Chièvre is attested (possibly) in the prologue to branche II of the *Roman de Renart* and in the prologue to the *Miracle d'une none tresoriere*, ed. G. Gröber, 'Ein Marienmirakel', in *Beiträge zur romanischen und englischen Philologie. Festgabe für Wendelin Förster* (Halle, 1902), pp. 421–39 (p. 428). Other goaty names are Mar*cabru*, and the '*Cabra* joglar' addressed by Giraut de *Cabra*ira. On 'Paien', see below.

[26] See P. Dronke, ' "Andreas Capellanus" ', *Journal of Medieval Latin* 4 (1994), 51–63.

(ii) Twelfth-century courts probably did not expect to provide a full-time livelihood for writers. In the Midi, at least, the non-noble troubadours were most likely courtiers or court servants of some kind. They were not 'writers' as such; indeed contempt for 'joglars', who make their living by composing and performing, is a standard topos of their poetry. Rather, such courtiers included the composition of courtly works among their other (diplomatic, secretarial, or administrative) services to their lord, frequently adopting a *senhal* to signal this change of role.[27] The following passage from *Erec* may be a similar expression of disdain by a court servant, using the *senhal* Crestïen, towards the activities of professional story-tellers:

> que devant rois e devant contes
> depecier et corrompre suelent
> cil qui de conter vivre vuelent.   (*Erec*, 20–22)
>
> (which those who want to earn a living from story-telling habitually fragment and corrupt in the presence of kings and counts.)

If there is no record of a 'Crestïen' attached either to Marie de Champagne's court or to that of Philip of Flanders, this may be because it was the name under which a court servant performed occasional literary services, and not because our romancer had no attachment to the courts concerned.[28]

(iii) The theme of pseudonymy, or variant names, while not uncommon in other twelfth-century texts (notably the *Tristan*), is central to at least three of the works ascribed to a 'Crestïen' (*Yvain, Perceval, Guillaume d'Angleterre*).

(iv) The 'name Christian' is a topos of saints' lives and 'Crestïen' is used as a pseudonym by characters in a number of examples from the second half of the twelfth century. (I return to this later.)

(v) There is such a clear association between changing name and baptism that 'to christen' is both 'to name' and 'to commit to a Christian identity'.[29] The name 'Crestïen', then, encodes within it the fact that it is a change of name: it is a pseudonym *par excellence*. (Note, though, that insofar as the name 'Crestïen' marks renunciation of worldly affiliation, it is at odds with the familiar portrait of a 'Chrétien' partisan with *clergie* against *chevalerie*.)

I think there is a strong case for seeing 'Crestïen' in some or all of its attestations as a pseudonym (a notion I shall refine later) but it is enough

---

[27] R. Harvey, '*Joglars* and the Professional Status of the Early Troubadours', *Medium Aevum* 72 (1993), 221–41.

[28] Cf. Benton, 'The Court of Champagne', p. 562.

[29] Holmes comments that Christianus is an uncommon name, and that it is associated, like the commoner Baptizatus, with converted Jews. See *Chrétien, Troyes and the Grail*, p. 53.

for me that it can be read as a description as well as a proper name. The next part of this paper glosses its use as a signature or attribution in the non-canonical texts. It asks what sense of 'Christian' is referred to and how a reader, alerted to this significance, might approach the canonical works ascribed to 'Chrétien de Troyes'. The third part then considers the use of the name 'Crestïen' by characters in saints' lives, and again relates this to the 'Chrétien de Troyes' of the modern academy. The final section of the essay looks at the name in the context of vernacular authorship in the twelfth century. How many 'Christians' produced these works? And how 'Christian' are they, after all?

2. *Signing oneself Crestïen*

'Cristien' and the Gospel

In the epilogue to one of three surviving Old French translations of the Gospel of Nicodemus the etymology of the name 'Crestïen' is transparent:

> Issi est finie l'estorie
> e en rumanz mise en memorie
> des ovraignes nostre seignur
> Jesu Crist nostre salveur.
> Jo, Cristien, l'ai translatée,
> de latin en romanz turnée.   (*Nicodemus*, 2181–6)

> (Thus is completed, and commemorated in the vernacular, the story of the works of Jesus Christ our lord. I Christian have translated it from Latin into French.)

'Jo Cristien' follows after and models itself on 'Jesu Crist', as the words follow and echo one another in the text, an echo reinforced by the framing repetition of 'rumanz'. Whereas André de Coutances, translator of another version,[30] names himself in the opening line of his translation,[31] Cristien explicitly refrains from putting his name forward at first. Strongly

---

[30] Compare this passage with the epilogue of André's translation of the same text, where the author's name leads to (and rhymes with) God:
    Ci faut le livre mestre Andreu.
    Or prions tuit ensemble Deu . . .   (2029–30)
[31] Here is yet another cleric claiming to have abandoned the secular literary amusements of his youth: 'Seignors, mestre André de Costances, / qu'a mout amé sonez & dances,/ vos mande qu'il n'en a més cure . . .' (1–3); advancing age summons him to perform good works and reconcile himself to God (4–10).

identifying with his text, he conflates its ending with his own by asking Christ to have mercy on him 'at the end':

> meis ne vol el comencement
> metre mun nun presentement,
> pur ço ke jo peccheor sui;
> mes par la grant pité de lui,
> lui requer ducement e pri
> k'a la fin eit de mei merci. (*Nicodemus*, 2187–92).

> (But I did not wish to present my name openly at the beginning, because I am a sinner; but through his great compassion I humbly beg and beseech him to have mercy on me at the end.)

The editors are uncompromising in their assertion that this translator cannot be identified with our 'Chrétien de Troyes'.[32] Yet the reader approaching the canonical 'Chrétien' romances with the mindset of the *Nicodemus* will be struck by correspondences between them. The *Nicodemus* comprises two stories: first the passion, crucifixion, burial and resurrection of Jesus, told in more detail than in the canonical Gospels (as regards the role of Joseph of Arimathia, for example), and second the eye-witness account by the sons of Simeon of the Harrowing of Hell. One or other of these stories is reproduced to a greater or lesser extent in all 'Chrétien''s romances. D. D. R. Owen has argued that the passion narrative transmitted by the Gospel of Nicodemus provides the framework of the false death plot in *Cligés*, and that the *Lancelot* offers, in the tale of Lancelot's victory over Meleagant and the release of the prisoners of Gorre, 'a diffuse parody' of the Harrowing of Hell.[33]

For Owen, the 'Cristien' of the Gospel translation is not to be identified with 'Chrétien de Troyes' and so he does not look for parallels between them.[34] Yet such parallels exist, even though they are not especially close. The heralding of the invincible Christ's arrival, for example,

> Envers lui ne pot contrester
> nule puissance ne durer   (*Nicodemus*, 1560–1)

> (No power can withstand him nor endure against him)

---

[32] There is no certainty as to the date of the translation. It is preserved in the same thirteenth-century manuscript as the *Vie de Saint Gilles*, a twelfth-century text. The editors suggest a date somewhere in the first half of the thirteenth century, and this is accepted by D. D. R. Owen, *The Vision of Hell. Infernal Journeys in Medieval French Literature* (Edinburgh and London, 1970), p. 99.

[33] D. D. R. Owen, 'Profanity and its Purpose in Chrétien's *Cligés* and *Lancelot*', *Forum for Modern Language Studies* 6 (1970), 37–48 (quotation from p. 42).

[34] 'Profanity and its Purpose', p. 42 n. 13; *The Vision of Hell*, p. 100.

resembles that of the fearless Lancelot:

> N'en ne lui puet contretenir
> passage ou il vuelle venir.   (*Lancelot*, 2297–8)

(No one can withhold access to him, where he wants to come.)

The hopes of the imprisoned souls in hell are like those of the captives in Gorre:

> Tut vivant a nus ci venistes
> pur ço ke tu nus vols oster
> de tenébres e delivrer
> e par ta sainte majesté
> sumes de la mort delivré.   (*Nicodemus*, 1876–80)

(You came alive to us here because you wanted to take and deliver us from darkness and by your holy majesty we are delivered from death.)

> Qu'an lor dist: 'Seignor, ce est cil
> qui nos gitera toz d'essil
> et de la grant malëurté
> ou nos avons lonc tans esté
> quant por nos fors de prison treire
> a tant perilleus leus passez . . .'   (*Lancelot*, 2413–16)[35]

(They were told: 'Lords, this is the man who will rescue us all from exile and the great misfortune where we have been so long, since he has passed through so many perilous places to release us from prison.)

Similar expressions of joy follow their respective liberations:

> Quant hors de cele tenebrur
> s'en issirent od lur seignur,
> David lur ad dit: 'Or chantez
> nuvele chansun; si loez
> nostre pére e nostre seignur,
> kar merveiles ad feit cest jur.' . . .
> Abacucs s'esdresce e parla:
> 'Beneeiz seit e eit honur
> cil qui vint el nun al seignur.'   (*Nicodemus*, 1893–8, 1908–9)

(When they issued forth from that darkness with their lord, David said to them, 'Now sing a new song; and praise our father and our

---

[35] Cf. 2303 where *delivrer* is used, and the quotation below.

lord, for he has wrought marvels on this day.' ... Habakuk rises and spoke: 'Blessings and honour on him who comes in the name of the lord.')

> Lancelot tuit beneïssoient
> et ce poez vos bien savoir
> que lors i dut grant joie avoir ...
> et dient tuit por ce qu'il l'oie:
> 'Sire, voir, molt nos esjoïmes
> tantost con nomer vos oïsmes,
> que seür fumes a delivre
> c'or serions nos tuit delivre.' (*Lancelot*, 3902–4, 3908–12)[36]

(They all blessed Lancelot, and you can be sure that there was to be great joy then ... and they all say so that he may hear, 'Lord, truly we all rejoiced as soon as we heard you named, for we were sure at once that we would all be free.')

A reader could be forgiven for confusing the 'Crestïen' of the *Lancelot* with the 'Cristien' of the *Nicodemus*: both are knowingly recasting a 'Christian' Gospel, whatever the differences between them.[37]

The narrative scheme of the Harrowing is likewise legible in *Yvain*, in the episode of Pesme Avanture, where again a group of people are liberated from captivity and deprivation; here Yvain's opponents, as in the Gospel, are explicitly demonic ('deus fiz de deable', 5271), while Yvain's role as Christ-figure is brought out when the captives are released:

> Ne je ne cuit qu'eles feïssent
> tel joie come eles le font
> de celui qui fist tout le mont
> s'il fust du chiel venus en terre. (*Yvain*, 5776–9)

(I don't think that they would have rejoiced as much over the one who made the whole world, if he were to come down from heaven to earth, as they do over Yvain.)

Indeed, already in *Erec* narratives of resurrection and redemption suggest themselves when the hero, apparently dead, returns to life in the castle of Death (Limors), vv. 4884–7. The *Perceval* too contains traces of a passion

---

[36] Without setting out the evidence for this at length, it was my impression that the Cristien *Nicodemus* was closer to the *Lancelot* than the other two translations.

[37] For a consideration of Lancelot as Messiah or anti-Messiah, see S. M. White, 'Lancelot's Beds: Styles of Courtly Intimacy', in *The Sower and his Seed*, ed. R. T. Pickens (Lexington, Kentucky, 1983), pp. 116–26.

narrative, hinted at by the lance and the Eucharist,[38] and indeed the whole development of the grail legend (although this is not explicit in the *Perceval*) depends on *Nicodemus* for the role of Joseph of Arimathia in transmitting the grail. The Crestïen of Arthurian romance is perhaps 'Christian' in his general reliance on Gospel narrative, just as is its 'Cristien' translator.

The most striking reminiscence of the *Nicodemus* material comes, however, not in works signed 'Crestïen' but in one claimed by the antonymically named 'Paien'. *La Mule sans frein*, the prologue of which names its author 'Paiens de Maisières' (14), recounts Gawain's terminating the reign of an evil enchantress and liberating the people under her thrall. These flock into the streets of the previously deserted town, rejoicing; and when Gawain asks the *vilain* – a major figure in this text, first introduced in the context of a 'beheading game' – for the *senefiance* of this (1015), he is told:

> Et or dïent en lor langage:
> Dieus les a par vos delivrez,
> e de toz biens enluminez
> la gent qui en tenebres estoient.
> Si grant joie ont de ce qu'il voient
> qu'il ne püent graingnor avoir.   (*Mule*, 1031–5)

> (And then they say in their tongue: God has delivered them through you and illumined with all good things the people who were in darkness. They rejoice so much at what they see that they could not rejoice more.)

Owen has noted that this evokes the Harrowing of Hell,[39] but not how it resembles 'Christien's' translation of that scene:

> La genz ki en tenébres fu
> clarté e lumére unt veu,
> e cil ki sunt el regiun
> de mort et de perdiciun
> la lumére sur els resplent.   (*Nicodemus*, 1431–5)[40]

---

[38] For a reading of the *Perceval* as a resurrection narrative, see also P. Duval, *La Pensée alchimique et le Conte du Graal* (Paris, 1979).

[39] See Owen's note to these lines in his edition and also 'Profanity', p. 46; *Visions of Hell*, p. 206.

[40] The greatest similarity comes in the rendering of Isaiah IX.2: 'Populus qui ambulabat in tenebris, vidit lucem magnam'. That is, the resemblance between the two Old French texts derives from the fact that both translate a common original. That does not detract from the reality of its presence, however.

(The people who were in darkness have seen brightness and light, and those who are in the realm of death and perdition, the light shines upon them.)

Owen's suggestion that 'Paien' is a further pseudonym adopted by 'Chrétien de Troyes' does not currently enjoy much support.[41] Paien is not in itself an uncommon name[42] but the possibility that it is a pseudonym fashioned in antithesis to 'Crestïen' is supported by the sardonic gloss on 'Troies/Troy' offered by 'maisières', which means 'walls', but especially 'tumbledown walls', 'ruin'.[43] The author of *La Mule sans frein* is thus a Pagan from the Ruins (a dig at the classical pretentions of *translatio studii*: Troy is in ruins, after all, as Conon de Béthune reminds his lady). Also, perhaps, he is an outsider from the thriving urban culture of modern Troies, stuck out in the Styx in the ruins of some former fastness. As Owen has shown, the prologue of *La Mule sans frein* looks like a pastiche of that of *Erec*,[44] their common ground being the use of peasant wisdom. In the case of *Erec*, however, the wisdom of peasants plays no role whatever in the subsequent romance, whereas in the *Mule*, as we saw, it is the *vilain* who expounds the *senefiance* of the adventure to the aristocratic hero. It looks as though the ruined 'Pagan' is giving the urban 'Christian' a lesson in understanding the Gospel. Is 'Paien', then, more Christian than 'Crestïen'? Just how serious is this joke?

'Crestïen' and the imitatio Christi of Christian Saints

The self-attribution 'Crestïens' figures twice in *Guillaume d'Angleterre*, both times in the prologue. First, Crestïens – the opening word of the text – boasts the text's fidelity to its source (which he says can still be found at Bury St Edmunds), the elaborateness of its rhyme, and its narrative pace

---

[41] D. D. R. Owen, 'Paien de Maisieres – A Joke that Went Wrong', *FMLS* 2 (1966), 192–6 and 'Two more Romances by Chrétien de Troyes?', *Romania* 92 (1971), 246–68. R. C. Johnston, co-editor with Owen of the Gawain romances, withdraws support for this view in 'The Authorship of the *Chevalier à l'épée* and the *Mule sans frein*', *Modern Language Review* 73 (1978), 496–8. See further the review of the question by Williams cited in n. 18 above.

[42] See J. Leclercq, 'Le poème de Payen Bolotin contre les faux ermites', *Revue bénédictine* 68 (1958), 52–86, esp. pp. 62 ff. Ducange's entry for PAGANI records the fact that the name Paganus was jocularly bestowed on children whose baptism was for some reason deferred.

[43] Maisières is also an extremely common toponym in France – see the editors' note to line 14 of the *Mule* prologue.

[44] In 'Paien de Maisieres – A Joke that Went Wrong'.

and direction.⁴⁵ (There is incidentally, a similar passage in the *Nicodemus*.⁴⁶) Then Crestïens introduces the protagonist, stressing his devout character:

> Crestïens dit, qui dire siaut,
> que an Angleterre ot ja un roi
> qui mont ama Dieu et la loi
> et molt esnora sainte yglise. (18–21)

> (Christian recounts, as he often does, that in England there was once a king who greatly loved God and religion and greatly honoured holy church.)

The suggestion of a connection between the piety of the tale and the narrator's name is confirmed when the hero's wife is soon afterwards described as 'moute bone crestïene' (36). How far does the name 'Crestïen' here invite a Christian reading?

There has been much debate whether *Guillaume d'Angleterre* derives from popular Byzantine romance (the tradition of *Apollonius of Tyre*) or from hagiography (the Eustace legend), since both these potential sources have narratives centring on the separation and reunion of a family.⁴⁷ The Eustace legend itself is so enmeshed in folklore that attempts to demarcate the hagiographic from popular culture are probably doomed.⁴⁸ There are,

---

⁴⁵ On the prologue to *Guillaume*, see L. Gowans, '*Guillaume d'Angleterre*. Prologue and Authorship', *French Studies Bulletin* 35 (1990), 1–5.

⁴⁶ Cf. *Guillaume d'Angleterre*:
> Crestïens se viaut antremestre,
> sans riens oster et sans riens mestre,
> de conter un conte par rime
> ou consonant ou lionime,
> aussin com par ci lou me taillie,
> mais que par lou conte s'an aillie.

with *Nicodemus*:
> Leucius le son escrit
> A Nichodeme, a Josep dit,
> bailla, et mut s'acordat bien
> a sun frére sur tute rien;
> une sillabe n'une lettre
> n'out plus en l'un k'en l'autre a metre. (2069–74)

⁴⁷ The fundamental study is G. H. Gerould, 'Forerunners, Congeners, and Derivatives of the Eustace Legend', *PMLA* 19 (1904), 335–448. See E. J. Mickel, Jr, 'Studies and Reflections on *Guillaume d'Angleterre*', *Romance Quarterly* 33 (1986), 393–406. On Apollonius, consult E. Archibald, *Apollonius of Tyre. Medieval and Renaissance Themes and Variations* (Cambridge, 1991).

⁴⁸ See J.-P. Martin, *Les motifs dans la chanson de geste. Définition et Utilisation (Discours de l'épopée médiévale, I)* (Villeneuve d'Ascq, 1992), pp. 36–51. See also S. Sturm-

though, two traits in the *Guillaume* which suggest that it is a significant reworking of the Eustace legend specifically: the different use made of the hero's two names, and the relocation of the crucial hunting scene.[49] I think, therefore, that the *Guillaume* hitches itself to a recognisably Christian narrative and joins the tradition of hagiographic *imitatio Christi*.

The saint begins life as a high-ranking Roman soldier called Placidas; he takes the name Eustace at baptism. The pious king Guillaume, once deprived of family and status, sheds half of his name and calls himself simply Gui. Since the text rhymes 'Guillaume' with 'roiaume'[50] this amputation of a syllable suggests that 'Gui' is the king ('roi') without a kingdom ('roiaume'). He is still referred to consistently as 'rois' by the narrator; his being remains that of a king, even when it is not recognised as such by others, nor reflected in his material surroundings. Thus the saint has a pagan name and a Christian name, whereas the king has a Christian name and an alias which both accompanies and signifies his loss of public standing. The different use made of the double names suggests that the *Eustace* is concerned more with spiritual identity, and the *Guillaume* more with the way identity is perceived within the world.

The saint seeks baptism as a result of a miraculous hunt in which a vision of Christ crucified appears to him on the antlers of a stag, and the stag then calls him to faith in the voice of Jesus. *Guillaume d'Angleterre* also starts with a divine summons, but this is a heavenly voice calling on the king to give up all his wealth and go into exile. So the one is called to Christianity, the other to renounce his worldly status. Living as a merchant, but at length reunited with his wife, Guillaume daydreams of a return to the aristocratic pursuit of hunting, takes to the hunt the following day, wanders too far, and is threatened with death. At this point he declares his royal identity, and his assailants turn out to be his long-lost sons. Thus the hunt reveals Jesus to the saint in the *Eustace* but the father to his sons in the *Guillaume*.[51] There is an *imitatio Christi* in Crestïen's text, but it has been relocated, the saintly king being the subject of the revelation, not its beneficiary. Again, what is

---

Maddox, ' "Si m'es jugie et destinee". On *Guillaume d'Angleterre*', in *The Sower and his Seed. Essays on Chretien de Troyes*, ed. R. T. Pickens (Lexington, Kentucky, 1983), pp. 66–80.

[49] See Heinz Klüppelholz, 'Zur Deutung der Jagdepisoden im *Guillaume d'Angleterre*', *Archiv für das Studium der neueren Sprachen und Literaturen* 227 (1990), 298–305.

[50] Cf. the rhyme in vv. 2039–40.

[51] Cf. *Guillaume*:
> Et dist, 'Seignor! mout vilainne oevre
> de moi ocirre feriiez,
> qu'un roi ocis i avriiez.'

and Eustace:
> O Placide quid me insequeris? [. . .] Ego sum Christus: quem ignorans colis.

at issue in *Guillaume* is recognition within a secular (here family) context. The supernatural character of the hunting episode in the *Guillaume* is confirmed when a purse which had been snatched from the king by an eagle immediately following the loss of all his family is 'miraculously' returned by the same eagle once they are all reunited.[52] The purse appears as a synecdoche of worldly possessions, its seizure punishing Guillaume's failure altogether to renounce them,[53] and its return marking his fitness to resume them.

These motifs of pseudonymy and the hunt lead me to believe that the *Guillaume* is rewriting the Eustace story. If so, then it has taken the further significant step of jettisoning the framework of conversion and martyrdom which surrounds the story of the loss and recovery of Eustace's family.[54] Eustace's *imitatio* culminates dramatically in his following Christ's passion, whereas the *Guillaume* opts instead for the less stark outline of a *vita*[55] in which the trials of life are patiently endured. For Guillaume, as a result, literal death is replaced by a pattern of metaphorical 'death' and 'resurrection' (compare the *Nicodemus*), whereby he loses and then regains his worldly identity.[56] Medieval readers who recognised this as 'Christian' would perhaps discern a similar fall and rise, played out before a public, in *Erec*, *Yvain*, the *Lancelot* and the *Perceval*; the hero's change of name during his 'fall' is particularly reminiscent of *Yvain*.

Guillaume's reinstatement is won because he renounces it. Offered a return to court life and the position of seneschal, he politely declines, pretexting the perils of fortune and the pain he might feel, if elevated again, at a fall from high office (2183–99). The paradox whereby what is lowly is exalted is familiar enough from Scripture; it is, indeed, explicit in the redemption narrative in Cristien's *Nicodemus* translation, where Christ's might comes precisely from his debasement (1727–32):

> [...] Intende Placidae: Ego sum Iesus Christus: qui caelum, et terram ex nihilo feci [...].

Cited from Bonitus Mombritius, *Sanctuarium seu vitae sanctorum*, 2 vols. (repr. Paris, 1919), I, p. 467, lines 30–48.

[52] On the admixture of the story of the 'treasure lost and found' to the Eustace story, see Gerould, 'Forerunners', pp. 392–406.

[53] Cf. the long monologue condemning cupidity that follows the eagle's snatching the purse from him and beating Guillaume with its wings, 889 ff.

[54] This jettisoning of the conversion narrative might be seen as discouraging for Holmes' and Klenke's view of Crestïen as a converted Jew. If he is prepared to allegorise a conflict between ecclesia and synagoga in *Perceval*, why not also represent it through the figure of the Roman convert?

[55] On the importance of the differences between *passiones* and *vitae* see C. F. Altman, 'Two Types of Opposition and the Structure of Latin Saints' Lives', *Medievalia et Humanistica* n.s. 6 (1975), 1–11.

[56] Cf. Mickel, 'Studies', p. 397.

> En forme de serf as victorie,
> nepurquant si es reis de glorie.   (1733–4)[57]

> (You secure victory in the guise of a serf, and yet you are the king of glory.)

This topos of high being low and vice versa becomes, through *imitatio*, one of the constants of saints' lives. It is also a common structuring principle in romances (such as *Le Bel Inconnu* or *Ipomedon*) and is regularly used by 'Chrétien de Troyes' to accompany the narrative of the loss and recovery of status which makes up the main plot of all the famous romances except possibly *Cligés*. The *Lancelot* provides especially clear examples of this 'low is high' topos when Lancelot is both reviled because of his ride on the Cart and elevated as redeemer, and later is exhorted to be both ignominious and supreme at the Noauz tournament. It is worth mentioning here a study of description in *Guillaume d'Angleterre* by Domenico d'Allesandro who finds it to be rather different from the canonical romances of 'Chrétien de Troyes'.[58] He notes,[59] however, a strong similarity between *Guillaume* 1762–69 and the *Lancelot* 6983–98, i.e. in the part of the work attributed not to 'Chrétien' but to Godefroy de Lagny.

Some have objected that the concern with status in *Guillaume d'Angleterre* is incompatible with its piety.[60] However, it would be a mistake to think that material wealth and status are not valued in *bona fide* hagiographic texts. All the saints who figure in such texts are cut out for brilliant worldly careers, which they can then renounce. As Ruth Morse has acutely observed: 'The schema thus enshrines precisely those values it pretends to deny.'[61] The Beatitude that the meek shall inherit the earth allows room for both the meekness, and the inheritance, to take material as well as moral or spiritual forms. In the Old French Eustace poems, for example, when the exiled Eustace is recognized by the imperial messengers, and his employers learn of their servant's former high status, they are chagrined by their social gaffe. The earlier, fragmentary, Alexandrine text[62] has them say:

---

[57] This contradiction is more marked in this translation than the other two.
[58] D. d'Allesandro, '*Guillaume d'Angleterre* e Chrétien de Troyes. Un'analisi comparata del descrittivo', *Annali dell' Istituto Universitario Orientale* 29 (1987), 349–56.
[59] p. 356.
[60] For example Holden, Introduction, pp. 10–11, maintains that there is a fundamental contradiction between the religious beginning of the poem and its materialistic ending.
[61] R. Morse, *Truth and Convention in the Middle Ages. Rhetoric, Representation and Reality* (Cambridge, 1991), p. 141.
[62] Ed. P. Meyer, *Romania* 36 (1907), 12–28. This text is thought to be from the twelfth century.

> Funt il, 'Cum poons estre tut mari *et* dolent
> quant si tr*és* vaillant home nus a si longement
> servi, nus, soffraitos, issi trés povrement.' (288–90)

(They say, 'How sad and afflicted we all should be, given that a man of such worth has served us for such a long time, reduced to need and in such great poverty.')

This is amplified in the early thirteenth-century octosyllabic version:

> Ha! fait cascun, que nel savoie,
> kant le servise rechevoie
> d'onme de si grant dignité!
> Ha, tant par en sui engigné!
> Mielz li deüson obeïr
> ke il a nos, e meulz servir. (1323–8)[63]

('Oh!', they all say, 'why did I not know it, when I accepted the service of a man of such high rank! Oh, how I have been misled! We ought to be humbling ourselves to him rather than he to us, and serving him.')

In the equivalent section in *Guillaume d'Angleterre*, when Guillaume humbly serves his merchant bosses as 'Gui', he too adopts a 'low' position from having been 'high', but the text represents this in non-material terms:

> S'aucuns le leideinge ou affite,
> ja por affit ne por losainge
> n'iert de lui servir plus estreinge,
> ains li ancline et sel deschauce.
> Qui s'umelie, si s'essausse,
> ice est droite veritiez,
> mont essauce home humilitez
> et molt l'eneure et mont lou lieve. (*Guillaume*, 1026–33)

(If someone insults or slights him, Gui will never, regardless of any slight or slander, be more reluctant to serve him, rather he will bow down to him and take off his footwear. Wheoever humbles himself is raised up, this is the strict truth, humility exalts a man and does him honour and raises him up high.)

On this comparison, the hagiographic texts appear more worldly than the *Guillaume*.

Perhaps what is paramount in this text is our attitude to the material

---

[63] *Le Vie de Saint Eustache. Poème français du xiiie siècle*, ed. H. Petersen (Paris, 1928).

(which we can control), rather than our involvement in it (which we can't).[64] As king, Guillaume accumulates wealth, and as a merchant he does so too; one cannot live without participating in a monetary economy. His reunion with his wife is effected through mercantile exchange: Guillaume buys a hunting horn that formerly belonged to him at an extortionate price; it is recognised by his wife who then goes on to spot her ring on his finger and demand that in tribute. In both cases, the characters excite reproof for placing sentimental over monetary value, but the fact remains they could not be reunited without the conventions of money and property within which they have to live.[65]

The difficulty of extrapolating the non-material (moral or spiritual) from the material hovers over the motivation for Guillaume's exile in the first place. Different scholars have constructed different faults for his departure to correct/atone for: presumption, attachment to the world, desire for control.[66] If the text presents a narrative of sin and expiation, then the character of the sin is left unclear; perhaps it has to be inferred from the way it is expiated. In this respect Guillaume's career is an adventure in which his future is the clue to his past. In the romances of 'Chrétien', too, secular adventures can be read as probing a moral failure, the nature and extent of which depend on our assessing to what extent the adventure was a success.

In sum, *Guillaume d'Angleterre* is (in my view) a saint's life in which the drama of conversion and martyrdom has been replaced by passive endurance of the extremes of social experience: status and servitude, wealth and poverty, family and isolation. Moral and spiritual issues are still at stake, but blurred as they become with the social and the economic, they lack the clear outlines of *passiones* (like that of Eustace), if not of *vitae*. In the *Guillaume*, the fundamental hagiographical tropes whereby high is low, and loss is gain, persist; and these tropes, even when their terms assume material forms, characterize the 'Christian' literature of the twelfth century.

---

[64] See works previously cited by Mickel and Sturm-Maddox in notes 47 and 48.
[65] Similarly some non-nobles are less materialistic than others. Guillaume's experience in the household of the merchant (who is not greedy but upright) is contrasted favourably with his sons' upbringing by peasants (who are greedy and stupid). At the end of the poem the *vilains* are given wealth, but the merchant is made a counsellor and his sons are knighted. See B. L. Callay, 'A Medieval Literary Stereotype. Noblemen in the Marketplace: Aristocratic versus Bourgeois Values in Old French Literature', *Michigan Academician* 14 (Winter 1982), 313–23.
[66] For discussion, see Klüppelholz, 'Zur Deutung der Jagdepisoden'.

'Crestïen', Christians, and Pagans

Alone of all the other works signed 'Crestïen', the *Philomena* inserts the name at its midpoint.[67] Tereus is hurrying Philomena towards a lonely house where he plans to seduce her:

> La meisons estoit an un bois
> – ce conte Crestiiens li Gois –
> loing de villes de totes parz
> et loing de chans et loing d'essarz,
> loing de chemins et de santiers.
> Parlant, gabant andemantiers
> or d'un or d'el, par traïson
> l'an a menee an sa maison ... (733–40)

(The house stood in a wood – so Chretiiens the Gois (?) recounts – far from villages on all sides, far from fields and reclaimed land, far from roads and tracks. Talking and joking of this and that along the way he treacherously led her to his house ...)

Immediately afterwards he solicits her favours and, on being repulsed, rapes her.

The puzzling words *li gois* which follow the name 'Crestiiens' in the majority of manuscripts appear as *li gais* in some others,[68] an alteration which has steered commentators in the direction of accepting *li gois* as an attributive construction. The meaning of 'Crestiiens li Gois/gois' continues to elude us, however.[69] It may be helpful to repunctuate:

> ... an un bois,
> ce conte Crestiiens; li gois
> loing de villes ...

---

[67] Other signatures may have been lost as a result of cutting the prologue and epilogue to fit its new setting in the *Ovide moralisé*. Attributions which may derive from a lost prologue and epilogue flank it on either side: 'Fors si com Crestiens le conte' (*Ovide moralisé* VI, 2212), 'Si com Crestiens le raconte' (*ibid.*, 3686 and 3842). All other works signed Crestïen are signed either at the beginning (*Guillaume, Erec, Charrete, Perceval*), at the end (*Nicodemus, Yvain*), or both (*Cligés*).

[68] Presumably by a process of *lectio facilior*. Variants are in de Boer's Paris 1909 edition. One manuscript has *li rois*, but with *li g* crossed out.

[69] For a review of the options under consideration, see H. F. Williams, 'Crestiiens li gois', *Bulletin Bibliographique de la Société Internationale Arthurienne* 10 (1958), 67–71, who opts for 'li gais' [the joyful] as a fourteenth-century interpolation and not a twelfth-century signature. 'Gois' has been undertood as a toponym based on a word for a vine-sickle; as a form of 'liégeois'; as deriving from *goz* and meaning 'dwarf'; and as deriving from English 'goat', and so translating the name 'La Chièvre'. U. T. Holmes thinks it means 'Goy' and reaffirms his view that Chrétien was a convert from Judaism: see his *Chrétien de Troyes* (1970), p. 53.

where *li gois* would mean 'Tereus's sport, his scheme' (< JOCUS); or even:

> ... an un bois,
> ce conte Crestiiens. Li gois
> ...
> parlant gabant ...
> l'an a menee ...

where *li gois* (in this case < GOSSUS) would refer to Tereus himself.[70]

I make these suggestions partly to ease the *impasse* on attributive *li gois*, but also because the contrast between the horrible actions of pagan Tereus and the Christian identity of the narrator may explain why the signature is inserted at this point; expressing the antithesis within a single line would give it greater emphasis. Soon afterwards, Tereus' own name will receive a sinister gloss. Reacting to Philomena's protestations that he stop pestering her ('teisiez vos an', 776 [be silent]) Tereus replies:

> Teirei, mes vos vos an teisiez. (777)

(I shall be silent, but you be silent about it.)

Tereus, of course, *is* finally silenced by Progné's revenge. The Christian teller (*qui conte*), then, wins out against the pagan malefactor (*qui taira*).[71]

Whereas the *Nicodemus* and the *Guillaume* present a narrator ('Crestïen') partisan with his narrative material (it is 'Christian'), the *Philomena* narrator is frankly antagonistic towards Tereus and Progné. On first seeing Philomena, Tereus falls in 'love' with her and hopes to possess her. His desire is condemned as *pechiez, mauvestié, folie,* and *vilenie* [sin, evil, madness, baseness] by the narrator (212–16), from whose point of view it is clearly incestuous (216–19). Pagans, the narrator says, are ruled only by their desires, to which their polytheistic religion gives full vent:

> Car uns lor deus que il avoient
> selonc la loi que il tenoient
> estali qu'il feïssent tuit
> lor volanté et lor deduit.

---

[70] = 'the cur'. If these lines are twelfth-century, the rhyme is not a Champenois one (it would imply *bos* for *bois*); that is, unless we admit the variant form 'gois' located by R. Levy, 'Old French *goz* and Crestiiens li Gois', *PMLA* 46 (1931), 312–20 (p. 315). For similar examples of *contre-rejet* to that which I propose here, see *Philomena* 44–5, 72–3, 107–8, 483–4, etc.

[71] W. Azzam, 'Le Printemps de la littérature. La "translation" dans "Philomena" de Crestiiens li Gois', *Littérature* 74 (1989), 47–62, writes interestingly about the task of the Christian reteller of a pagan fable extracting truth from the mendacity of his source.

> Tel loi lor avoit cil escrite
> que quanqu'il lor plest ne delite
> pooiot chascuns feire sanz crime.
> Itel loi tenoit paiennime. (216–28)

(For one of the gods they had according to the religious code to which they held laid down that they should all do their pleasure and their will exactly. The code that he had written was such that all could do without reproach whatever pleases or delights them. Such is pagan religion.)

In fact, says the narrator from his Christian standpoint, the Devil holds Tereus in his grip (462), and fills his mind with wicked subterfuges to achieve his purpose. His love, his religion, and his rhetoric are all as false as each other. Progné too is confined within her deadly pagan practices. Told that Philomena is dead, she curses her gods (978) and performs elaborate rituals designed to release her sister's soul from 'hell' (1031–2). Desire for revenge makes her perform the unnatural act of killing her own child, whose cooked flesh is served to his father as the best available form of redress.[72] Like Tereus, she is acting on the Devil's counsel (1298, 1331). Her child-sacrifice is a parody of the redemption, where the father (Tereus) is put in the role of humanity; for the death of the Son is provoked by his resemblance to his Father and by his Father's sin:

> 'Ha,' fet ele, 'chose sanblable
> au traïtor, ou vil deable!
> Morir t'estuet de mort amere
> por la felenie ton pere.
> Sa felenie conparras,
> por son forfet a tort morras.' (1299–1304)

('Oh, how you resemble the traitor, the vile devil! You must die a bitter death because of your father's crime. You will pay for his crime and die unjustly for his wrongdoing.)

Contrast this passage with the episode in *Guillaume d'Angleterre* where Guillaume, echoing Christ's words, offers his own flesh to his starving wife rather than that she devour her new-born children:

> Racheter vuel la mort mon fil
> et de ma char et de mon sanc. (536–7)

(I mean to redeem my son's death with my body and my blood.)

---

[72] Cf. E. J. Burns, *Bodytalk. When Women Speak in Old French Literature* (Philadelphia, 1993), pp. 132 ff.

The 'Christian-ness' of both texts is brought out through their divergent rewriting of the Eucharistic sacrifice.[73]

In *Philomena* an effect of the 'pagan-ness' of Teresus and Progné is to make Philomena and her father Pandion appear less alien. Pandion speaks of having lived longer than the patriarchs (360–1) and Philomena advises Tereus to follow 'la costume as François' (280).[74] The falsity of Tereus's swearing on his gods is denounced by Philomena:

> Traïtres, mes peres te crut,
> qui ta traïson n'aparçut,
> por ce que devant lui ploroies
> et por ce que tu li juroies
> sor toz les deus an cui tu croiz.
> Ou sont li deu? Ou est la foiz?
> As tu les ja mis an obli?   (817–23)

> (Traitor, my father believed you, and didn't realise your treachery, because you wept in front of him and swore on all the gods in whom you believe. Where are the gods? Where is your faith? Have you forgotten them?)

Philomena's question 'ou sont li deu' echoes the challenge issued by Christian martyrs to their pagan tormentors. Described as beautiful, intelligent, nubile, her portrait recalls that of the virgin martyrs Fides or Catherine, whom pagan kings likewise interrogate, attempt to seduce, and then destroy with sexually charged torments. Philomena is not literally killed by Tereus, but he claims that she is dead, and as with the martyred saints her bodily suffering is transmuted into a text which makes her torments legible to others.[75]

But while there are concessions made to soften the portraits of Philomena and Pandion by making them less 'pagan' than Tereus and Progné, their distance from the 'Christian' narrator is still palpable. Pandion abandons his first daughter to an unsuitable partner with little thought (13) and only hangs on to the second from self-interest; Philomena, though not responsible for his murder, helps cook Itis. The transformation of all three principals into birds at the end demotes them from humanity. Only when Philomena

---

[73] On the child-eating as a pagan 'Last Supper', see Azzam, p. 59, and Azzam's reference to a paper by Méla, p. 48 n. 5.

[74] But see E. Schulze-Busacker, '*Philomena*: Une révision de l'attribution de l'oeuvre', *Romania* 107 (1986), 459–85, who suggests (p. 469) that the narrator is drawing attention to his use of a specifically French proverb, rather than a gnomic saying.

[75] A striking parallel is the Occitan *Chanson de Sainte Foi d'Agen*, ed. A. Thomas (Paris, 1974), in which the dead virgin's blood forms a picture, and her memory is later inscribed in marble (413 ff.).

is dead can she be transformed into the 'courtly' nightingale, and enjoin 'courtly' restraint rather than transgressive or violent attitudes towards women:

> Ancore, qui crerroit son los
> seroient a honte trestuit
> li desleal mort et destruit
> et li felon et li parjure
> et cil qui de joie n'ont cure
> et tuit cil qui font mesprison
> et felenie et traïson
> vers pucele sage et cortoise ... (1454–61)

(To this day, if one were to believe the nightingale's advice, those who are disloyal, criminal, or perjuring would be shamefully killed and put to death, and so too all those with no regard for joy, and those who act wrongly towards a wise and courtly girl ...)

The 'Crestiien' of this text outdoes Marcabru in the ferocity of his condemnation of sexual cupidity and deceit passed off as 'love'.[76]

The reader of *Philomena* is led to inquire what suspicion of pagan eroticism may lurk in other texts signed 'Crestïen'. Does *Erec*, the only text with the self-attribution 'de Troie', set out to improve, as well as 'translate', antique matter through comparing its hero and heroine with Aeneas and Lavinia? What of the parading and updating of Ovidiana in *Cligés*, in which the self-attribution to Chrestïen figures, with unique emphasis, at both beginning and end? We have been accustomed in recent years to see 'Chrétien de Troyes' as a scholar-poet revelling in the humanist renaissance of the twelfth century, but the Crestïen of the *Philomena* at least is more resistant to than complicitous with the heritage of antiquity.

Crestïen, Carestia, and the Love Lyric

The phrase 'de Troies' in *chansonnier* rubrics 'Crestien de Troies' finds so many parallels among other trouvère names (Conon *de Béthune*, Guiot *de Dijon*, Raoul *de Soissons*, etc.) that it is unlikely medieval readers would view it as referring to anything other than a town in Northern France.[77] The

---

[76] This point is made by Rossi, 'Chrétien de Troyes e i trovatori', p. 38, n. 43.
[77] The sigla used here to refer to *chansonnier* manuscripts are the standard ones established by A. Jeanroy, *Bibliographie sommaire des chansonniers français du moyen âge* (Paris, 1918). Songs are attributed to a 'crestiens (cresteien, croistien, crestiiens, crestijens) de troies' in four manuscripts: *C* (= Bern, Bibl. Mun. 389), *R* (= Paris, BN fr. 1591), *T* (= Paris, BN fr. 12615), and *a* (= Rome, Vat., Reg. 1490). (Some of the songs attributed to him in these manuscripts are also found, but with different or no attributions in other

sense of a poet continuing – or combatting – a pagan past is then not one which the lyric context endorses. The name 'Crestien', however, is another matter, given that several other trouvères have what look very like sobriquets (cf. *Blondel* de Nesle, *Moniot* d'Arras).

The absence of an author miniature makes it impossible to know how *chansonnier* compilers represented the referent of this rubric to themselves. *T*, the most richly illuminated of the manuscripts to contain 'crestijen' attributions, and so the most likely to have contained a portrait, does not include one. Furthermore, it includes only songs whose authenticity is rejected by Zai: *Quant li dous estez decline* (R1380) and *Joie de guerredons d'Amors* (R2020). Both are predominantly secular in tone, the first exploiting the metaphor of the prison of love, the second rehearsing themes of fidelity and reward, suffering and death, and the superior position of the lady. *R*, likewise organised by author, contains only *D'amors qui m'a tolu a moi*. Manuscript *a*, another author-based collection whose author portraits are largely lost,[78] follows the text of *D'Amors qui m'a tolu a moi* with that of a rondeau *Soufrés, maris, et si ne vous anuit*, apparently with the same rubric, or at least without a change of rubric.[79] The manuscript with the greatest number of 'Crestïen' songs, *C*, orders its contents alphabetically rather than by author. It contains *Amors tençon et bataille, D'Amors qui m'a tolu a moi*, and (though not in an ancient rubric[80]) *De joli cuer chanterai* (R66), a short (three-stanza) text expressing submissive and cheerful service. The song surviving in the most copies (twelve in all) is *D'Amors, qui m'a tolu a moi*, but of these twelve, only four attribute it to a 'crestien de troies'.[81] The trouvère 'Crestïens de Troies' is thus a shadowy figure, his corpus small and ill-defined, his identity never clearly represented. If the 'Crestien' of the *chansonniers* is a sobriquet, then, it isn't easy to ascribe much significance to it.

Our purchase on a trouvère Crestïen comes rather from the dialogue between him and the troubadours Raimbaut d'Aurenga and Bernart de Ventadorn, as conducted in the songs *D'Amors qui m'a tolu a moi, Non chan per auzel ni per flor*, and *Quan vei la lauzeta mover*. In *Non chan*, Raimbaut addresses a 'Carestia', now widely accepted as an anagram of

---

manuscripts.) Note that 'troies' is always spelled with final -*s*, which would confirm identification with Troyes in Champagne over ancient Troy (OF Troie).

[78] See S. Huot, *From Song to Book. The Poetics of Writing in Old French Lyric and Lyrical Narrative* (Ithaca, 1987), p. 48.

[79] Zai, p. 47. N. van den Boogaard, *Rondeaux et refrains du xiie siècle au début du xive* (Paris, 1969), where this rondeau figures as no. 193, says it is a later addition.

[80] See Zai, p. 120.

[81] i.e. *a, R, T, C*. There is no rubric in *HLP²UV*, and the song is given to Gace Brulé by *KNP¹X*. (See Jeanroy's *Bibliographie sommaire*, reference in note 77, for locations of these manuscripts.)

Cristia(n), the Occitan form of Crestien.[82] As a common noun, *carestia* means both 'dearth' and 'preciousness' (cf. OF *chierté*) and is etymologically related to 'caritas'. It thus opens up an intriguing web of associations:[83] religious (charity), ethical value (the 'precious' sense of *chierté* is usually abstract), material indigence (its 'dearth' acceptance is usually concrete) and poetic (*car* is a term for a poetic style using rare words or rhymes, elsewhere espoused by Raimbaut). This range is reinforced through the antonymic *senhal* used elsewhere of Raimbaut, 'Linhaure', which invokes material wealth (*aure*) and splendid family (*linh-aure*) combined with physical loss (Ignaure was castrated) and rhetorical show (a gilded style). The third *senhal* in the trio, 'Tristan', used by Bernart, holds a phonetic mirror up to 'Cristia(n)', the mock-innocent shift *Crist*- to *Trist*- effecting a major shift in meaning.[84] The career of Tristan is repudiated in *D'Amors qui m'a tolu a moi* (whose first person explicitly rejects the idea of the philtre) but embraced in *Non chan per auzel ni per flor* (in which Raimbaut thinks a bit of adultery *à la* Tristan would suit him rather well). Bernart's sorrowful representation of himself as a tragic lover (*trist*-an) contrasts with the cheeky cheerfulness (-*baut*) of Raimbaut and with the long-suffering patience advocated in the 'Crestien' song, especially in the lines which seem to accept and gloss the *senhal* 'Carestia' as finding value in lack:

> Cuers, . . .
> Ja, mon los, plenté n'ameras
> ne pour chier tans ne t'esmaier;
> biens adoucist par delaier,
> et quant plus desiré l'auras,
> plus t'en ert douls a l'essaier. (37–45)
>
> (Heart, if you follow my counsel you will not love abundance nor be dismayed by scarcity. Delay makes sweet and the longer you have desired the sweeter the experience will be.)

The significance of *D'Amors qui m'a tolu a moi* has always been sought in its capacity to confirm or qualify readings of the canonical romances, specifically *Cligés*.[85] What meaning might a reader bring to the signature Crestïen as a result of an encounter with 'Carestia'? In *D'Amors qui m'a*

---

[82] See A. Roncaglia, 'Carestia', *Cultura Neolatina* 18 (1958), 121–37. Other contributions on this subject are reviewed, most recently, in M. L. Meneghetti, *Il Pubblico dei trovatori*, 2nd edn (Turin, 1992), pp. 101 ff.
[83] Much of this is based on Luciano Rossi, 'Chrétien di Troyes e i trovatori'.
[84] It is perhaps worth noting that the interversion 'Cristia' to 'Carestia' recalls that of 'Tristan' to 'Tantris'.
[85] E.g. G. Zaganelli, *Aimer, sofrir, joïr. I paradigmi della soggettività nella lirica francese dei secoli xii e xiii* (Florence, 1982), pp. 25–65.

tolu a moi we find another example of paradox reminiscent of the Beatitudes, this time that lack is gain: the *chier tans* of 'carestia' is better than *plenté*. This might lead to an association, rather than with *Cligés*, with the *Perceval*, the romance in which lack (the land laid waste) and plenty (the grail) form a structured pair, and whose prologue is informed by 'carité'. The themes of lack and plenty are also vital to *Guillaume d'Angleterre* in which the sacrifice of wealth serves as a necessary preparation to its resumption. The term 'carestia', furthermore, suggests a resolution of the paradox through recourse to hierarchy: lack (on the material level) conduces to gain (on a higher one). Did Raimbaut d'Aurenga point the way to reconciling the contradictions of low and high, loss and gain, in the para-biblical and para-hagiographical writings of Crestïen?

The name Crestïen features, then, as signature or attribution in a range of medieval contexts other than the romances canonically attributed to 'Chrétien de Troyes'. Traditionally, scholars of Old French have been concerned to argue whether, as a matter of historical fact, they refer to the same person. This survey has sought to show how reflecting upon the name in its textual contexts can spark connections between these works of uncertain attribution and the canonical romances, and amongst these non-canonical works themselves. In all cases, these works can be read as probing what it might mean to be called 'Crestïen'. The content of the two devotional texts (*Nicodemus* and *Guillaume d'Angleterre*) is not only 'Christian' in itself but also relies on recognisably 'Christian' narrative structures which can also be discerned in other works. Of the more profane texts, *Philomena* is informed by a 'Christian' attitude to pagan writings, while the transformation of the name Cristian to Carestia may reflect engagement with 'Christian' patterns of thought. That does not, of course, exclude the possibility that the name may also be read ironically in some of these contexts, and that some of these texts nurture ideas and sentiments contrary to religious orthodoxy. It does mean, however, that 'Christianity' is invoked in all of them as a point of reference with respect to which interpretation can be situated.

3. *'Lo nom Crestien' in Lives of the Saints*

One of the arguments advanced in the dispute over the authorship of the works signed 'Crestïen' is that it is an uncommon name.[86] However, there is one genre in which it is quite the reverse, namely hagiography. The early third-century *Passio* of St Perpetua, cited as epigraph to this paper, shows

---

[86] Holmes and Klenke, *Chrétien, Troyes, and the Grail*, pp. 53–6.

the antiquity of this motif. As Dronke puts it, 'she has chosen the name "Christian" because that is what she now is – she may even imply that the choice of name makes her what she is.'[87] The oldest surviving vernacular hagiographic text, the sequence of St Eulalia, has the saint embrace death rather than lose 'lo nom christiien',[88] and this remains, implicitly or explicitly, a constant of hagiography. There are, in particular, two twelfth-century lives in which this topos of 'lo nom Crestïen' is prominent: those of Becket and of St Alexis. Elucidating the significance of the name in these texts will suggest how a late twelfth-century audience would respond to the name 'Crestïen', and so refine the understanding gleaned in the last section of this paper.

The *S* text of the Life of St Alexis (the earlier of two OF versions in decasyllabic *laisses*) dates from the twelfth century.[89] It is an expanded version of *L* (the famous Hildesheim *Alexis*), material having been added in order, apparently, to make the story more realistic. Anticipating the objection 'Why, during the seventeen years he lived beneath his family's staircase, did no one ask Alexis who he was?',[90] *S* has Alexis's father ask the saint just that:

> Biaus crestïens, ne savons vostre non.
> Faut vous conrois? De coi aiés besoing?   (795–6)
>
> (Fair Christian, we do not know your name. Do you need anything? What might you need?)

To which Alexis replies:

---

[87] Dronke, *Medieval Women Writers*, p. 5. The Latin text reads: 'Et ego dixi ei: "Numquid alio nomine vocari potest quam quod est?". Et ait: "Non". "Sic et ego aliud me dicere non possum nisi quod sum, Christiana." ' *Passio SS. Perpetuae et Felicitatis*, ed. C. I. M. I. van Beek, 3, 2–3.

[88] 'Il [Maximien] li enortet, dont lei nonque chielt,
quēd elle fuiet lo nom christiien.'   (13–14)

[89] A. Goddard Elliott, *The 'Vie de Saint Alexis' in the Twelfth and Thirteenth Centuries: An Edition and Commentary* (Chapel Hill, 1983). The sigla of manuscripts containing versions of the *Alexis* are those established by G. Paris and L. Pannier, *La Vie de saint Alexis: Poème du XIe siècle et renouvellements des XIIe, XIIIe et XIVe siècles* (Paris, 1872): *S* = Paris, BN fr. 12471, *L* = Hildesheim, *M¹* = Paris, BN fr. 1553, and *M2* = Carlisle, Cathedral Library; the *Q* version contains 7 further manuscripts, of which details in Elliott. Elliott records (p. 70) a Lyons chronicler speaking of Peter Waldo (founder of the Waldensians) being converted as a result of hearing a Life of St Alexis performed in 1173. See also U. Mölk, 'La *Chanson de saint Alexis* et le culte du saint en France au XIe et XIIe siècles', *Cahiers de Civilisation Médiévale* 21 (1978), 339–55.

[90] Cf. Elliott, p. 30; she suggests that other questions answered by the *S* text are 'What were the names of all of the other characters?' and 'How did his bride react when Alexis told her he was leaving?'.

> 'Sire,' dist il, 'Crestïens ai a non,
> e trestout cil qui levé sont des fons.
> Qui cest non garde s'en a bon guerredon,
> et qui nel fait, mor[t] morians a non.
> [. . .]
> Par mon droit non, sire, m'avés noumé,
> se tant sui bons que m'en puisse garder.
> En s[aint] baptesme, en fons, me sui donnés,
> mais jou criem perdre par mal siecle mener.'   (797–806)

('Sire,' he said, 'my name is Christian, as for all those who are baptised. Whoever preserves this name is well rewarded for it, and whoever fails to do so bears the name of mortal death. [. . .] You have called me by my rightful name if I am good enough to ward it off (i.e. damnation). I have given myself in holy baptism, at the font, but I fear to lose it by living wrongfully in the world.')

The father addresses Alexis as 'crestïens', using the word as a common noun; but Alexis receives it as a name, thereby renouncing his identity as his father's son and heir, in order entirely to subsume his identity to that of 'nostre signour'. The name 'Crestïen' is common to all who have been baptised, Alexis stresses, and so (for a Western Christian audience) it is a universal name, a kind of 'Everyman'. Yet Alexis also points out that it offers a moral challenge which not everyone can meet, since there is a danger of failure to live up to the name of 'Christian', and consequent risk of forfeiture.

Guernes de Pont-Sainte-Maxence's life of Becket was composed soon after Becket's death in 1170, probably between 1172 and 1174.[91] There is no doubting, in this case, that the text is contemporary with our 'Chrétien de Troyes'. After initially making a brilliant career at the court of Henry II, and becoming archbishop of Canterbury, Becket is depicted as incurring the envy of other courtiers, and then, through his uncompromising defence of clerical prerogatives, the anger of the king as well. Becket further inflames Henry's wrath by denying that he owes him service; he will acknowledge none but Christian bonds (see 1883ff).[92] As a result he is branded a traitor, threatened with imprisonment, and flees the country. This episode is recounted with an abundance of Christological motifs. Becket says to his enemy the archbishop of York, 'Satanas, fui d'ici' (1870); his detractors are compared to the Jews who called for the crucifixion (1936ff); before leaving

---

[91] Guernes de Pont-Sainte-Maxence, *La Vie de Saint Thomas Becket*, ed. E. Walberg, CFMA (Paris, 1936), Introduction, pp. iii–v.

[92] Earlier he had spoken out for the indissolubility of the sacraments:
> Co que Deus a sacré ne puet nuls dessacrer,
> ne nul cristïen humme nuls descristianer.   (1271–2)

he eats a 'last supper' (1976ff); like Alexis, he is referred to as 'li huem Deu' (2007). In his flight, Becket assumes disguise and changes his name:

> Gris dras d'un frere ad pris, k'il puisse estre celez:
> or est Thomas changiez, Cristïens est numez.   (2059–60)
>
> (He took the grey robes of a lay brother, so that he might be concealed; now has has changed his name from Thomas, he is named Christian.)

This name is retained until he reaches safety in France (cf. 2095).[93] Later the text will reveal that he was originally named after Doubting Thomas, on whose feast day he was born (5856–9). The name 'Cristïen' marks Becket's first experience of destitution, and assimilates his sufferings to those of Christ against those who doubt him. Like Alexis, his worldly identity is stripped away leaving him identified with his service of Christ.

In both texts, then, the name 'Crestïen' signals a particular conception of incognito: one which involves not merely the renunciation of a name, but of all the worldly associations that accompany it. Previously I spoke of 'Crestïen' as possibly being a pseudonym, but a better term might be the neologism 'anonym':[94] a renunciation of all identity other than the spiritual and ethical aspirations of the Christian. Alexis reaches the name 'Crestïen' from a background in aristocracy and Becket from one in *clergie*, but in the name these contrasting paths meet. The name 'Crestïen' is a description, but one that is founded not on the bearer's own attributes, rather on his or her acknowledgement of those of Christ. It does not flag adhesion to a particular interest group (knights or clerks) but acceptance of a common subjection to a higher Law. This is very different from the current image which we have of the ironic courtier 'Chrétien de Troyes'.

Each of these hagiographical texts offers an interesting purchase on the canonical writings of 'Chrétien de Troyes'. Becket's career has a similar pattern to those of Erec and Yvain, since he like them experiences an initial and astounding success which is quickly reinscribed as a failure. His brilliance as a courtier and his diplomatic efforts as archbishop are his undoing; he must then forfeit his identity and lead a prolonged exile before being permitted to return to England. The 'anonym' Crestïen recalls especially the willing acceptance of anonymity by Yvain.

Alexis's story is more reminiscent of the *Lancelot*. Nichols, speaking of the *L* redaction, points out that when Alexis is living in Edessa, it is a statue of the Virgin that confers on him the generic name 'saintly man' (*ume Deu*); like a Chrétien hero, he gives up his personal name for a description, and

---

[93] Later there is a pun on 'cristïenté': see v. 2688.
[94] Ruth Morse, personal communication.

as if in commentary on the *Lancelot* he prefers the name bestowed by the Virgin to that of an earthly love.[95] In *S* the description of the statue is much amplified as compared with *L* (see *S* 366–75). The scene where the statue speaks (*S* 515ff) bears the influence of Mary miracles, many of which involve the miraculous intervention of a statue of the Virgin.[96] The competition between earthly and heavenly bonds is brought out by the statue's praise of Alexis for abandoning his family, and by Alexis's tale of leaving his fiancée.

It might be objected that these two hagiographical texts are too marginal to have any impact on potential audiences of works signed 'Crestïen'. Each of them is, however, representative of a substantial tradition. Guernes' *Vie de Saint Thomas Becket* runs parallel to an abundant Latin literature on Becket, several of the texts of which reiterate this motif of his adopting the name Christianus.[97] It is unlikely that many people remained in ignorance of the details of Becket's misadventures, when his assassination was such a *cause célèbre*. The *S* version of the *Alexis*, meanwhile, is connected with further vernacular redactions *M* and *Q* (both thirteenth-century) which retain and amplify the incident of the renaming as Cristïen. M^2 665–74 reiterates *S* 795–806 (quoted above), and then adds this scene where Alexis's fiancée asks him his name:

> 'Comment as non, biau frere pelerin?'
> 'Crestiens, dame, ensi le vos plevis.'   (708–9)
>
> ('What is your name, fair brother pilgrim?' 'Christian, lady, I assure you.')

In her note to these lines, Elliott observes that this vignette is more developed in M^1 than M^2 and is taken up again in *Q*.

In the later twelfth and early thirteenth centuries there was, then, a reasonably substantial and influential body of texts which would support the idea that the name Crestïen was a form of saintly incognito or 'anonym'. The contexts in which this anonym appears invite comparison with romances of 'Chrétien de Troyes' in which anonymity plays a key role. In particular, the theme of travelling incognito occurs in the *Lancelot* and in

---

[95] S. G. Nichols, 'Amorous Imitation. Bakhtin, Augustine, and *Le Roman d'Enéas*', in *Romance. Generic Transformation from Chrétien de Troyes to Cervantes*, ed. K. Brownlee and M. S. Brownlee (Hanover and London, 1985), pp. 47–73 (p. 57).

[96] See Adgar, *Le Gracial*, ed. P. Kunstmann (Ottawa, 1982), nos. XIV, XXXVIII, XL, XLIV, XLV.

[97] See E. Walberg, *La Vie de Saint Thomas le Martyr par Guernes de Pont Sainte-Maxence* (Lund, 1922), Introduction, p. lxxix. The chroniclers in question are Roger de Pontigny, Herbert of Bosham and Gervase of Canterbury. The motif is not found in the other vernacular lives of Becket, however.

Yvain, as well as episodically in *Cligés*. Indeed, a play with anonymity informs the conventions of romance-writing generally, not only in the works we ascribe to 'Chrétien' but also in *Li Biaus Desconnëus, Ipomedon*, and *Partonopeu*. These connections between romances and saints' lives are only now beginning to be explored. How 'Christian' they all are has yet to be evaluated, but it seems to me that 'Christian' conventions form an important part of the interpretative grid through which they would be read.

4. 'Crestïen' and Authorship in the Later Twelfth Century

It is not just the characters of twelfth-century texts who are anonymous. The authors are so too for the most part. The ones most securely identified are chroniclers. The *chansonniers* of troubadour and trouvère songs are eager to attribute songs, but frequently disagree on who the authors are. Rubrics prefacing narrative works usually introduce them by their subject matter (*ci commence du* . . .) not author, but some romances, and pious texts like saints' lives, include an inscribed author figure. When they do, it is striking how names recur, or, to put it another way, how few names there are. Thus, in addition to the handfuls of texts signed by or attributed to a Wace, a Crestïen, or a Marie, we have three Thomases (*Tristan, Horn,* and *Alexander*), two Berouls (*Tristan* and a *Patrick's Purgatory*),[98] and some number of Beneits (authors of lives of saints Brendan, Eustace, and Becket, as well as of the *Roman de Troie* and the *Chronique des ducs de Normandie*). It is presumed that at least some of these last were so called because they were Benedictines.[99] That being so, perhaps the name 'Crestïen' signals a less narrow adhesion, a belonging to the Christian community that comprised both clergy and laity. The name 'Marie', in that case, might be the female equivalent of 'Crestïen'. As 'anonyms', they would mark a staging post between complete authorial anonymity and a historically identifiable signature. This is not to suggest that an author using an 'anonym' would be literally unknown to his audience, of course, but that a part of his self-presentation as an author would be the assumption of a position bordering on anonymity.[100]

I have elsewhere elaborated the idea that 'courtly literature' and the

---

[98] Owen, *Visions of Hell*, pp. 66–9.
[99] Benedeit, *The Anglo-Norman Voyage of St Brendan*, ed. I. Short and B. Merrilees (Manchester, 1979), Introduction, p. 5: 'It is quite possible that the title [*danz*] refers to a Benedictine monk.' The Beneit responsible for a tail-rhymed life of Becket was, for his part, a monk of the Benedictine foundation at St Albans. A third(?) hagiographer named Beneit is the author of the Eustace fragment referred to earlier. Benoît de Sainte-Maure identifies himself as a cleric, but not as a monk.
[100] Foucault in the essay cited seems to me to be overly confined within the author-function he is analysing when he assumes that anonymity and the author-function are

discourse of 'courtly love' arose in an atmosphere of repressed conflict between the clerical and lay members of aristocratic courts, and that the pervasive irony and euphemism of 'courtly love' poetry were a means of negotiating and palliating tension.[101] Viewed in this context, the sobriquets chosen by troubadours are typically self-deprecating and disarming. The names 'Crestïen' and 'Marie', though more self-consciously elevated, may likewise be intended to forestall conflict, since they would be rallying points for both laymen and clerks. Such names may be an implicit reproof to the clerical factionalism of the 'Benedicts'. Perhaps, then, we should envisage the existence of a 'generalist' school of writing (with authors styling themselves 'Crestïen' or 'Marie') as opposed to to more 'particularist' groups (Benedicts) or individualists (?Beroul).

A striking feature of the texts in the 'Crestïen' camp is the many echoes between them. Previous scholarship, bent on establishing the corpus of 'Chrétien de Troyes', has been little interested in the relations among themselves of the non-canonical texts. Putting them in the foreground as I have done here brings out the similarities between them. I summarise here from section II of this paper:

(i) The *Nicodemus* echoes or is echoed by *La Mule sans frein*.

(ii) The claims made by the narrators of *Guillaume* and *Nicodemus* about their metrical command are similar (see note 46), and they treat the theme of 'low is high' in a similar way.

(iii) *Guillaume d'Angleterre* and *Philomena* share the theme of the eucharistic sacrifice.

(iv) Descriptions in *Guillaume* resemble those of 'Godefroi de Lagny'.

(v) The rebuttal of 'pagan' passion and enjoining of restraint in the lyric *D'Amors qui m'a tolu a moi* recalls the parti-pris of *Philomena*.

If – as seems likely – these texts are not all by the same man (whether or not we call him 'Chrétien de Troyes'), then why do they share these common features? Was there a concerted effort of imitation by a larger or smaller group of writers? And why do they all use the same name?

Holden suggests that the author of *Guillaume d'Angleterre* sought to appropriate the name and fame of 'Chrétien de Troyes'.[102] Linda Gowans goes further down the same road, suggesting that he used the name in order

---

incompatible. In much medieval poetry, anonymity is precisely a constituent of the author-function.

[101] S. Kay, 'The Contradictions of the Courtly Lyric and the Origins of Courtly Love: The Evidence of the *lauzengier*', *The Journal of Medieval and Early Modern Studies* 26 (1996), 209–53.

[102] *Guillaume d'Angleterre*, Introduction, p. 35.

to satirize the famous romancier.[103] Given my view that 'Crestïen' is less a pseudonym than an 'anonym', I think this unlikely. On my reading of the name, it does not offer the basis for a personal attack. A more fruitful hypothesis may be that 'Crestïen' functions like a reciprocal *senhal* among the troubadours, a signal of friendship and participation in poetic exchange.[104] The presence of similar material in the various works signed 'Crestïen' could be seen as resulting, then, not from common authorship but from allusion or citation. The practice of reciprocal *senhals* suggests a willingness to forego individual identity for the sake of solidarity or group identity. Sharing the name 'Crestïen' might represent the elevation of such solidarity into an ideal of Christian brotherhood which it would be difficult for other poets to surpass: a kind of *nec plus ultra* of reciprocal *senhals*.

We might then consider whether the shared patterns which have always been discerned in the canonical romances might also be perceived as arising from mutual imitation between poets using the same *senhal*. For instance, could the Crestïen of *Yvain* be in debate with the Crestïen of *Erec*, which is, after all, the only narrative work ascribing itself to a Crestïen de Troie? Or could the Crestïen of the *Lancelot* be in dialogue with the Crestïen of *Cligés*, and/or with the Crestïen of *Yvain*? The *Lancelot* has long been seen as a text in debate with itself, given its apparent inscription of two different authors. In recent years the view has been aired that the 'Godefroiz de Leigni' of the epilogue is an alias adopted by 'Chrétien de Troyes' in order to provide an 'author function' for one strand in this debate.[105] If indeed the two names are co-referent, then I would propose that it is 'Godefroi' which identifies a historical figure and that 'Crestïen', which is so much the more likely of the two names to be a *senhal*, is his alias or anonym. If Marie de Champagne's court recognised 'Crestïen' as the *nom de plume* of a figure they knew in daily life as 'Godefroi', then Godefroi's assertion that he worked not in competition with Crestïen but with his full support (7104–7) would have raised a smile.

This paper assumes that the name 'Crestïen' acts as a description as well as a proper name, and argues that all of the texts which bear it as a signature or attribution can be referred to some understanding of what it means to be 'Christian'. This understanding will vary from one text to another, and from one reader to another. The suggestions advanced here should not be taken

---

103 '*Guillaume d'Angleterre*: Prologue and Authorship'.
104 S. Stronski, 'Les Pseudonymes réciproques', *Annales du Midi* 25 (1913), 288–97; more recently, see W. E. Burgwinkle, *Razos and Troubadours Songs* (New York, 1990), p. xxviii.
105 D. Hult, 'Author/Narrator/Speaker: The Voice of Authority in Chrétien's *Charrete*', in *Discourses of Authority in Medieval and Renaissance Literature*, ed. K. Brownlee and W. Stephens (Hanover, 1989), pp. 85–95.

as justifying an orthodox Christian interpretation of any of these works, such as those advanced by D. W. Robertson or Jacques Ribard. At most, I provide a context for readings such as theirs. Establishing the 'Christian' as a reference point for interpretation opens up a range of options from the devout to the sacriligious. The inversion of 'Crestïen' as 'Païen' – if such it is – suggests that medieval readers were ready to read the name ironically. Did some audiences of the canonical romances think their author was 'Christian' in embracing so many of the aspects of human life? Did they rather think that – in the words of yet another contemporary to invoke the topos of 'le nom crestïen' – he was a Christian in name alone?

> De sul le nun ert crestiens.
> S'il servi Deu, le glorius,
> pur quei fud il dunc orguillus?
> Se il servi le autur de chasteé,
> pur quei fud il dunc si desvé
> entur femmes, entur folie?   (*Le Gracial*, XVII, 118–23)

(He was Christian in name alone. If he served the God of glory, why was he so arrogant? If he served the author of chastity, why was he so mindless about women and about foolish behaviour?)

In a society where heretical beliefs were a burning matter, and where the stakes – so to speak – were high, the invocation of Christianity might serve as a cover for all sorts of ideas, and the use of a self-effacing 'anonym' dispense from all sorts of reponsibility. Conversely, invoking what one flouts might be seen as courting disaster. We cannot know. *A fortiori*, then, we cannot answer the question, 'Who was Chrétien de Troyes?' By speculating so brazenly on this subject, however, I hope to have drawn attention to the role of conjecture in what now tends to pass for historical fact and, to paraphrase Scripture, where there was light, to have shed some darkness.

II

IRONY AND GENDER PERFORMANCE IN
LE CHEVALIER DE LA CHARRETE

Nick Corbyn

I wish to intervene in the debate as to what Lancelot represents, to suggest how he is a key figure in medieval literature, and, obliquely, why he might be such a contentious and enduring object of critical debate. Against those critics in the past such as Topsfield[1] and, more recently, Bruckner[2] who have argued that Lancelot represents a new model of improved knighthood, I shall argue that Lancelot is a figure for a subjectivity in crisis and for a crisis of subjectivity. Bruckner, for example, argues that Lancelot embodies a new concept of *chevalerie*, a reconciliation of the competing demands of love and prowess.[3] I shall contend that this and other such arguments are flawed on two accounts. Firstly, because they run counter to the ironic textual presentation of Lancelot's subjectivity;[4] and, secondly, because such views rely on a substantive notion of subjectivity, a notion which the text can also be seen to trouble. Basing my argument on close textual reading, I shall

---

[1] 'The truly devoted *fis amaire*, humble, obedient, courageous, is finally so purified of self-love that he personifies the Goodness for which he fights symbolically against Meleagant.' L. T. Topsfield, *Chrétien de Troyes* (Cambridge, 1981), p. 112.
[2] M. Bruckner, *Shaping Romance* (Philadelphia, 1993), pp. 94–108.
[3] Bruckner, *Shaping Romance*, p. 95
[4] For 'ironic' readings of the *Charrete* as an indictment of adultery and 'courtly love' see: E. Baumgartner, *Chrétien de Troyes: Yvain, Lancelot, la charrete et le lion* (Paris, 1982), pp. 80–81; R. W. Hanning, *The Individual in Twelfth-Century Romance* (New Haven and London, 1977), pp. 228–33; P. Haidu, *Aesthetic Distance in Chrétien de Troyes: Irony and Comedy in Cligès and Perceval* (Geneva, 1968), pp. 10 and 160, n. 119; P. S. Noble, *Love and Marriage in Chrétien de Troyes* (Cardiff, 1982), pp. 65–69; D. D. R. Owen, 'Profanity and its purpose in Chrétien's *Cligès* and *Lancelot*', *FMLS* 6 (1970), 37–48; D. J. Shirt, 'Chrétien and the cart', in *Studies in Medieval Literature and Languages in Memory of Frederick Whitehead*, ed. W. Rothwell, W. R. J. Barron, D. Blamires and L. Thorpe (Manchester and New York, 1973), pp. 279–301; R. H. Thomson, 'The prison of the senses: *fin'amor* as a confining force in the Arthurian romances of Chrétien de Troyes', *FMLS* 15 (1979), 249–54.

analyze the ironic presentation of Lancelot as founded upon a split in his subjectivity. I shall then proceed to argue, using Judith Butler's idea of performance, that these internal contradictions are not unfortunate mishaps that befall a stable and preexistent subject, to be synthesized into a new concept of *chevalerie*, but that they are precisely constitutive of his subjectivity. That is, the conflicting demands made upon Lancelot as a knight within the text, demands which are deployed to ironic effect, are also to be seen as a playing out of the inessential nature of subjectivity itself.

There are three main assumptions underlying this essay. Firstly, that ideology is fundamental to any notion of the subject and its formation. Secondly, that an ideological tension between *clergie* and *chevalerie* is fundamental to a reading of romance.[5] Thirdly, that this ideological tension relates to an opposition between *chevalerie* and *clergie*, best understood as different discursive strategies for dealing with the world, and is intimately bound up with subjectivity. That there was tension between knights and clerics is undoubted, the most famous example being the struggle between Henry II and Beckett. However, the appeal of understanding *chevalerie* and *clergie* as discursive strategies, rather than as categories representing classes, is twofold. On the one hand class alone provides an unsatisfactory basis for the analysis of the tension because high-ranking clerics were often from the same families as knights, and therefore in theory just as aristocratic.[6] On the other hand, viewing *chevalerie* and *clergie* as discursive strategies allows of a more nuanced and productive analysis, capable of accounting for the position of a cleric who, as a producer of romance, however critical his stance, is by definition fully participant in courtly cultures, and for the position of the knight in a romance who deploys it and benefits from it.[7]

However, if romance represents clerics talking about knights, it seems reasonable that the way the former talk about the latter in a text might reflect in some way the relation between them outside the text. I would therefore

---

[5] See S. B. Gaunt, *Gender and Genre in Medieval French Literature* (Cambridge, 1995), pp. 71–121. The second assumption is drawn from Gaunt, although he uses it as a springboard to analyze the gender constructions underlying *chevalerie* and *clergie*, while I am focusing on a more general critique of the notion of the subject itself. For different views on what constitutes the core of romance fictionality, see Bruckner; and D. Maddox, *The Arthurian Romances of Chrétien de Troyes. Once and Future Fictions* (Cambridge, 1991), pp. 35–53. Bruckner sees repetition as the core of fictionality, while for Maddox it is customal intrigue, where Chrétien's romances are seen to play out the claims of competing medieval customs.

[6] As social categories *chevalerie* and *clergie* were not discrete since individuals passed back and forth between them, and individuals in religious orders inevitably began their lives in secular society.

[7] For an example of a knight who uses *clergie* discursively, see *Flamenca*, 1416–21 and 1795–1800. I am grateful to Simon Gaunt for discussing this point with me.

contend that textual irony in the *Charrete* performs precisely this function. That is, the ideological tension between *chevalerie* and *clergie* outside the text finds its representation inside the text in the systematic ironization of the knight protagonist, Lancelot.[8]

If this seems relatively straightforward, things begin to become more interesting when we consider exactly how this ironic function operates, how Chrétien ironizes Lancelot. As a story about a knight, Lancelot, the *Charrete* can be seen as a meditation on the interrelation of *chevalerie* with the world.[9] The *Charrete* has two narrative threads: the chivalric, Lancelot's dispute with Méléagant and his struggles to rescue the Queen and the people of Logres; and the amorous, his pursuit of Guenevere. That is, if one will, the doctrine of *chevalerie* is exercised in two different ways in the world, ways which can be summarized as follows. *Chevalerie* at its simplest means the ability to fight well. In the realm of sex relations, conventionally the best warrior knight becomes the best catch, a fight for the right to a night, as it were, an assumption exemplified by the ladies who organize the tournament of Nouaz. It is this version of *chevalerie* and therefore knightly identity, following the first assumption, which is at stake in the chivalric quest. In contradistinction to this, *Amors* is apparently an agenda set by women. The virtue of the lover is not how deftly he wields a lance but the sincerity and loyalty of his service to his lady.[10] It is this version of *chevalerie* and knightly identity which is at stake in Lancelot's amorous pursuit of Guenevere. Thus *chevalerie* reveals different things in different contexts. Knightly identity appears to be a moving target. In this regard the cart scene (vv. 320–77) is crucial, for in it the shifting values of *chevalerie* come quickly to an unambiguous head. As Lancelot hesitates in front of the

---

[8] For a reading that relies on the union of cleric and knight in both class and desire, see R. Krueger, *Women Readers and the Ideology of Gender in Old French Verse Romance* (Cambridge, 1993). Her reading of the often self-conscious displacement of female desire within romance, including the *Charrete*, is conducted against a background of unitary male desire. Bruckner in her tripartite reading between intra-, extra-, and intertext, also relies on the union between *chevalerie* and *clergie* in the mirroring she detects between intra- and extratext (narrative and frame).

[9] *Le Chevalier de la Charrete*, ed. C. Méla (Paris, 1992). All subsequent references to this edition will be given in the text. English translations are from *Chrétien de Troyes: Arthurian Romances*, trans. D. D. R. Owen (London, 1987)

[10] I say apparently because while *Amors* could be seen to sanction female subjectivity, to set an agenda which men and especially Lancelot struggle to understand, it could equally be said that the *Amors* agenda is men doing what men think women want, the penis eye view, given that it is men who produce the texts and the problematic nature of courtly love in other romance texts. But this is a moot point in the current context of the enabling moment of the text. Whether the courtly love code is actually or only apparently set by women does not preclude the possibility of incontrovertible contradiction of the chivalric code by the courtly love code. Krueger (p. 61) describes this process but sees it as part of a subsequent problematization of this mystification through its overt textual visibility.

cart he is faced with a choice between the chivalric and the amorous versions of *chevalerie*. His love service to Guenevere demands that he mount the cart, while his status as fighting knight requires him to do no such thing. To mount the cart is, in knightly terms, an act beyond the pale. As the felon's mode of transport, the death cart as Topsfield terms it, it taints him as a chivalric pariah and irrevocably undermines his status as a knight. So from the point of view of the role of ideology in identity, the cart, in opposing chivalric *chevalerie* to the amorous, represents a crisis in Lancelot's subjectivity.

This point has been a springboard for the positive readings of Lancelot. For Topsfield, mounting the cart is a break with the formal, courtly limitations of Arthur's world, and, possibly, of his audience. Gauvain refuses to mount the cart because he believes in the appearance of prestige which is *vaine gloire*, related only to the convention of Arthur's court. Lancelot, in contrast, reveals himself in mounting the cart as a person guided by a higher purpose and a virtue other than that of Arthur's court. It is a sign of his humility, of self-knowledge apart from courtly society. The text bears Lancelot out, for Gauvain is unequal to the task at hand, while it is Lancelot alone who in his devotion to his Lady is able to rescue her and free the prisoners. Bruckner, too, sees love as the force that leads Lancelot to his greatest triumphs, and Lancelot himself as the superior norm, showing up as flawed the value system that judges negatively such a successful figure. Indeed, if one isolates his achievements it is difficult to view Lancelot as other than a hero: he rescues the Queen; he frees the prisoners; he defeats Méléagant; and he shows up the limitations of Kex, Gauvain and Arthur.

Yet while clearly advanced as such by the text on one level, on another level it is just this heroic figure that Chrétien's narrative is designed to unseat. The cart incident also allows us to glimpse the basis of the text's ironic function. The combination of the two narrative threads, amorous and chivalric, pulls *chevalerie* into a fateful contradiction. Stepping on the cart sets the text in motion because it pulls the chivalric rug out from under Lancelot's feet. To mount the cart is apparently to be faithful to *Amors*, but in chivalric terms such an act taints Lancelot as a knightly pariah, an abject state, I shall argue, from which he spends the rest of the text trying to recover. A process of recovery which provides Chrétien with manifold opportunities to ironize Lancelot.

However, if the basis of Chrétien's irony is the disjunction in *chevalerie* between its chivalric and amorous functions, and if this is to be read as indicative of a constructed subjectivity in crisis, why then is the debate at this pivotal moment one between *Amors* and *raison*? *Raison*, which means 'speech' as well as 'mind' and is explicitly stated to reside in the mouth in Lancelot's speech, is a clerical quality and not a knightly one, usually associated with *clergie* and not *chevalerie*. I would suggest, however, that it is made to do service on behalf of the chivalric formulation of *chevalerie* against the amorous, as represented here by *Amors*. In other words, *clergie* is being employed chivalrously. This use of *clergie* to be chivalrous, as it were, adds a second dimension to the conflicting pulls exerted on *chevalerie* in its encounter with *Amors*.[11] For not only is the knight damned for getting it wrong and obeying *Amors* but he is lampooned in the narrator's eyes for the way he gets it wrong, namely by trying to reason like a cleric. Perhaps this is precisely why Lancelot mounts the cart, because he tries to think clerically. This emerges as a consistent source of irony for generally when Lancelot sticks to action, traditional (chivalric) knightly virtue, he is borne out by the text as efficacious, but, as this example can show, any attempt to engage with thought is met with dire results. Another example of this is the duel at the ford into which Lancelot blunders through such committed endeavour to thought that he comically fails to hear the challenge issued.

To return now to the opprobrium of the cart, the reader is left in no doubt as to the shame of Lancelot's actions.[12] Interestingly enough, Lancelot seems remarkably blind to the implications of the cart; at least no direct questioning of or regret for his decision is ever attributed to him and it is left to the other characters' reactions to mark the shame of the cart. The lady who first offers Gauvain and Lancelot a bed for the night is dismissive of the knight, who in her opinion is forever shamed for having mounted the cart (vv. 484–7). The courtiers busily playing on the meadow where Lancelot will (not) dispute his lady companion against her young admirer censure themselves from continuing in his presence. But the clearest-cut condemnation of the cart comes from the mystery knight whose head will subsequently be presented to Méléagant's sister:

>   Tu? Tu? Comant tu l'osas panser?
>   Einz te deüsses apanser   2590
>   Que tu anpreïsses tel chose
>   A quel fin et a quel parclose
>   Tu an porroies parvenir,
>   Si te deüst resovenir
>   De la charrete ou tu montas.   2595
>
> (You? You? How did you dare think of it? Before undertaking such a thing, you should consider how you might finish and end up; and you should remember the cart into which you climbed.)

This neatly points out the extent to which Lancelot's knightly status is

---

[11] It might also provide an interesting example of the discursive use of *clergie*.
[12] Once again, Bruckner's reading is very different; see footnote 13 for a summary of the differences.

undercut by the cart and how as a result his very ability even to undertake the subsequent rescue of the Queen is brought into question. The two narrative strands and associated character values are intimately linked and to undermine one is to question the very possibility of the other. After all, what queen wants to be loved by a knight with the social status of a convicted felon? But the same defeated knight puts the situation in even more explicit terms, saying that he would rather die than mount the cart (vv. 2774-6).

If the disjunction between the amorous and chivalric values of *chevalerie* is the key ironic structuring potential, set in motion by mounting the cart, then the examples above raise interesting questions which I believe can be resolved by drawing together earlier references to the protagonists' inability to think and positing a second key ironic device, namely that of their lack of self-consciousness and comprehension of the issues at stake. For logically by the terms of my argument and as the quotation and reference above show, following the edicts of *Amors* can undercut a knight's status so completely as to preempt any successful status as a courtly lover. However Guenevere's action at Nouaz seems specifically to contradict this in that she wants Lancelot to humiliate himself for her. The reason, I believe, for this contradiction lies in Guenevere's inconsistency in this regard. At her first encounter with Lancelot she completely snubs him. She later tells herself that this was madness and that she did it for a joke. She then tells him that it was because of the cart, implying that she wants his knightly virtue/status intact, and then at Nouaz she demands that he humiliate himself. Such inconsistency seems to imply an inability to grasp the terms of the debate or even a lack of awareness of the debate in the first place. It is interesting to note that, while the text focuses on Lancelot's subjectivity, the Queen as other in his amorous persona becomes implicated in the ensuing irony, that is, as soon as she cares about Lancelot as both knight and love servant she falls prey to similar irony.[13]

Lancelot himself appears in a similar light. After his attempted suicide Lancelot berates the Fates for his ill fortune, betraying as he does so an apparent inability to grasp the conflicting claims of the chivalric and the amorous. The monologue starting at line 4318 and lasting some seventy-eight lines is by far Lancelot's longest and contains a diversity of conflicting positions. He initially berates Death for her failure to accept him after his

---

[13] Compare Krueger who argues (p. 61) that this treatment of Guenevere works to trivialize her responses, but reads this in the context of a narrative that calls attention to such displacements as part of the problematization of female desire, its inscription as an issue within medieval discourse. Compare also Bruckner (p. 78) who reads Guenevere's contradictory answers as part of a process of repetition and variation, by which standards her responses at the tournament reveal her to have learnt the virtue of delay, so conspicuously lacking in these hasty exchanges.

inept suicide bid (vv. 4336–41). Death, to which we shall return later, is a necessary consequence of Guenevere's snub for which he admits there must have been some adequate reason although he does not know what it is. Then a couple of lines later on, almost as an afterthought, he adds:

> Bien cuit que espoir ele sot   4348
> Que je montai sor la charrete.
>
> (I think she perhaps knew I climbed into the cart.)

So it seems he does after all have some inkling of why it might be that Guenevere paled at the sight of him. There then follows a lengthy and impassioned invocation of *Amors* as the authority by which to judge his actions, an authority by which it is impossible to do wrong. The invocation becomes ever more heightened until it is claimed that *Amors* should welcome all faithful actions, including mounting the cart. This second admission of the cart as cause is followed by an acknowledgement of the calumny he has heaped on himself. 'Ce geu dom an me blasme', is how he describes the cart after making reference to the 'honte et reproche et blasme'. But the repeated invocation of *Amors* and denigration of those who criticize him as 'cez qui d'amor rien ne sevent' leaves one with the impression that whilst, after all, he may not be oblivious to the reactions of those around him, he cannot be said to give any indication of comprehension of the disjunction between *Amors* and chivalric *chevalerie*. Indeed one can see the narrative as Lancelot's unconscious in this regard, conveying what the hero cannot about himself. As I have said, Lancelot struggles to a dim awareness of the implications of the cart while the narrative repeatedly marks its shame.

Thus the ideological tension outside the text between *clergie* and *chevalerie* is transformed into a space within the text between the protagonist and the narrative, between the chivalric and amorous values of *chevalerie*. A corollary of this is that male obeys female and begets irony.[14] In fact Chrétien even alerts us to the potential deployment of this irony by promoting the contrast between his relationship to his patron Marie de

---

[14] See Bruckner for a diametrically opposed interpretation: 'there is total synchrony (at least until the night of love) between Lancelot's service on behalf of the Queen and his role as liberator for the citizens of Logres' (p. 95). As stated in footnote 8, by equating cleric with knight, Bruckner is able to read the frame as mirroring the narrative. Then, by reading against the intertext of the Tristan, love and chivalry are seen to be harmonious where they are at odds. Lancelot still functions to show up the competing demands of different value systems (p. 101), but any such tension left unresolved by appeal to the intertext is swept up by her reading of romance as open-ended, as being precisely about the fact of those competing value systems per se, not their resolution, whereas I have attempted an interpretation of one such conflict.

Champagne and that of Lancelot to Guenevere. Two passages in particular at the start and towards the end of the text echo the Prologue. As Lancelot hesitates in front of the cart,

> Mes Reisons, qui d'Amors se part,   365
> Li dit que del monter se gart,
> Si le chastie et si l'anseigne
> Que rien ne face ne *anpreigne*
> Dom il ait honte ne reproche.

> (But Reason, who is at odds with Love, tells him to avoid getting in, warning and instructing him to do and engage in nothing that might bring him shame or reproach.)

The use of *anpreigne* so soon after the Prologue recalls a similar use in line 2. If one accepts the parallel the implication is clear. Lancelot is exhorted by Reason not to undertake any shaming act as Chrétien is exhorted by Marie to undertake the telling of this story, the difference being that Chrétien will avoid the ignominy of submitting entirely to the *sen* and *matiere* of his lady by ironizing Lancelot's progress whilst Lancelot himself will cover himself in shame and ignominy by obeying explicitly Love's exhortations. Much later on during the tournament of Noauz when Guenevere sends word to Lancelot to do his worst, his reply is described in the following terms,

> Si li dit que molt volontiers,   5656
> Com cil qui est *suens antiers*.

> (Hearing this, he replies 'Very willingly!' in the manner of someone who is entirely hers.)

As numerous critics have noted, this description of Lancelot as entirely at the command of his lady is exactly that used by Chrétien about himself in relation to Marie de Champagne.[15] If we compare the subsequent derision with which Lancelot's behaviour is greeted with Chrétien's ability to slip his narrative bonds on a structural level in the writing out of the text of Marie by the time of the Epilogue, and the replacement of the male-female dyad (Chrétien/Marie) with a male-male dyad (Chrétien/Godefroi), then the implication may be clear: that Lancelot in his often uncomprehending and slavish devotion to Lady Love is a hostage to fortune while Chrétien the cleric is master of his own fate.[16]

---

[15] This has been pointed out by numerous critics, see Bruckner (p. 84), Krueger (p. 62) and D. Hult, 'Author/Narrator/Speaker', in *Discourses of Authority in Medieval and Renaissance Literature*, ed. K. Brownlee and W. Stephens (Hanover, 1989), pp. 76–96 (p. 90).

[16] The significance of the male-male bond is forcefully stated by Gaunt. For him it is one

This completes the analysis of the ironic function so endemic to the *Charrete*. The following conclusions about irony in the text emerge. The first strand is the split in Lancelot's subjectivity due to the competing demands of amorous and chivalric *chevalerie* as crystallized in the cart scene. The second is the hero's (and heroine's) lack of awareness of the problem he (she) faces, a vague awareness that something is wrong and that something needs to be done but an inability to pinpoint exactly what it is or what he has done wrong. The third is the contrast drawn by Chrétien between his relation to Marie in the frame and Lancelot's to Guenevere in the narrative. But if the key ironic function is a subjectivity in crisis, how is it that this might be read as a crisis of subjectivity, as a playing out of the constructed nature of the subject? The answers, I believe, are to be found in Judith Butler's theory of performance, as advanced in *Gender Trouble*.[17]

The main thrust of Butler's book can be seen as an answer to her own question, 'To what extent do regulatory practices of gender formation and division constitute identity, the internal coherence of the subject, indeed, the self-identical status of the person?' (p. 16). Butler argues, through Nietzsche and Foucault, that gender identity is never the innocent given, the essential foundation that it has historically been taken to be. This means that the supposed facts of existence, of a sexed subject, born male or female, a subject preexistent at some basic level, however infinitesimal, to the cultural meaning of gender, of masculine or feminine, subsequently assigned to it, is a reification, the arbitrary and fictitious posing as the natural and essential. If gender has, since de Beauvoir, been acknowledged as a cultural construction, here for Butler sex is always already gender.[18] Moreover, gender, as one key discourse among many in the formation of identity, is a social construct and effect of signifying systems which masks the power relations inherent in its (gender's) production, by posing as the inevitable constellation of discrete and precultural givens.

The invocation of power will make it obvious that the ways in which this process occurs are far from arbitrary. Gender as it follows (or not) from sex serves to instantiate, enforce and naturalize an arbitrary binary classification

---

of many instances which reveal the real hero of Chrétien's romances as the clerical narrator (p. 100). See also Krueger (pp. 34–66) and Hult, 'Author/Narrator/Speaker'. For Krueger, the visible male bond both mystifies women by writing them out of the text and demystifies them in its self-consciousness by calling attention to that very process, thereby inscribing female desire as a problematic issue within romance discourse. Hult's position is given in footnote 24.

[17] J. Butler, *Gender Trouble* (New York, 1990).

[18] Gender as it is used by Butler and in this exposition thus takes on a far more sweeping function than mere cultural inscription, the 'cooking' of the 'raw'. It designates the very process of subject formation via insertion into power relations.

of male and female which has as its goal a matrix of compulsory heterosexuality.

The pervasiveness and all-encompassing nature of this construction is repeatedly emphasized by Butler. This is a genealogical critique of the very formation of the subject, for these processes of gender formation thus critiqued span and delimit the very meaning of the 'human'. The fact of being is always already a being in power relations, relations that serve compulsory heterosexuality. The concept of the natural is then seen to be a regulatory device, enabling those subject formations which fail to conform to the model prescribed by compulsory heterosexuality to be designated unnatural.

But if the illusion of the sexed and gendered self is an effect of an historically contingent and specific set of power relations that naturalizes itself through the illusion of a natural and developmental teleology, then the self, that bedrock of the classical liberal and existential model of freedom, is therefore seen to be performative. That is, the self in no way predates the acts that constitute it in accordance with this regulatory framework. The self comes into being through the very acts that it is said to preexist and thus comes to have meaning in time.

It is Butler's great insight to pursue the implications of the subject as a signified, as the result of signifying practices, and of the repeated approximation of gender coherence. At one stroke the radical decentering of the subject implied by the theory of performance that would preclude any conventional notion of agency provides the ground for the subversion of this determinist vision:

> The subject is not determined by the rules through which it is generated because signification is not a founding act, but rather a regulated process of repetition that both conceals itself and enforces its rules precisely through the production of substantializing effects. [...] 'agency,' then, takes place within the possibility of a variation on that repetition.   (p. 145)

For Butler the proliferation of identity categories and practices such as camp and drag that do not conform to the fiction of gender coherence expose that fictionality by displaying the utterly inessential link between physical anatomy (let alone the inessential grid of anatomy itself), gender, sexual orientation and object, resignifying the very notion of identity, hitherto based on the discrete binary opposition of male and female, such that identity might very well be said no longer to exist as a category.[19] This is a

[19] The notion of consciousness or agency seems to be Butler's source of trouble in her own theory. For Butler to argue that there is no stepping outside the system which creates us and that therefore the only viable source of action against oppression is a redeployment of those systems leaves her ambiguously dependent upon a concept of conscious volition

radical move for it enables those subject formations which, as I said above, fail to conform to the model prescribed by compulsory heterosexuality to be seen as no different to the hegemonic heterosexual, performative and signified as both are. This is the possibility of agency, of variation on that repetition. It therefore becomes possible to resignify the homosexual as anything other than unnatural, and the heterosexual as anything other than natural and essential, because both formations are ontologically indistinct.

The three aspects of Butler's thought most relevant to the discussion of irony in the *Charrete* and which enable a subjectivity in crisis to be seen as a crisis of subjectivity are as follows: firstly, subjectivity is performative. The subject comes to have meaning in time and does not preexist the acts which then form it. Crucially, the ways in which subjectivity is performed are regulated such that some formations and acts are acceptable and some are not. Compulsory heterosexuality is one key regulatory discourse which wields binaries such as natural / unnatural, culturally intelligible / unintelligible to enforce its strictures. Secondly, the pervasiveness of the power relations of compulsory heterosexuality ensures that this coding of performed identity as natural / unnatural, failed / successful, and so on, is obscured from view, so deeply does it reside at the heart of subjectivity. We abut here against the very limits of the thinkable. The subject is created along the line of binary sex, the body created 'human' accordingly, and gender ensues causally, all in the service of compulsory heterosexuality. Thus to 'fail' to perform accordingly is to be culturally unintelligible, to undermine that very subjectivity. If cultural intelligibility is valued, then acts coded as failure by the hegemony of compulsory heterosexuality invoke a recuperative drive to restore a stable sense of acceptable, natural identity. Finally, the shift to subjectivity as performance and signification enables censured acts and formations to be resignified as indistinct from dominant normative acts and formations. For example, homosexuality is

---

or agency. On the one hand, conscious volition is ruled out as formed and conditioned by, and thus participant in, the very structures it seeks to oppose; yet on the other, Butler seems, logically at any rate, to enlist its support in formulating and deploying these subversive repetitions. If we are to understand subversive repetition as independent of conscious thought and volition, then how can it constitute a viable programme for political action? Without conscious control, does such a programme owe more to probability theory than orchestrated action? What are the chances of enough people repeating subversively? What constitutes enough? And if enough people repeat subversively, in camp or drag, for example, how can we be sure that instead of proliferating identity categories, these subversions do not simply replace existing identity categories? Finally, of what use is such a theory against the monolithic hegemony of compulsory heterosexuality; does it help for someone encountering homophobia to know that, really, they were performing subversively?

often deemed unnatural by hegemonic heterosexuality. If we reinterpret this as performance, then it is a failed performance. But as a failed performance it is still as much repetition (having meaning in time) as successful performances like heterosexuality. With repetition it becomes unfounded to distinguish between failed and successful performances, as all identity, however dominant, becomes an approximation of an absent original.

To return to our earlier question, if the key ironic function is a subjectivity in crisis, how is it that this might be read as a crisis of subjectivity? First of all, Butler allows us to theorize the split between amorous and chivalric *chevalerie* which causes a crisis in Lancelot's subjectivity. She enables us to see the moment at which the contradictions internal to *chevalerie* are revealed, mounting the cart, as a failed performance, as transgressive of a hegemonic identity regime.

If we align *chevalerie* in its chivalric, fighting version with heterosexuality and *chevalerie* as subtended by the doctrine of *Amors* with homosexuality, then Butler's theory of performance allows us to view Lancelot's action in mounting the cart as a failed performance. Lancelot's pursuit of *Amors*, motivated by his private and transgressive desire to sleep with the Queen, is transgressive of his knightly identity in the way that in the terms of Judith Butler's argument homosexuality is transgressive of strictly demarcated heterosexuality.[20]

This equation of transgression bears closer scrutiny. If homosexuality is defined as the desire for someone of the same sex as opposed to someone of the opposite sex, then *Amors* instates an inverse opposition in that it requires Lancelot to submit to the female agenda rather than to the male one of the chivalric code. Clearly one could not literally equate the dominant, normative ideology of the heterosexual with that of the chivalric value of *chevalerie*. The chivalric only applies to a portion of medieval society whereas the heterosexual is specifically constructed to be universal but the effect of transgression within knightly circles is nevertheless quite as damning as in the heterosexual. This is not to equate Lancelot's transgression or lapsed performance with actual homosexuality but rather to point out that his knightly identity is irredeemably damaged by the attraction of *Amors*. In a sense whether he is/ was/ will be in love with Guenevere becomes irrelevant. The key is that in stepping on to the cart he exposes his

---

[20] Within the terms of Butler's theory, homosexuality is fully within the system of compulsory heterosexuality, within the system as its constitutive outside. Homosexuality is a desire both manufactured and prohibited by this system to enforce adhesion to the prescribed mode of being. It follows from this that *Amors* is fully within 'compulsory *chevalerie*'.

knightly status to an irresolvable contradiction, just as the married man would do to his heterosexual status if he were to sleep with a man.

To return to the importance of this for Lancelot within the text, the subject neither experiences itself as performative nor the regulated nature of that performance. Butler is acute about the functioning of compulsory identity regimes that compel compliance and that base cultural intelligibility itself on such adhesion. As far as Lancelot is concerned, riding the cart is a failed performance – Lancelot has shamed himself as a knight – and a performance which must be recuperated, a fact which is betrayed by his acute anxiety to do so.

Thus the grounding conditions of the text, that Lancelot compromises chivalric *chevalerie* with the amorous, exemplified in the mounting of the cart, and that he and Guenevere lack self-awareness, can be read as initiating not only a rich seam of potential irony but also a recuperative drive to restore a lost sense of stable knightly identity. The trauma of mounting the cart can be seen to have a deep effect on Lancelot. His taciturnity, rudeness and quasi-autism as he rides towards the ford with the lady companion resemble the stunned, repressed response of someone who has just suffered a profound shock or loss, the full implications of which he is struggling to come to terms with. He is so withdrawn that he is oblivious to his companion, to the challenge of the knight guarding the ford and this latter's actual attack, until he finds himself on his backside in the water.

Yet it is perhaps the obsession with performance that most marks the *Charrete* as Lancelot pursues the Queen. Note that performance is not being used here in Butler's genealogical sense but rather from the uncritical subject's point of view to denote Lancelot's obsession with how he is perceived. Lancelot betrays a consistent concern less with what he is doing rather than with how he is doing it. For example, in the fight with the guardian of the ford:

> Tant que la bataille a ce monte 865
> Qu'an son cuer en a molt grant honte
> Li chevaliers de la charrete
> Et dit que mal randra la dete
> De la voie qu'il a enprise,
> Quant il si longue piece a mise. 870

> (... until the combat has lasted so long that the knight of the cart feels great shame in his heart, saying he will do scant justice to the expedition he has undertaken when he has needed so long ...)

The shame comes from the time he is taking to despatch the opposition, from the fact that his performance as a knight is not up to standard. The implication is that if he keeps on performing like this, he feels, he will not be successful in his quest to win the Queen and / or salvage his reputation/performance.[21] Similarly in the fight with the mystery knight it is only when Lancelot realizes that the others are looking at him that he feels ashamed. The shame is then linked to a conscious relation to performance and identity and wish to control.

The clearest hint that Lancelot's quest has at least as much to do with the knightly performance of saving the Queen as it does with the Queen herself is given by Bademagu, who assesses Lancelot's ambitions thus:

> Il la doit mialz avoir sanz faille   3240
> Par bataille que par bonté,
> Por ce qu'a pris li ert conté.
> Mien escient, il n'an quiert point
> Por ce que l'an an pes li doint,
> Einz la vialt par bataille avoir.   3245

(He would certainly rather have her through combat than through kindness, because that will enhance his reputation. In my opinion he's seeking her not in order for her to be handed to him peacefully, but in the hope of winning her in combat.)

Perhaps the battle with all the overtones of violent performance it entails is the focus of Lancelot's ambitions. Equally well, in the redemptive nature of Lancelot's performance one can catch more than passing overtones of Charles Méla's comparison of Lancelot with Christ.[22] He crosses the *Pont de l'Espée* with bare hands and feet bleeding profusely and there is repeated equation of suffering and pain with pleasure.[23] It is as if in the act of 'redeeming' his people Lancelot is taking the opportunity to redeem himself of his own 'sins' not in the next life but in this one here and now. The stakes are raised in his attempted suicide and as he berates Death he seems to want to die:

---

[21] For a fascinating philological account of the non-identity of the OF. *avoir honte de* and the Mod. Fr. *avoir honte*, see D. Hult, 'Lancelot's Shame', *Romance Philology* 42 (1988), 30–50. Hult starts with the observation that '*honte* maintains a strong connection with the sort of ethos developed in warrior societies – that is, signifying physical injury or assault as well as the dishonor that results from it'. (p. 32). This coincides with my sense of chivalric *chevalerie* and the use of *honte* to describe Lancelot would thus seem all the more appropriate. His analysis also lends itself to my use of performance: 'The Knight of the Cart is aware that his performance is not what it should be and, naturally, he feels inwardly the sense of his inadequacy . . . But however much he experiences the inadequacy within himself, its cause is the present fight and the distance which Lancelot perceives between his actual performance and what he feels is expected of him.' (p. 35).

[22] See the introduction to the *Charrete* (p. 24).

[23] Compare Topsfield, *Chrétien de Troyes*, p. 143.

> Ce voel je bien qu'il soit tex,   4268
> Et se Deu plest, je an morrai
>
> (I'm very content that it should be so, and please God I shall die of it.)

If Lancelot is in thrall to Thanatos it is perhaps because he realizes that it is in death alone that he can fix his performance.

It will by now be increasingly obvious how, once we read the ironic function through Butler's theory of performance, a subjectivity in crisis becomes grounds for a crisis of subjectivity. The shift by Butler to analyze subjectivity as an effect of signifying practices allows identities which transgress hegemonic norms to be seen as ontologically indistinct from those norms. To consider the cart scene, because its ontological status as repetition is precisely the same as that repetition which performs sanctioned modes of identity, it reveals Lancelot's identity always to have been a 'failed' performance. That is, *chevalerie* in its chivalric incarnation is just as much a performance, an insubstantial approximation of an absent original as the *Amors* value which transgresses it. If we transpose these ideological variants back into the terms of Butler's original argument, the heterosexual is just as much of a performance as the homosexual. The fact that one repetition, the homosexual, is designated a failure, a transgression, is the result of power relations, of the construction of the system in favour of a compulsory heterosexuality. Ontologically, as performance, the two are identical, neither is any less (or more) insubstantial than the other.

It is this aspect of the failed heterosexual, or to retranspose the terms back into medieval textuality, of the failed chivalric *chevalerie* which the existence of the competing value of *chevalerie* signals. Whereas the positive view of Lancelot sees in the competing demands the impetus for a new model of knightly identity, I see the competing demands as figures for an inessential subjectivity; competing models, each jostling to occupy the position of original, to subjugate the other to the role of copy. In fact, as we see from Butler, both are copies.

There are two points I would like to make by way of conclusion. The first concerns what the text tells us about the functioning of hegemonic identity regimes above and beyond the notion of a performed subject; and the second has to do with the relation of inessential subjectivity to the critical debate that continues to swirl around the *Charrete*. I ended the first half of this essay by describing Chrétien's expert self-conscious narrative as it contributed to a third ironic function. We can now come full circle and in turn analyse this as performance, a clerical and an equally problematic one. The clerical narrative performance becomes problematic with the inception of the epilogue and a second clerical voice, that of Godefroi de Leigni. Much has been made of this clerical double act, with opinion divided as to whether Godefroi is historical figure or textual construct. I prefer to see Godefroi as a textual fiction, a device to allow Chrétien to write Marie out of the text.[24] Within the dynamic of the prologue, epilogue and text it is significant, as I have said, that Chrétien starts off in his Lady's service, ridicules Lancelot for his service to women and then writes Marie out of the prologue to form a male-male clerical bond with Godefroi. It is the status of the highly visual male-male bond that is problematic and which threatens to undermine the clerical ironic exercise.

Seen in this light, we can discern three pairings: Chrétien and Marie, in the frame; Lancelot and Guenevere, in the text; and Chrétien and Godefroi, in the frame. My point is that Chrétien slipping out of his bond with Marie is meaningful only in contradistinction to Lancelot's continued eroticized relationship with Guenevere. The self-conscious comparisons drawn by Chrétien are testament enough to this. If the frame dynamics take on a specific meaning in relation to an explicitly eroticized text, then there is, I would contend, at the very least an implicit and oblique eroticization of the frame. One is, I believe, justified in positing an erotics of association between text and frame, such that one erotic dyad of Lancelot and Guenevere parallels another obliquely erotic dyad of Chrétien and Marie.

We must then logically inquire as to the status of the visible homosocial male bond we were left with above. If Chrétien and Marie is an eroticized bond, albeit obliquely, and it is significant, as I have said, that Chrétien replaces this with a homosocial dyad, could this latter also be sexualized, and, if so, what would the implications be thereof? For a view of the latter as always already sexualized, we must turn to Sedgwick. Her theory of male homosocial desire posits a continuum between ' "men-loving-men" ' and ' "men-promoting-the-interests-of-men" ', between the homosexual and the homosocial. For her, the homosocial is always sexualized. This is in no way to say that the homosocial bond between Chrétien and Godefroi is homosexual, rather that the sexual is not something artificially to be hived off and added later like a culinary ingredient. It is always present, but in

---

[24] For a good exposition of these opposing arguments, see Hult, 'Author/Narrator/Speaker' and K. Brownlee, 'Transformations of the *Charrete*', *Stanford French Review* 1 and 2 (1990), 161–78. While Hult argues in favour of seeing Godefroi as Chrétien's textual construct, and Brownlee for Godefroi as an historical figure, it is interesting to note that in either case the main point from which they start is the calling of attention to a break in the text by the epilogue, and that in this respect their arguments are interchangeable. For the record, Hult concludes that the self-conscious break is a clerkly ruse allowing Chrétien to 'fuse the political narrative with the exaltation of the love service' (p. 92), representing the triumph of courtly rhetoric and the poet over the restraint of his *matière*. Brownlee, on the other hand, sees Godefroi as the paradigm of continuation, he who simultaneously continues, rewrites, imitates, and transforms Chrétien's story.

different forms, more or less sublimated and acceptable. The most we would want to say about the bond of Chrétien and Godefroi is that it is homoerotic. But why might such a sexualized bond be problematic? It is problematic because a sexualization of chivalric *chevalerie* can be seen as the basis of Chrétien's ironization of Lancelot. If Chrétien's own clerkly bond is sexualized then it is as potentially transgressive of clerical discourses of homophobia[25] as Lancelot's desire is of chivalric *chevalerie* and Chrétien's bond is exposed to the same ironic dynamic that so undermines Lancelot. Homosocial bonds are not in themselves ironic but they are exposed to this possibility when the sexualization of a discourse is ironically exploited.

Let us weave this into the fabric of the essay as a whole. The main ironic device of the text as I have formulated it lies in the conflicting demands made of *chevalerie* as it is pulled this way and that by its chivalric and amorous values. I have also, following Gaunt, sought to found this irony in an extratextual ideological tension between knight and cleric, between *chevalerie* and *clergie*. While the use of Butler allows one to see *chevalerie* and therefore knightly identity as always failed, its advantage lies in its explication of the cart scene, of how a dominant hegemonic formulation of identity, chivalric *chevalerie*, designates as transgressive any act, here amorous *chevalerie*, which does not meet its strictures. The point in turning the Butlerian spotlight on Chrétien is that, while it reveals *clergie*, like *chevalerie*, like heterosexuality, as an ideological formation to be always failed, it also reveals Chrétien's bond with Godefroi, whether real or phantasmatic, to be potentially similarly transgressive of the hegemonic identity structure of *clergie*. Note that in this regard we do not actually need to know exactly what is or was the hegemonic identity structure of *clergie*, merely that it would preclude any sexualization of male bonds, and that one might reasonably align this to a greater or lesser extent with clerical discourses of homophobia. An offence against the dominant identity category of *chevalerie*, however constructed *chevalerie* itself may be, that so troubles Lancelot, could return to trouble Chrétien in relation to *clergie*, either in his relation to Godefroi or in their relation to the clerical whole.

Thus it is that we come full circle and find Chrétien hoist on his own petard. But at this moment an intriguing thought comes to mind. Is this circularity coincidental or significant, and could it be precisely related to identity as performance? I would like to suggest that the idea of performance and the working of irony within the text allow the *Charrete* to be read as a meditation on the functioning of compulsory identity regimes. I have already observed that it is Lancelot's commitment to the concept of discrete identity categories as manifested in his desire to redeem his knightly status

---

[25] The homophobia of the clerical world was well documented, as exemplified by Alain of Lille's *Complaint of Nature*, almost exactly contemporaneous with the *Charrete*.

that prevents him from doing so, or rather, from approximating 'agency'. One can add that it is a similar commitment to discrete categories which allows Chrétien to ironize Lancelot and which then enables the tables to be turned, and the clerical performance to be ironized. One might therefore see this as paradigmatic of the insidious functioning of compulsory identity regimes, whether of textual *chevalerie* or, reading back to the original theoretical context, compulsory heterosexuality. That is, the ironization of Chrétien illustrates how a subscription to the terms of an identity matrix (the irony at Lancelot's expense only works if one has a stake in discrete identity categories) ensures its survival, for even as Chrétien appears to be in control, it is the matrix that ultimately controls him.

The second and final point to be made by way of conclusion draws on the meta-debate, as it were, as to why opinions are so divided over the *Charrete* and over Lancelot. What, in the light of this essay, might that debate represent? Is it too fanciful a notion that what is at stake in the argument over Lancelot is nothing less than the naturalization of the performative subject? That is, those who see in Lancelot the figure of all things good and improved implicitly unify and harmonize the founding dissonances and disjunctions of subjectivity, and therefore support the mystifying strategies of compulsory identity regimes.

III

A NEW FRAGMENT OF THE *FIRST CONTINUATION* OF THE *PERCEVAL* (LONDON, PRO, E122/100/13B)[1]

Lisa Jefferson

An additional witness, even if fragmentary, to a text known only from two manuscripts must be welcome, and it is thus a pleasure to report an identification of a bifolium containing two sections of the *First Continuation* of the *Perceval* of Chrétien de Troyes, often referred to as the *Continuation-Gauvain*. Its text is that of the 'mixed' redaction as edited by William Roach.[2] The first section is from the episode of the Chastel Orguelleus numbered by Roach as IV, 11, lines 11503–11742; the second contains most of the episode VI, 1 and about half of VI, 2, the episode named after Gauvain's brother Guerrehés, lines 14147–14389.

The chief interest of this new fragment of the *First Continuation* lies in its great similarity to the manuscripts *T* and *V* of this text, recently the subject of a study by Keith Busby.[3] The close relationship between these two manuscripts – Paris, Bibliothèque Nationale, fonds français 12576 (*T*) and Paris, Bibliothèque Nationale, nouvelles acquisitions françaises 6614 (*V*) – has long been recognised, and Busby has recently proposed that the

---

[1] I should like to record at the outset my most grateful thanks to Dr David Howlett who first sent me to see the unidentified fragments at the Public Record Office, and to Dr R. M. Ball who recorded this and other fragments he found in the course of his work at the PRO. (Almost all were fully identified by him, but this and one other French romance, which I have also been able to designate, eluded his efforts.) I thank also all the staff at the PRO in Chancery Lane who have been so helpful, and Mr Mario Aleppo, the Head of Conservation at Kew, who promptly ensured conservation and protection of the manuscript. I thank also Dr Stewart Gregory who generously spared the time to examine the language of this fragment and comment upon it and upon a draft of this article.

[2] *The Continuations of the Old French Perceval of Chretien de Troyes*, 5 vols. (Philadelphia, 1949–83), I: Redaction of MSS *T V D*, pp. 312–18 and 384–91.

[3] K. Busby, 'The scribe of MSS *T* and *V* of Chrétien's *Perceval* and its *Continuations*', in *Les Manuscrits de Chrétien de Troyes / The Manuscripts of Chrétien de Troyes*, ed. K. Busby et al., 2 vols. (Amsterdam, 1993), I, 49–65.

same scribe worked on both. He discusses the valuable insight into scribal methods provided by this identification, particularly the degree of freedom from an exemplar felt permissible. The new PRO fragment would seem without any doubt to have come from a third manuscript made at the same time as *T* and *V*, the second half of the thirteenth century, and in the same workshop or scriptorium, displaying the same Picard (Pas de Calais) colouration of language, and it was written, I believe, by the same scribe as that identified by Busby as a second hand in manuscript *T*.

Full details of manuscripts *T* and *V* are given by Terry Nixon in his 1993 catalogue.[4] The following description of the PRO fragment will allow comparison. This fragment has all the appearance of being part of a much larger manuscript, and it would be a reasonable hypothesis that it contained originally the full span of the Grail texts, as do its siblings. It is not impossible that more fragments may one day be found: the Public Record Office in London is a vast storehouse of documents, some of which are consulted frequently by scholars, others less so, perhaps never. Catalogues, calendars and indexes to its holdings exist, but entries are often very brief, and do not mention fly-leaves or wrappers taken from earlier manuscripts.

The *First Continuation* fragment is a bifolium bound as a wrapper around a Customs book, the ledger of Valentine Goodwyne, Collector of Customs and Subsidies at King's Lynn, Norfolk for the years 1 Mary and 1 and 2 Philip and Mary (1553–5);[5] its present shelf-mark is E122/100/13B, and it was until recently kept in a parchment bag along with the ledger book of the Controller of Customs at Lynn for the same years (E122/100/13A). This has a fragment of a liturgical manuscript wrapped around it.[6] The bag housed both documents with their surrounding parchment bindings since the sixteenth century, it being the standard practice for the documentation of the transactions and accounts of the Customs in England to be brought to the Exchequer in London in these parchment bags.[7]

The bifolium dates from the thirteenth century and is of clean and almost undamaged parchment, each folio measuring approximately 300mm x 225mm. There are a few small stains and a slight tear in the lower margin of the first folio (approx. 20mm), but its protective parchment bag kept it from real damage. The manuscript had however been folded in four for so

---

[4] T. Nixon, 'Catalogue of Manuscripts', *Les Manuscrits de Chrétien de Troyes*, II, 1–85; no. 23 = T = BN f.fr. 12576; no. 24 = V = BN n.a.fr. 6614; several plates of illustrations of these two manuscripts are found in both volumes.

[5] It is dated from Easter 1. Mary to Michaelmas 1 & 2 Philip & Mary at the top of the first folio and 19 October 1555 is given at the end for the date it was delivered.

[6] It is listed by Dr Ball as a fourteenth-century breviary; the Office of the Dead; Incipit: *lacionis uiuificabis me*; with a note to see *Breviarium Sar*. ii, 272, 275–76.

[7] See the introductory note to the PRO Index to Exchequer: King's Remembrancer: Particulars of Customs Accounts: E122.

long that it was initially almost impossible to lay it straight; the Conservation Department have now rectified this, and have, after careful conservation treatment, placed it with its enclosed sixteenth-century document within a strong protective folder.

The written area is approximately 252 x 185mm and the text is written in 3 columns, each approximately 252mm in length, with 40 lines per column (the ruling is not visible, but the first line of writing does appear to be above the first ruled line), and approximately 50mm wide including the offset first letter of each line, which is separated with a space of approximately 5mm. Decorated initials are used, alternately red or blue with the other colour being used for a little very basic pen-flourishing with straight lines issuing from the initial up and down the margin to the side; all are two lines high except for the initials 'L' on f. 1r and f. 1v which are both three lines high. Brown ink has been used and the script is a neat and careful small early gothic text hand. It is similar in every way to the hand shown in plate 132 (p. 439) of the second volume of *The Manuscripts of Chrétien de Troyes*, which illustrates the second hand identified by Busby as at work on manuscript *T*. General features of hands of this period such as juncture, the form of **d**, an **s** extending below the line in final position, a round **r** after bowed letters, the letter **i** ticked in minim groups, and the crossing of the tironian note are all present,[8] as are the more individual points noted by Busby as common to the first hand of *T* and to *V*: 'the backward descender under the small **h**, the final ascender on some of the small **r**'s in final position, and the way the initial stroke of the tironian note **et** abbreviation sometimes extends far into the left-hand margin when in initial position'.[9] Points of difference between the first and second hands of *T* and of similarity between this second hand and that of the scribe of the PRO fragment are the placing of the abbreviation mark beside an offset capital **Q** (it is at a half-way point whereas the first hand of *T* places it higher), the more open capital **S** with a longer final backward stroke, and what one could perhaps term a greater tendency to 'crabbedness'. The hands are however extremely similar and not easy to distinguish.

Catchwords on f. 2v: '*autre chose redist aprez*', indicate that this was the outer bifolium of a quire, a supposition that one might in any case have made from the amount of text between the two folios. 2405 lines of the text edited by Roach from manuscripts *T* and *V* lie between the end of the first and the beginning of the second folio here, and with 40 lines to the column

---

[8] See Nixon, 'Catalogue', p. 50 for the presence of all these in *T*.
[9] Busby, 'The Scribe...', p. 53. There is no noteworthy use in this fragment of the writing of a final letter suprascript and of the carrying over of the last part of a line into the next for reasons of space: these occur (v. lines 11569), but not in the distinguishing fashion noted by Busby (pp. 53–4).

it is clear that this quire at least was formed of 12 folios.[10] No quire number is visible on f. 1r, but there is some slight damage, some small black marks, in the lower right hand corner.

The bifolium would appear to have been considered as scrap parchment from before the time it was used as a wrapper: a number of scribbles appear on it, apparently made at a time contemporary with that of the enclosed Customs document: at the lower left-hand edge of f. 1v are some abacus-type figures giving a sum of money (this type of sum also appears in the pages of the Customs document). At various other places, in the blank spaces between columns and in the margins, sometimes upside down to the text, a sixteenth-century hand has scribbled amounts of money, e.g. 'lxij li. xiij s. iiij d. / lxxij li iij s. iiij d. / xli xix s. iiij d. / xxx li.'. It has then been used to label the contents: on f. 2v, upside down to the main text and across the lower margin is written: 'lynne pro ultima mese anni'. It is impossible to say how long the manuscript from which the fragment was taken had been in England.

Comparison of the language of all three texts brings out both identical and dissimilar usages. Busby noted for *T* and *V* the non-elision of **que** before a vowel producing a hypermetric line, and this is frequently found in this fragment (siglum *J* in the edition below) also, suggesting that this is not simply an individual 'scribal peculiarity'. A detailed comparison of orthographic differences between the text of *T* and *V* as edited by Roach and that of this fragment does however reveal some noteworthy standard differences; for instance, *Dex* is used in J each time where T has *Diex*; *segnor* is used in J each time where T has *seignor*; J regularly prefers *capele* to *chapele* and *castel* to *chastel*; J has *couchierent / couchent* where T has *colchierent / colchent*. The apparatus to the text below allows full comparison of these two sections of the text, which can also be compared to the results of Busby's study of the points of difference between T and V over the 3098 lines of Chrétien's *Perceval* preserved in V. It would appear that Busby has not noted any regular differences between the two for most of the examples he gives, although his presentation makes this unclear.[11] He notes however (p. 58) a strong divergence between the use of *le* and *la* as the feminine singular definite article (but does not indicate which manuscript employs which), and the use of the dialectal form *aiue* in *T* against *aide* in *V*; Busby comments that 'these two features may suggest that the

---

[10] Manuscript T is composed in large part of quires of 12: see Nixon, p. 50.

[11] Note 27 on p. 55 states: 'Only a few examples have been selected from each category below. The first form given is usually that of *T* and the second, that of *V*; when more than one instance of a variant is noted, both directions are possible. The order of listing is generally the order of appearance.'

dialect of the scribe stands in a fluid relationship to that of his exemplar or vice versa' (p. 58).

The appearance of this third witness of a text copied in the same place and at the same time from what must have been the same exemplar shows again that a scriptorium producing three very large manuscripts of the same texts over a fairly short period of time had trained its scribes to write in almost identical fashion, but that no undue worry constrained these scribes to copy letter-by-letter. An additional point of interest to note is that whereas Busby points out (p. 52) that T and V frequently agree on the positioning of decorated initials starting a new paragraph, yet in this fragment they often occur in different positions. Statistically, this may or may not be significant, and the question deserves further investigation in detail, as was done by Roger Middleton for the manuscripts of another of Chrétien's works.[12]

Comparison of the format of all three manuscripts is also of interest. The production of three manuscripts containing the same text(s) in the same workshop at the same time has led to similarities such as the three-column format, but the layout is not identical. Each manuscript would appear to have been tailor-made, perhaps deliberately differentiated to ensure that each was distinguished from its sibling.[13]

In the edition of the fragment that follows I have followed all the usual conventions for the expansion of abbreviations (which are indicated by italics), the addition of the acute and cedilla accents, the use of the apostrophe, the differentiation of u/v and i/j according to pronunciation, and the addition of punctuation, in which I follow Roach. Roach used T as his base manuscript and gives variants for V, and variant readings also from the German version (D) as edited by Karl Schorbach.[14] All the variants given below are based on Roach's edition and are thus given for T as edited by Roach and for V as he gives the reading in his apparatus; in the absence of a variant reading for V one should assume that it agrees with T (Roach gives no variant), but I have preferred to cite as T only since I have not myself checked the manuscripts. In view of the great interest in being able to compare these three versions in precise detail, I give far more variants than might be thought usual, omitting only the use of single or double letters (e.g. *iluec* / *illuec*). I have corrected the text here only in cases where the

---

[12] R. Middleton, 'Coloured capitals in the manuscripts of *Erec and Enide*', *The Manuscripts of Chrétien de Troyes*, I, 149–93.

[13] Busby points out differences in the illustration and decoration of T and V, commenting that 'the more lavish decoration of T is presumably due to the requirements of the customer' ('The Scribe . . .', p. 54), but the minor differences in format are also noteworthy.

[14] *Parzival von Claus Wisse und Philipp Colin (1331–1336), eine Ergänzung der Dichtung Wolframs von Eschenbach, zum ersten Male herausgegeben* (Strassburg, 1888: Elsässische Litteraturdenkmäler aus dem XIV–XVII Jahrhundert, 5).

manuscript reading is an impossible one; these are indicated by the use of square brackets; all rejected readings are placed in the footnotes and J has been used as the siglum (it was necessary to find a letter not already employed by Roach).

f.1 col. 1

Si laverent et si mangierent,	11503
Et quant liy[15] fu si se couchierent.[16]	
A grant joie et a grant deduit	11505
Passerent ensi cele nuit,	
Mais molt lor ot corte duree,	
Car la Pentecoste ert passee	
Et fu aprez le Saint Jehan,	
Qui[17] sont plus cortes qu'en tot l'an.	11510
A l'endemain fu li matins	
Et li solaus [si][18] clers et fins,	
Car molt par fist bel tans et cler;	
Et quant il fu tans de lever,	
Li rois, qui fu au paveillon,	11515
Se leva et si compaignon.	
La premiere [cose][19] qu'il firent,	
A le[20] capele messe oïrent.	
Puis fu li mengiers[21] aprestez,	
Car matins mengiers[22] est santez	11520
A ceus[23] qui ont foible[24] cervel.	
Disner orent molt riche et bel,	
Si sont asis molt liément,	
Et si mangierent vistement.	
Lardez orent de venison[25]	11525
Qu'il en prenoient a foison,	
Et lués que il furent levé[26]	
Si ont le camberlent armé	
S[i][27] richement le seignor del[28] Lis	
Sor une querite de samis,[29]	11530

[15] 11504 lius T
[16] 11504 colchierent T
[17] 11510 Qu'el T
[18] 11512 fu J
[19] 11517 messe J; chose T
[20] 11518 la chapele T
[21] 11519 li disners T
[22] 11520 matin mengier T
[23] 11521 cels T
[24] 11521 feble T
[25] 11525 venoison T
[26] 11527 disné T
[27] 11529 Si om. T, V
[28] 11529 de T
[29] 11530 sor un samit qui fu treslis T, V

Et li rois meïsmes sanz faille
Li a lacié[30] le[31] ventaille.
Puis est montez et l'escu prent
Et a son col molt bel le pent.
La lance ou ert ses gonfanons   11535
A prise, et fiert des esperons
Tot droit al[32] pré que bien savoit.
De la porte del castel[33] voit
Grant oirre issir .j. chevalier
Desor .j. sor bauchant destrier;   11540
Estoit armez trop cointement,
Et vint el pré delivrement

col. 2

Ou mesire Bran de Lis fu.
Si tost com il se sont veü
Si poignent lués delivrement.   11545
Si vos di bien[34] veraiement,
Sor les escus si s'entrefierent
Que totes les lances froissierent
Et tant vienent[35] de grant vertu
Que il se sont entr'abatu.[36]   11550
Mais ne[37] jurent pas lengement,[38]
Ains relievent[39] molt vistement,
Et traient nues les espees,
Dont il se donent grans colees
Par desor[40] les elmes luisans,   11555
Dont li pires est[41] molt vaillant.[42]
Mais molt durement ert[43] grevez
Cil del castel[44] qui ert navrez.
Et Bran[45] de Lis toz sains estoit
Et delivres, sel requeroit.   11560
Si durement le vait[46] hurter

[30] 11532 lachie T
[31] 11532 la T, V
[32] 11537 au T
[33] 11538 chastel T
[34] 11546 Bien le vos di T, V
[35] 11549 vinrent T, V
[36] 11550 Qu'el pre se sont entre abatu T, V
[37] 11551 n'i T, V
[38] 11551 longuement T
[39] 11552 saillent sus T, V
[40] 11555 Amont sor T, V
[41] 11556 Toz li pires ert T, V
[42] 11556 vaillans T
[43] 11557 est V
[44] 11558 chastel T
[45] 11559 Brans T
[46] 11561 va T

Qu'en nul liu nel lait ester;
A force s'est ajenoilliés,
Et ains qu'il se fu[47] redrechiés,[48]
Li a fait fianchier prison,   11565
Si l'en amaine au paveillon.
Le roi le done et il le prent
Si l'en mercie durement.[49]
Puis fait[50] lués faire une ramé
De rains bele et encortinee;   11570
Dedens couchent[51] le chevalier
Qui de repos avoit mestier.
Et li rois et si compaignon
Desarmerent el paveillon
Le segnor[52] del[53] Lis liément,   11575
Puis le fist vestir errament[54]
Et font grant joie tot[55] le jor.
Quant vint le soir a la froidor
Si sont alé esbanoïr[56]
Desoz l'ombre d'un olivier.   11580
Tot entor le roi sont asis
Li vaillant chevalier de pris,

col. 3

Por escouter chiax qui cornoient
Molt durement et fresteloient;
N'ainc nus tel[57] estrument ne fist   11585
Qui a gaite point[58] convenist
Qu'el castel[59] n'oissiés soner
Et molt grant joie demener.
Li rois en veilloit plus les nuis
Et plus[60] li plaisoit li deduis   11590
Des bons gas que[61] s'entredisoient
Les gaites qui la nuit cornoient.
Lez le segnor del[62] Lis seoit

47 11564 fust T
48 11564 redreciez T
49 11568 Puis l'en merchie bonement T, V
50 11569 fait fait J
51 11571 colchent T
52 11575 seignor T
53 11575 de T
54 11576 errannment T

55 11577 tout T
56 11579 esbanoier T
57 11585 cel V
58 11586 poinst V
59 11587 chastel T
60 11590 Car molt li plaisoit T, V
61 11591 quil V
62 11593 de T; del V

K. qui les gaites escoutoit.
Adont por rien ne se tenist 11595
Por nule chose c'avenist[63]
Que il ne deïst son avis:
'Segnor',[64] fait il, 'Par Saint Denis
Je quit la joste est oubliee[65]
Qu'encor ne fu anuit rovee. 11600
Li rois n'a compaignon ne per
Que[66] l'aie oï encor rover.
Il n'en [ont][67] ore nul besoing.'
'Ké', fait li rois, 'je [la][68] vos doing'.
'Sire', fait K., 'par Saint Martin, 11605
J'amaisse mix a le matin
Une haste hochié en cras
Que je vostre joste ne fas.[69]
Ja ne vos en mercierai[70]
Mais tote voie[71] le ferai 11610
Quant il vos plaist, sire, demain,
Foi que doi monsegnor[72] G.'.
Grant joie demainent et font
De ses dis cil qui illuec sont.
Et quant l'orent asez gabé, 11615
Au paveillon sont retorné.
   La nuit ont trespassee ensi.
Au matin quant fu esclarci,[73]
Anchois[74] que prime fust sonee,
A li rois le messe [escoutee].[75] 11620
Et lués que il orent disné
Si ont le senescal[76] armé.

f. 1v
col. 1

Puis est montez, son escu prent,
Et d'ax se part hastivement.

[63] 11596 qu'avenist T
[64] 11598 Seignor T
[65] 11599 oblïee T
[66] 11602 Cui T, V
[67] 11603 ont om. J
[68] 11604 la om. J
[69] 11608 fais J (with the *i* underdotted for erasure)
[70] 11609 merchïerai T
[71] 11610 toutes voies T
[72] 11612 monseignor T
[73] 11618 esclarchi T
[74] 11619 Ainçois T
[75] 11620 cantee J
[76] 11622 seneschal T

Mais plus tost ne fu il es prez 11625
C'uns chevaliers molt bien armez[77]
Ist del castel[78] molt tost poignant
Et vient el pré tot maintenant.
Sor les escus s'entreferirent,
Qu'andoi a terre[79] cairent,[80] 11630
Et molt vistement sus resaillent
Et as espees qui bien taillent
Felenessement se requierent
Et parmi les hiaumes se fierent.
Li chevaliers ireement 11635
Va Ké ferir et il l'atent;
Et cil .j. grant colp[81] l'a feru[82]
Parmi le pene[83] de l'escu.
Son colp[84] estort, li brans brisa,
Et li chevaliers le hasta. 11640
Si durement le va hurter
Que le[85] bosne li fist passer
Que li iiij olivier tenoient
Qui au coron del pré estoient.
Lor s'aresta[86] li chevaliers; 11645
Enmi le pré ert ses destriers,
Et il vint la, si est montez.
Au cheval Ké en est alez,
Et il le prist sans contredit,
Si l'en mena car bel le vit. 11650
K.[87] est arriere repairiés
Ne set mot[88] que soit engigniés[89]
Ains quide avoir trestot le pris.
Mais cil l'a assez mix conquis.[90]
Au roi dient si compaignon: 11655
'Sire, por Deu, et c'or alon

[77] 11626 Cuns grans chevaliers toz armez V
[78] 11627 chastel T
[79] 11630 Si fort que a terre T; Que andoi a terre V
[80] 11630 chaïrent T
[81] 11637 cop T
[82] 11637 Que molt grans cop li a feru V
[83] 11638 la penne T, V
[84] 11639 cop T
[85] 11642 la T, V

[86] 11645 Lors aresta T; Lors s'aresta V; (cf. lines 14385 Lor)
[87] The initial offset letter here is an *O* underdotted for erasure.
[88] 11652 Ne set pas T, V
[89] 11652 quil soit ensaigniez V
[90] 11654 The scribe has omitted this line in its proper place, has realised his mistake, and has then placed it at the end of the column with an indication of the error.

Encontre Ké por lui gaber;
Trop le feroit bien desgigler".[91]
Li rois l'otroie, encontre vont.
Trestoz premerains les semont.   11660
Devant trestoz[92] en va li rois
Qui molt ert sages et cortois.

col. 2

'Ké', fait il, 'Venez vos de loing?
Avez vos dont eü besoing?'
Et K., qui toz est aprestez   11665
De mal dire, s'est arestez
Et dist: "Sire, laissiés me ester;
Ne me devez pas ranprosner.
J'ai .j. de chiax[93] laiens[94] vencu,
Mais il m'a mon cheval tolu.   11670
Li chans est miens, je l'ai conquis,
Et cil en va qui n'a le pris.[95]
    Chascuns se tent que ne rist mie.[96]
'Sire, avez vos mestier d'aïe?'
Ce li dist Tor[97] li fix Arez.   11675
Li autre li ont dit apréz:
'Senescal,[98] estes vos blechiés?"
'Ce m'est avis que vos clochiés.'
Ce li dist mesire Gavains,
Adont li dist mesire Yvains: 11680
'Ké, c'or me bailliés vostre escu.
Bien avez l'estor maintenu,
Merveilleus cols[99] ferir vos vi
Bien l'avez fait, la Deu merci.'[100]
L'escu li baille et il le prent   11685
Par le guige,[101] a son col le pent.
Chascuns le gabe a son pooir,
Et il le set trestot de voir.
Lors dist a monseignor Y.:

[91] 11658 desjogler T, V
[92] 11661 trestous T
[93] 11669 chiaus T
[94] 11669 dela T, V
[95] 11672 Qui n'ot le pris T, V
[96] 11673 Chascuns se teut, qu'i[l] ne rist mie T
[97] 11675 Thors T; tors V
[98] 11677 Seneschal T
[99] 11683 cops T
[100] 11684 la Dieu merchi T
[101] 11686 guiche T

65

'Sire, je vos doins a demain 11690
Autant com j'ai hui gaaignié.
Le[102] joste et le camp[103] vos doins gié
Por mon escu que vos portez.
Bien faites quanque[104] vos volez.
Certes je vos reservirai 11695
D'autel mestier quant je porrai.'
Cil qui ce li oïrent dire
Ne se porent tenir de rire;
Ensi gabant l'en ont mené
Au paveillon et desarmé. 11700
Et li sires de Lis li dist:[105]
'Biax sire Ké,[106] se Dex[107] m'aït,

col. 3

Vos passastes trestoz premiers
Le bosne[108] des iiij oliviers;
Et celui qui en ist avant 11705
Claiment, ce m'est vis, recreant."
K. li respont: 'Ce puet bien estre,
Foi que je doi au roi celestre.
Sire, se vos savez l'entree
Et l'issue, autretant m'agree. 11710
Ensi va; li .j. entreront[109]
D'une part et li autre istront."
Atant sonerent el castel[110]
Es mostiers par trestot isnel
.j. glas si bel et si tres grant 11715
C'on[111] n'oïst[112] pas Deu[113] tonant.
Li rois enquist et demanda
Por coi li glas si grans sona,
Et li sires de Lis li dist:[114]
'Jel vos dirai dusc'a[115] petit. 11720

[102] 11692 la T
[103] 11692 champ T
[104] 11694 quanques T
[105] 11701 dit T
[106] 11702 Keus T
[107] 11702 Diex T
[108] 11704 Les bones T, V
[109] 11711 enterront T
[110] 11713 chastel T

[111] 11716 The abbreviation for "con" has been added later after the illumination for the initial below had erased most of the letters 'con', of which traces remain including the whole letter 'n'.
[112] 11716 n'i oïst T, V
[113] 11716 Dieu T
[114] 11719 dist T
[115] 11720 dusque a T; dusqua V

Biax sire, il est hui semmedis,
Ja puis que passe mïedis
Ne fera nus, je vos di bien,
La dedens nulle ovre[116] por rien
Ains i est molt bien celebree   11725
La mere Deu[117] et honeree,
Plus qu'en tote crestienté,
Ce sachiés bien de verité.[118]
Ja verrez aler as mostiers
Les dames et les chevaliers   11730
Et les borjois[119] et l'autre gent,
Apareilliés trop richement.
Tot vont les vespres escouter
Por la haute dame honerer.[120]
Et ensi tot le semedi   11735
Dusques a tierce del lundi,[121]
Que par le castel[122] sont sonees
Totes[123] les messes et cantees.[124]
Adont commenchent[125] lor labor[126]
Li menestrel tot li plusor.[127]   11740
Si vos di bien, sanz nulle faille,
Que devant la n'arez bataille.'

f. 2r
col. 1

N'ot pas illuec granment esté,   14147
Quant a veü[128] une clarté
Loins en la mer qui se sambloit[129]
Une estoile, et vers lui venoit;   14150
Si s'esmerveilloit durement
Que vers lui vient si droitement.
Et quant il vit qu'ele aprocha,
As .ij. camberlens, demanda:
'Veez vos rien en cele mer?"   14155

---

[116] 11724 oevre T
[117] 11726 Dieu T
[118] 11728 par verité T, V
[119] 11731 borgois T V
[120] 11734 honorer T
[121] 11736 tierche le lundi T, V
[122] 11737 chastel T
[123] 11738 Toutes T
[124] 11738 chantees T; chantes V
[125] 11739 comencent T
[126] 11739 labour T
[127] 11740 pluisor T
[128] 14148 veue V
[129] 14149 resambloit T

'Sire, ne[130] vos devons celer:
Une clarté i veons grant,
Et si vient vers nos aprochant."
'Voire", fait li rois, "vez le la
Prez de ci.[131] Dex,[132] que ce sera?" 14160
Lors va avant, si a veü
Li rois que ce[133] .j. calans[134] fu
De riches porpres bien bendez;
Desor ert toz encortinez,
Mais n'i ont veü rien vivant 14165
Fors .j. cisne[135] qui vient devant,
Qui le calant atraïnoit.
.j. anel d'or el col avoit
Ou une caïne ert fremee,[136]
D'argent molt sotilment[137] ovree. 14170
Li autres chiés en retenoit
Al chief del calant qui venoit.
Soz les loges est arivez.
Molt en est li rois trespensez.
   Adont commencha a crïer 14175
Li chisnes fort et halt[138] et cler.[139]
Estrangement se[140] merveilla
Li rois, et tantost commanda
As camberlens[141] a deffermer
Le posterne desus[142] la mer. 14180
Cil ont fait son commandement
Et il i va tot[143] droitement
Por savoir qu'en la nef avoit.
Ens est entrez; adonques voit
As .ij. chiés .ij. chierges ardans, 14185
Ainc mais n'avoit veü[144] si grans.

---

[130] 14156 ne T, V, J; Roach amends to ne[l] from other MSS which coincide at this point.
[131] 14160 chi T
[132] 14160 Diex T
[133] 14162 che T
[134] 14162 chalans T
[135] 14166 chisne T
[136] 14169 fermee T
[137] 14170 soltilment T; soltiuement V
[138] 14176 haut T
[139] 14176 chisnes molt haut et molt cler V
[140] 14177 s'en T, V
[141] 14179 chamberlens T
[142] 14180 desor V
[143] 14182 tout T
[144] 14186 veus T, veu V

col. 2

Soz la¹⁴⁵ cortine s'abaissa,
Et ens enmi le tref ala,¹⁴⁶
Et vit .j. chier paile¹⁴⁷ roé
Tot¹⁴⁸ a fin or fait et ovré   14190
Estendus, qui trop biax estoit.
Et desoz¹⁴⁹ le paile¹⁵⁰ gisoit
.j. chevaliers mors estendus,
Qui parmi le cors¹⁵¹ ert¹⁵² ferus
Haut el tenrun¹⁵³ de le poitrine.   14195
D'un riche covertor¹⁵⁴ d'ermine
Avoit covert trestot le cors
Trusc'al trols¹⁵⁵ qui paroit de fors.
Li rois le voit, s'en ot dolor.
Ainc mais n'avoit veü nul jor   14200
Nul si tres bel mort chevalier.
Lors va avant sans atargier,
Tot le covertor¹⁵⁶ li osta
Et sa grant biauté remira.
Cil avoit .j. porpoi[n]t¹⁵⁷ vestu   14205
D'un chier samit a or batu
Et d'un siglatun¹⁵⁸ miparti.
'Dex',¹⁵⁹ fait li rois, 'ainc mais ne vi
Si bel home en crestïenté
Ne si richement adoubé.   14210
Trop li siet bien cil auquetons.
Vez com il a gens esperons,
Car de fin [or]¹⁶⁰ sont, ce m'est vis.
Dex!¹⁶¹ tant mar fu quant il n'est vis,
Que trop par a¹⁶² riches joiaus.   14215
Vez com il est et gens et biax.
Certes si est a desmesure

---

145 14187 le T
146 14188 ala om. T; le nef ala V
147 14189 pale T
148 14190 Tout T
149 14192 desoz T, V, J; Roach amends from M: desor
150 14192 pale T
151 14194 le ch cors J (with 'ch' underdotted for erasure).
152 14194 est V
153 14195 tendrun T
154 14196 covertoir T
155 14198 Dusqu'al troz T
156 14203 Tout le covertoir T
157 14205 porpoit J; porpoint T, V
158 14207 sciglaton T
159 14208 Diex T
160 14213 or om. J
161 14214 Diex T
162 14215 ot T, V

De grant riquece[163] sa chainture.'[164]
Si vos di bien de s'amosniere[165]
Que ele estoit molt bele et chiere.[166]   14220
Por le grant biauté qu'il i vit,
Ensi comme li contes dit,[167]
Vint avant li rois, si le prent.
Unes letres par dedens sent.
Tot errament[168] overte l'a,   14225
Les letres prist, se's[169] desploia,

col. 3

Et les porvit de chief en chief.
Oiez qu'il ot el premier chief:
Les [letres][170] le roi saluoient
Et molt francement[171] li prioient: 14230
'Rois, cis cors fu rois; qui ci gist,
Avant que fust [mors],[172] te requist
Que tu le laiaisse[s][173] ester
Enmi ta[174] sale et demorer,[175]   14234
Tant que .j. chevalier venrra
Qui del cors li errachera[176]
Le troz[177] qu'il a parmi le cors.   14235

163 14218 richece T
164 14218 çainture T
165 14219 s'almosniere T
166 14220 Que ele ert molt et bele et chiere T; Quele estoit molt bele et molt chiere V
167 14222 dist V
168 14225 errannment T
169 14226 ses J; se T, V; Roach amends: se[s]
170 14229 detres J
171 14230 franchement T
172 14232 The scribe has himself corrected here, by writing the omitted word at the end of the line, preceded by a symbol, and by marking the place where the word is to be inserted with the same symbol.
173 14233 laissasses T
174 14234 te T
175 142234 En te sale et tant demorer V
176 This couplet is omitted in Roach without comment, although the passage makes no sense without it; the other redactions differ considerably in phrasing at this point. T and V are evidently in difficulties at this point for lines 14237–40 are also omitted: see next note. The later German version, cited by Roach, clearly follows the reading of J here: *mitten in üwerme palas, seht, bitz ein ritter ziehe us dem toten man daz trunsel mit dem ysin gar.*
177 14235 trous T

A NEW FRAGMENT OF THE *FIRST CONTINUATION* OF THE *PERCEVAL*

Quant le fer en ara trait fors,[178]
. . .
. . .
. . .
. . .
Se celui ne fiert autresi   14241
Qui parmi le cors le feri,
Et par icel liu droitement,
Et de cel fer meïsmement.
Rois en .j. sarcu le metez.   14245
Richement soit embalsumez,[179]
Que plus d'un an bien i sera
Li cors que ja fla[ir] ne fera.[180]
Se li troz ne li est ostez
Anchois[181] que li ans soit passez,   14250
Si[182] le porrés faire enterer,
Que ja puis n'en orrez parler.
S'il est vengiés, bien ert seü
En vostre cort quels hom il fu,
Dont il ert et de quel païs,   14255
Et com il fu a tort ocis.'
Adont ploia le brief ariere,
Si le remist en l'amosniere.[183]
Tot[184] autresi com le troverent
En la nef quant il i entrerent,   14260
Le fist li rois apareillier;
Desoz son chief .j. oreillier
Li mist, et puis le[185] recovri

---

[178] 14237–40 Roach supplies 4 lines here: [*Tout ausi soit icil honnis / Et de son cors avilenis / Que Guerrehés fu el vergier, / Qui le troz osera sachier,*]. The lines have been taken from a later repetition of the passage, lines 14391–94. See Roach's note pp. 440–41. The later German version might seem to indicate that somewhat more practically explicit words had been in the lost French passage here: *der ritter, ders uz zühet, joch muoz er mit dem selben ysin doch ginen stechen, der in stach, und durch die brust sam disem geschach, alse men in gestochen siht; anders würt er gerochen niht.*
[179] 14246 soit enbalsemez T, V; Roach emends *soit* to *est*.
[180] 14248 ja flairs n'en istra T; ja flair ne fera V; ja flart ne fera J
[181] 14250 Ainçois T
[182] 14251 Se V
[183] 14258 saumosniere T; laumosniere V. At this point Roach prints 2 lines from the German version, but does not include these in the line-numbering system: [*und hies in tragen in den sal / mit siner gezierde über al.*]
[184] 14259 Tout T
[185] 14263 li V

71

Du[186] covertor[187] tot[188] autresi
Com l'ot trové premierement. 14265
A ses camberlens[189] molt deffent
Que ja par aus[190] ne soit seü
Rien qu'il aient illuec veü.

f. 2v
col. 1

Adont li rois se remua,
Et a[s] fenestres[191] s'apoia[192] 14270
Por le cisne[193] que il oï,
Qui cria et braist et feri
Tant fort ses eles en la mer
Si que il en a fait torner
Le chalant molt isnelement 14275
O[194] le grant caïne[195] d'argent
Qui en la neff saudee[196] estoit,
Que il entor le col avoit.
Le roi encline par samblant
Puis si s'en va sa nef traiant, 14280
Et crie et maine grant dolor,[197]
Ce resamble, por son segnor.[198]
Li rois en[199] est trop merveilliés[200]
Vint a son lit, si est couchiés.[201]
Tote[202] nuit veilla, je vos di, 14285
Dusc'al demain[203] qu'il s'endormi.
Quant on sona par la cité,
Si com on ot acoustumé,[204]
As capeles[205] et as mostiers,
Mesire Gavains toz premiers 14290
Se vesti molt tost et leva
Et ses compaignons apela,

[186] 14264 Dun V
[187] 14264 covertoir T
[188] 14264 tout T
[189] 14266 chamberlens T
[190] 14267 als T
[191] 14270 affenestres J
[192] 14270 s'apuia T
[193] 14271 chisne T
[194] 14276 od T; A V
[195] 14276 chaine T
[196] 14277 saldee T
[197] 14281 sa dolor T; grant dolor V
[198] 14282 seignor T
[199] 14283 sen V
[200] 14283 merveilliez T
[201] 14284 colchiez T
[202] 14285 Toute T
[203] 14286 Dusqu'al matin T, V
[204] 14288 acostumé T
[205] 14289 chapeles T

Toz cels qui avec lui estoient.[206]
Del chevalier quant il le voient
Se merveillierent durement   14295
Et quidierent[207] tot vraiement[208]
Del chevalier que il dormist.[209]
'Dex',[210] font[211] il, 'qui est la qui gist?'[212]
Lors sont si prez del dois venu
Qu'il esgardent, si ont veü   14300
Que c'est .j. chevaliers ocis.
Molt l'esgardent enmi le vis,
Mais nus d'ax toz ne le connut.[213]
La novele, si comme dut,[214]
En vait molt tost par la cité.[215]   14305
Si vos di bien par verité
Que por la merveille esgarder
I veïssiés grant gent aler.

col.2

G. li preus nel[216] remua,
Anchois[217] trestot[218] coi le laia,[219]   14310
Et dist que ja n'ert remuez
Devant que li rois ert levez.
Puis en va en la cambre[220] droit,
Le grant merveille que il voit
En la sale a au[221] roi contee.   14315
Et li rois, qui l'avoit trovee,
Fait sanblant tot a escïent
Comme s'il n'en seüst noient.
Lors s'est isnelement levez,
Et quant il se fu atornez   14320
De si tres riches vestiment[222]
Comme a cors de tel home apent,
Si vint[223] en la sale manois.

206 14293 Tot cil qui od lui la estoient V
207 14296 cuidierent T
208 14296 Si quidierent certainement V
209 14297 Que li chevaliers se dormist V
210 14298 Diex T
211 14298 fait V
212 14298 qui est qui la gist T, V
213 14303 nus dals ne le reconut V
214 14304 come il dut T; come dut V

215 14305 chité T
216 14309 le T; nel V
217 14310 Ainçois T
218 14310 trestout T
219 14310 laissa T
220 14313 chambre T
221 14315 al T
222 14321 riche vestement T
223 14323 vient V

Molt trove gent entor le doïs,
Mais la presse f[ont]²²⁴ departir   14325
Cil qui le roi voient venir.
Lors vait²²⁵ avant, et si a pris
Le keutepointe de samis²²⁶
Et le paile²²⁷ soz²²⁸ coi gisoit,
Et le porpoint que il avoit   14330
Si riches et si nobles fu.
'He Dex',²²⁹ fait il, 'tant mar i fu
Cil chevaliers quant il n'est vis.'
Lors va avant, et si a pris
Le covertor,²³⁰ sel descovri.   14335
'Seignor,' fait il, 'ainc mais ne vi
Si bel home de mere né.
Si ne quit en crestienté
En fust nus si de joie plains
Com cist²³¹ quant il ert vis et sains,   14340
Ne si amez que²³² il estoit.
Bien pert as joiax²³³ qu'il avoit,
Car onques mais nus chevaliers
N'en ot tant biax ne de si chiers.
Bien pert qu'il amoit hautement,   14345
Et qu'il ert nez de haute gent.
Dex,²³⁴ com biax ex,²³⁵ si beles mains,
Si²³⁶ biax dois, si lons et si plains,

col.3

Si droites jambes, si vols piés
N'ot ainc mais nus. Et si²³⁷ sachiés   14350
Qu'il ert cointes a desmesure,
Et bele et riche sa chainture.'²³⁸
Lors prent maintenant l'aumosniere;
Bien savoit tote²³⁹ la maniere

---

²²⁴ 14325 fait J; font T, V
²²⁵ 14327 vait om. V
²²⁶ 14328 Le colte pointe de samis T; Le covertoir sel descovri V (cf. 14335)
²²⁷ 14329 pale T
²²⁸ 14329 soz T; sor V (Roach prints sor)
²²⁹ 14332 Diex T
²³⁰ 14335 covertoir T
²³¹ 14340 cil T
²³² 14341 come il T, V
²³³ 14342 joiaus T
²³⁴ 14347 Diex T
²³⁵ 14347 oex T
²³⁶ 14348 Com T, V
²³⁷ 14350 Et se V
²³⁸ 14352 çainture T
²³⁹ 14354 tout[e] T (with Roach emendation)

D'unes letres que il trova.　　　　　　　14355
Lors les trait hors, si esgarda,
Et quant il les ot bien leüees,
Et de chief en chief porveües,
Mesire G. li a dit:
'Sire, c'avez[240] trové escrit　　　　　　14360
En ces letres, dites le nos?'
'Par cele foi que je doi vos,
Biax niés, nel[241] vos celerai mie;
En talent ai que jel vos die.
　Cil[242] cors ci a molt grant fiance,　　14365
Ce dist li briés, de sa vengance,
En chaus[243] de la Table Roonde
Plus s'i fie qu'en tot[244] le monde.
Cest trols[245] qu'il a parmi le cors
Vauroit,[246] ce dist, que il fust[247] fors　　14370
Mais ainc nus ne l'osa oster.
Chaiens[248] sont li bon[249] bacheler,
Se Deu[250] plaist, qui li osteront.[251]
Trestoz les emprie et semont.
Si m'a cist[252] cors el brief requis　　　　14375
Qu'en iceste[253] sale soit mis
En .j. sarcu.[254] Toz sui certains
C'un an et .j. [jor],[255] plus ne mains,
I veut[256] estre, c'est veritez,
Avant que il soit enterrez,　　　　　　　14380
Se ne li est ostez anchois[257]
Li troz del cors. Et si fu rois,
Si com je voi es letres chi.
S'il n'est[258] vengiés, bien le vos di,
Lor[259] sarons tote[260] l'aventure　　　　14385

[240] 14360 qu'avez T
[241] 14363 ne V
[242] 14365 Cist T
[243] 14367 ciax T
[244] 14368 tout T
[245] 14369 troz T
[246] 14370 Volroit T; Valroit V
[247] 14370 fu T (Roach corrects to fu[st])
[248] 14372 Çaiens T
[249] 14372 buen T
[250] 14373 Dieu T
[251] 14373 hosteront T
[252] 14375 cis T
[253] 14376 Qu'enmi ceste T, V
[254] 14377 sarc T (Roach amends: sarc[u])
[255] 14378 jor om. J
[256] 14379 velt T
[257] 14381 ançois T
[258] 14384 Sil nest T; Sil est V; Roach prints as V.
[259] 14385 Lors T, V
[260] 14385 toute T

De sa mort, ce dist l'escr_i_pture.
Segnor,[261] il est de haute ge_nt_,
B_ie_n[262] p_er_t a son atornem_ent_.

(catchwords [line 14389]:
                    autre chose redist[263] ap_re_z)

---

[261] 14387 Seignor T
[262] 14388 P_ar_ bien J (with the P_ar_ underdotted for erasure).
[263] 14389 redit T, redist V

IV

THE GLASTONBURY LEGENDS

Aelred Watkin

(The following is the unrevised text of a lecture given by Dom Aelred Watkin, OSB, titular abbot of Glastonbury Abbey, at St Andrews University in the 1950s. Since that time there has been a great deal of research on Glastonbury, primarily involving the re-editing of medieval texts, but this beautifully written and coherently argued lecture remains a remarkably comprehensive and relevant summary of the various strands.* Neither dismissive nor credulous, Watkin's piece thus provides an excellent introduction to the Glastonbury legends, to the mingling of history and romance which ultimately led to the promulgation of a late-medieval cult of St Joseph of Glastonbury. More specifically, it serves as an introduction to the 'Magna Tabula', itself the focus of Jeanne Krochalis's study in this volume of *Arthurian Literature*.)

The child who defined a sieve as 'holes surrounded by wire' could well have been a student of early Glastonbury history, for the historian who has the courage to attempt an examination of the origins of Glastonbury is faced by problems of peculiar difficulty. First, he is confronted by a complex of fact and legend. He has to try to distinguish between the two and he must not forget that legend itself is an historical fact and that fiction has its history as much as has real event. Again, he has to submit to a necessity peculiarly distasteful to the trained judge of events, the necessity of admitting that there is much that he can never know. Thirdly, he has to avoid the dangerous and facile transition which turns possibility into probability, that almost imperceptibly substitutes 'may it not be?' for 'it may be', and then, unaware of the difference of emphasis, seeks, by repeating 'may it not be' sufficiently often, to arrive at 'it is'. Finally, there is the age-old difficulty of the burden

---

* Footnotes have been added by James Carley to editions of primary texts, and several recent articles relating to materials analysed in detail by Watkin have been cited.

of disproof, the impossibility of refuting statements not intrinsically impossible but for which no tittle of real evidence has been adduced.

All these difficulties are ones which historians have frequently to face, but Glastonbury presents problems of its own. Excavation has shown there has been a religious house there from at least the fifth century and that means that the place stretched back largely beyond recorded history. Glastonbury was open to every form of Celtic influence and when, later on, it became what Dr Armitage Robinson has called 'a temple of reconciliation between Saxon and Celt', it became also the repository of the earliest traditions of the new-comers. Saxon, Dane and Norman arrived to find Glastonbury already in existence, mysterious, ancient and unknown.

We have, therefore, to try to distinguish the stages by which inevitable legend grew; for the earliest traditions of Glastonbury were not so much fashioned by herself but rather grew up slowly with her like the imperceptible petrifaction of a stalactite in a cave. Charles Plummer castigated Glastonbury's pre-eminence in the field of 'monastic lying', but rather it was that eagerly she snatched at anything that could explain her to herself. Belief that forged evidence and emulation that inspired invention – two very different impulses that, unfortunately, are often confused in the minds of historians – added to and remoulded ancient tradition. But, as if that were not enough, at Glastonbury throughout the centuries, from the sixteenth to our own day, traditions have constantly been added unknown to earlier ages. The Glastonbury thorn is now said to have sprung from the staff of Joseph of Arimathea; Wirral was originally Weary-all Hill where Joseph rested; Joseph brought the Holy Grail with him to Glastonbury; the Christ Child walked the neighbouring hills; Chalk Well was Chalice Well which flowed red from the Grail; Excalibur flashed amid the reeds at Street Bridge ...

The very beauty and multiplicity of these legends, the patent sincerity of many of their evangelists and the fascination of the place itself – all of these have tended to create a sense of awe which seems to make evidence an irrelevance and doubt a vulgarity. And yet each year adds fresh legends and consolidates further newly discovered 'ancient traditions'. Supplemented and endorsed by 'voices' from the past relayed by the planchette or ouija board, errors long refuted by serious scholars are given fresh leases of life in a plethora of books and pamphlets in which theory passes for fact, assertion for proof and analogy for logical connexion. The unfortunate historian, who has first to find his way through the cloud-cuckoo-land of Celtic dreams and has then to endeavour to discover what facts lie behind the beliefs of the medieval monks, is now faced by a *corpus* of legend which in the extravagance and variety of its claims makes the Celt appear cautious and the monk modest.

Yet the historian who endeavours to discover the real story of one of the oldest and most sacred spots in Britain is surely occupying himself with a task that is potentially of a most rewarding character and it is clear that the first beginning of any such history must stem from a study of the early legends. Here, we must all be pupils of Dr Armitage Robinson's *Two Glastonbury Legends* (Cambridge, 1926), for Dr Robinson by, as it were, taking these legends to pieces and tracing their growth and their appropriation by Glastonbury, has shown once and for all the method which later scholars must employ.

For our sources we must first turn to what Glastonbury has to tell us about herself and then see how far we may trace her legends elsewhere. Our first source, then, is William of Malmesbury's *De antiquitate Glastoniensis ecclesie*.[1] Written about 1135 as an attempt to trace the story of the abbey from the earliest times, it received lengthy interpolations sometime between 1171 and 1247. Fortunately Robinson and W. W. Newell in brilliant essays have managed to separate fairly completely the original work from the later additions.

Next we have the chronicle of Adam of Damerham.[2] Adam was a prolific writer; one of his holograph manuscripts remains at Longleat and his chronicle, which has never yet been printed in full, was built up from smaller studies and records composed over a period of about thirty years and covers the history of Glastonbury from 1171 to about 1291. Finally, we have the fourteenth-century chronicle of John of Glastonbury.[3] John managed most skilfully to combine the interpolated Malmesbury and the work of Adam with much matter of his own. These three sources tell us practically all we know of what was believed at Glastonbury about Arthur and Joseph of Arimathea by the year 1400. Beyond an account of some miracles attributed to St Joseph, and a mention of the Glastonbury thorn, this corpus of legend remained unaltered, as far as we know, up to the time of the dissolution. The Holy Grail, Chalice Well and the burgeoning of Joseph's staff into the thorn, all these are additions of more recent times.

We turn, then, first to the story of Arthur and see what the interpolator of William of Malmesbury has to say about him. The first mention of the king occurs in a section headed *de nobilibus Glastonie sepultis* and it plunges us at once into the heart of our enquiry. We read here (i) that Arthur lies buried in the monks' cemetery between two pyramids with his wife and many princes of the Britons. (ii) That Arthur was in the year 542 wounded

---

[1] *The Early History of Glastonbury. An Edition, Translation and Study of William of Malmesbury's 'De Antiquitate Glastonie Ecclesie'*, ed. and trans. J. Scott (Woodbridge, 1981).
[2] *Adami de Domerham Historia de Rebus Gestis Glastoniensibus*, ed. T. Hearne, 2 vols. (Oxford, 1727).
[3] *The Chronicle of Glastonbury Abbey. An Edition, Translation and Study of John of Glastonbury's 'Cronica Sive Antiquitates Glastoniensis Ecclesie'*, ed. J. P. Carley, trans. D. Townsend (Woodbridge, 1985).

iuxta fluvium Camlan by Mordred and taken to the isle of Avalon to be healed of his wounds. (iii) That Arthur died at Avalon in the summer round Pentecost, being a hundred years old or thereabouts. Leaving aside the first statement, which we will discuss later, let us examine our second and third assertions: that Arthur, wounded in battle, was taken to Avalon to be cured and there died.

The story of the wounding of Arthur and of his transportation to Avalon seems gradually to have been expanded from an entry in the tenth-century *Annales Cambriae* under the year 539 which states simply that Arthur and Mordred fell in the battle of Camlan. Geoffrey of Monmouth in his *Historia regum Britanniae* of about 1138 says that Arthur was carried to Avalon to be cured of his wounds, as does the *Vita Merlini* of about 1150, though here Avalon is called the *insula pomorum* or isle of apples. Gerald of Wales in *de instructione principum*, written about 1194, repeats the same story, but he identifies Avalon with Glastonbury, calls Avalon the *insula pomifera* and adds that in the British tongue it has been called Inisgutrin, that is the isle of Glass. In his *Speculum ecclesiae*, written some twenty-five years later, he adds further that Avalon might be derived from Avallo or Vallo, a former ruler of the island; a name which the interpolator of Malmesbury renders as Avalloc, stating that Avalloc was said to have dwelt there with his daughters on account of the retired nature of the spot.

Gerald, then, would seem to have been the first author to have identified Avalon with Glastonbury. But it is not quite so simple as that. Gerald also identified Glastonbury with Inisgutrin, the isle of glass, and this identification can be traced much further back. William of Malmesbury in his *Gesta regum Anglorum* quotes a half-decipherable regum Anglorum, no longer extant, charter of the year 601 in which a king of Dumnonia grants five hides to the old church situated in the land called Ynyswitrin; and Caradoc of Llancarfan, writing in the 1130s, states that Glastonbury was originally called Ynis gutrin, that is (he says) the isle of glass. We have thus two separate equations:

(i) Glastonbury = Ynyswitrin (601) = isle of glass (Caradoc *c.* 1135 and Gerald *c.* 1194).
(ii) Avalon is an island (Geoffrey of Monmouth *c.* 1138) = isle of apples (Merlin *c.* 1150 and Gerald *c.* 1194) = isle of Avallo (Gerald *c.* 1219) or Avalloc (pseudo-William).

It is these two equations that are combined by Gerald *c.* 1194. Glastonbury = isle of glass = isle of apples – isle of Avalon – isle of Avallo or Avalloc.

At first sight these epithets may seem very disparate, but there is one factor that is common to them all, namely a reference in some form or other to a Celtic underworld or beyond-world, a magical abode of healing and of peace. Thus behind Caradoc of Llancarfan with his story of Meluas, the king of the summer land, of Meluas' seizure of Arthur and Guinevere and the siege of the city of glass, is the Welsh tradition enshrined in the *Spoils of Annwfn*, which is probably earlier than 1050 and which describes a voyage of Arthur to a fortress evidently representing Annwfn, the Celtic underworld. Arthur's purpose is to carry off a magic cauldron kindled by the breath of nine maidens and Caer Wydr, the fortress of glass, is also mentioned. In the Arthurian romance of Chrétien de Troyes, *Erec*, written in the second half of the twelfth century, we find the same Welsh myth in which Maheloas is described as lord of the 'isle de Voirre', or isle of glass.

Nevertheless the so-called *Dialogue of Arthur and Gwenhyfar* suggests that in the original story Arthur and Guinevere had visited Meluas' land and he had fallen in love with her there. Thus the author of *Culwch and Olwen* – almost certainly earlier than 1100 – speaks of this underworld, but introduces a fresh character when he states that God had set in Gwyn the spirits of the devils of Annwfn, Gwyn's wife was stolen and Arthur retained her. Further, in the legend of St Collen – the date of which it is impossible to determine – we find Gwyn, Annwfn and Glastonbury all together. St Collen made a cell on Glastonbury Tor and there heard men talking about Gwyn ap Nudd and saying he was king of Annwfn. The saint then destroyed Gwyn's stronghold.

From all this it will be seen that, though the part played by Arthur has changed, there is a common factor in the Celtic underworld, the land of Annwfn or the kingdom of Gwyn, which Caradoc in the 1130s has identified with the isle of glass and Glastonbury. Where, then, does the isle of apples come in? Here we have the same notion of a world beyond our own, but now the stress is more upon immortality, the enchanted orchard of the Hesperides, Eden with its Tree of Life, the land of eternal summer where the fruit conferring immortality is always in season – 'nor never can those trees be bare'. Nevertheless, the underworld of Annwfn appears to be identical with the isle of apples; the magic cauldron of Annwfn was, as we have seen, kindled by the breath of nine maidens and the *Vita Merlini*, our first reference to the isle of apples, states that there it was that Morgan and her eight sisters cured Arthur of his wounds. Therefore, by the middle of the eleventh century, the underworld has been identified with the isle of glass, by *c.* 1140 Caradoc has equated it with Glastonbury and now by 1150 the author of *Vita Merlini* has identified the underworld with the isle of apples. To identify, therefore, the mythical isle of apples with Glastonbury was now obvious and inevitable.

What then of Avalon? The author of *Vita Merlini* stated that it was to the isle of apples that Arthur was taken; in 1138 Geoffrey of Monmouth had already said that Arthur was taken to the isle of Avalon to be healed. Thus it is clear that by 1150 the isle of Avalon and the isle of apples are considered to be identical, and here again we are on the verge of the identification of

Avalon with Glastonbury. Finally, the connexion is made yet again when both Gerald of Wales and the interpolator of Malmesbury derive Avalon from Avallo or Avalloc, for this brings us back to Avalloc or Avallach who seems to be have been, like Gwyn, a deity of the underworld and who appears in later Arthurian romances as Evalach.

It may seem odd that the mythical isle of the *Vita Merlini* can be identified with an actual place. Indeed, this seems to have occurred to at least one Glastonbury author, for John of Glastonbury gives an interpolated form of part of the *Vita Merlini* in which lines are added calling the isle of apples the New Jerusalem and stating that it is a holy burial-place which promises salvation to all who rest there. Nonetheless, the connexion cannot have been purely adventitious. The isle of Glastonbury may have been the site of a Celtic monastery at least by the fifth century and stretching back beyond written record were the wattle-church and the holy cemetery, and it is, therefore, by no means a fanciful conjecture to suppose that it had earlier pagan associations as an isle of the dead, both as an actual burial-place and as a supposed passage to the underworld. No grave of any of the lake villagers who dwelt nearby has yet been discovered and it would seem not unlikely that it was to the isle of Glastonbury that their bodies were transferred. It is dangerous, perhaps, to conjecture in this way, but there must have been some factor which led Caradoc to bring Meluas and Arthur to Glastonbury, that impelled Geoffrey to take Arthur to Avalon to be cured of his wounds. There is more in this than merely the romancing of monks or the wishful thinking of an age-old community pondering its forgotten youth. Granted the existence of Arthur and granted that Glastonbury was a kind of Westminster Abbey of Celtic times, his burial there is not impossible. Geoffrey of Monmouth, however, does not speak of Arthur's burial but of his being cured of his wounds; yet, if he is recording a tradition (and it is a big 'if'), it may well be that to the Celtic mind the healing of wounds and burial were one and the same thing. For if death be the approach to the underworld and the renewing of life, burial is the gateway to healing. In the words of M. Dolben:

> In some mysterious Avilon,
> Beyond the years, some consummate hereafter,
> A fount of healing springs for all alike.

To return, then, to our original entry in the interpolated William of Malmesbury. Arthur, wounded at Camlan by Mordred, is taken to the isle of Avalon to be healed of his wounds and he died at Avalon in the summer around Pentecost, being about a hundred years old. The reference to the summer seems to be an echo of Caradoc who calls Meluas king of the summer region – either a periphrasis for Somerset or a reference to the enchanted garden – while the age of a hundred years appears to be based on the *Vita Merlini* which states that all who live in the isle of apples attain to the age of a hundred or more. For light upon the statement of the pseudo-William that Arthur lies in the monks' cemetery between two pyramids we have to move on to the next stage of our enquiry, which must be an examination into the alleged exhumation of Arthur at Glastonbury in the early 1190s.

There are four accounts of this exhumation and it will be well to go through them before commenting upon them. Gerald of Wales in his *De instructione principum*, written between 1192 and 1199, states that certain writings, certain letters on the pyramids, certain visions and revelations but, most of all, King Henry II, who had heard of Arthur's presence at Glastonbury from a Welsh bard, impelled the search which led to the discovery of the bodies of Arthur and Guinevere at a depth of sixteen feet between two pyramids in the monks' cemetery. The body was in an oaken coffin and lay below a stone which was itself under the ground. Under the stone was a leaden cross stating that this was the body of Arthur. In his *Speculum ecclesiae* of *c.* 1216 Gerald amplifies this description by saying that Henry II, inspired by the tales of the Britons and their bards, told Abbot Henry de Sully to undertake the search. The pyramids are said to have been erected in memory of Arthur and the stone is now said to have lain at the depth of seven feet.

Ralph of Coggeshall in his *Chronicon Anglicanum* under the year 1191 gives a simpler version of the story. He states that the pyramids were indecipherable but that Arthur's tomb was found because a monk had expressed a desire to be buried at that spot. He mentions the leaden cross but not the stone. Adam of Damerham, writing after 1277, says that Abbot Henry de Sully had frequently been urged to move Arthur's body to a better resting-place and, on a certain day, the spot was surrounded by curtains and the digging began. The bodies were found and the leaden cross, but, again, no mention is made of the stone. Adam states that Arthur had laid 648 years in the cemetery, the pseudo-William makes Arthur die in 542 and this, therefore, would make 1190 the year of the discovery.

We must now examine the alleged discovery in detail. With regard to the date, Ralph puts it in 1191 and Adam in 1190. Henry II died in July 1189 and Abbot Henry de Sully was appointed by Richard later that year. To account for the confusion which makes Henry II speak to Abbot Henry, we should, I think, incline to the earlier of the two dates.

The place of the discovery was in the ancient cemetery of Glastonbury, between two pyramids. These tall inscribed stone crosses were described minutely by William of Malmesbury *c.* 1135. It is impossible here to go into their history but it seems abundantly clear that there was nothing in the inscriptions on the pyramids which could have conduced to the search for

Arthur. Indeed, at a slightly later date the writings upon them were thought to be a list of the companions of St Patrick. Nevertheless, the question remains: why dig at that particular spot? Was it merely, as Ralph says, that a monk wished to be buried there? This seems unlikely, and we shall have to return to this point later on.

Arthur was said to have been buried sixteen feet down and, according to Gerald, there was found a stone seven feet below the surface and under the stone a leaden cross. Whatever we may decide about the exhumation itself it seems clear that the cross was an over-ingenious forgery. Fortunately the cross itself existed in the time of Camden who gives a reproduction of it. The inscription ran: *His iacet inclitus Arturius in insula Avalonia*. We may note the otiose mention of Avalon and we shall probably feel the inspiration of this inscription is to be found in the eleventh chapter of Geoffrey's *Historia* in the phrase '*sed et inclytus Arturus letaliter vulneratus est, qui . . . ad sananda vulnera sua in insulam Avalloniam evectus etc*'. But the fact that the cross was forged does not necessarily make the discovery itself suspect.

What prompted the search? According to Gerald it was the stories of the Welsh bards which reached Henry II, who in turn urged the search. Gerald also speaks of visions and the writings on the pyramids. Ralph adds the story of the monk. It is certainly likely that the identification of Avalon with Glastonbury had by then already been made; it is possible that this identification reached the ears of Henry II and that the king suggested the search. If this is so, the exhumation of Arthur was suggested to the monks from outside, and, the suggestion once made, the pyramids were scrutinized, documents were read and revelations pressed into service. But what actually happened on the spot itself?

Let us first examine the possibility that the entire exhumation was fraudulent. We have the undoubtedly forged cross, we have the incredibly large bones exhumed at an unnaturally great depth below a concealed stone and the excavation itself is carried out behind curtains hiding it from public view. All these are suspicious features. Further, we have the story of an earlier and legendary excavation which took place a few miles from Glastonbury and on land which once belonged to the abbey, a story which can almost be proved to have been known at Glastonbury by about 1180. This tale is that of the wonder-working cross of Waltham in Essex which was said to have been found at Montacute Hill in consequence of a vision vouchsafed to the local smith. The cross was alleged to have been buried forty cubits into the soil, it lay below a large stone and the excavation was carried out behind curtains. Indeed, the parallel is so close that we may well wonder if the story served as a model for the exhumation of Arthur.

On the other hand, in favour of the genuineness of the events of 1190 we do in fact know that the level of the monks' cemetery was heightened by several feet at the time of St Dunstan, and the stone, therefore, could have been an earlier grave stone then covered over. The cross, though fraudulent, may have replaced a grave-cross less precise in wording, for to establish that the grave was certainly that of Arthur the written identification of Glastonbury with Avalon had to be made. Such a cross could well have begun with the words *Hic iacet sepultus*. We are, of course, again in the field of conjecture. That evidence was manufactured to support the burial of Arthur is clear, but it does not follow that there was not an earlier tradition. The perplexing point is the actual situation of the grave. Why dig between the two pyramids? Let us take the question the other way round and ask ourselves why, if Arthur existed and was buried in the cemetery, the pyramids should have been erected upon either side of his tomb. The pyramids were certainly of Saxon date and there is evidence, though by no means conclusive, that they were erected under the influence of St Wilfrid and his friends from the north to mark the introduction of the Benedictine rule into Glastonbury about the year 677. Such an introduction meant the union of Saxon with Celtic Glastonbury and if there existed the tradition that a great Celtic leader was buried at a particular spot in the cemetery the obvious plan to record the reconciliation of the new with the old would be to erect the two great memorial crosses on either side of his tomb. And if we wonder why no claim was made to Arthur's tomb before the twelfth century, we should not forget that the Arthur of the hagiographers – the Arthur of the lives of SS Cadog, Padarn and Gildas – was no saint, but an immoral tyrant. The presence of his corpse would not then be an asset to be claimed and his memory would be one best forgotten. The impulse that in later years caused the stones of Avebury to be buried may have been similar to that which allowed Arthur to lie deep and unrecorded below the soil of Glastonbury.

We must now return to the interpolator of William of Malmesbury. Leaving aside a marginal note of uncertain date which occurs later in John of Glastonbury, there is not much. First there is a story that records the knighting of Ider, son of Nuth. At *Mons ranarum*, which is identified with Brent Knoll, Ider killed three giants. Arthur found him in a collapsed condition and attributed this to the delay in carrying him to Glastonbury. We find this story again in John of Glastonbury, but the place is now called *mons de Areynes* and said to be in North Wales. We may well think that the confusion between frogs and spiders betrays a Latin original in which *Mons Ranarum* and *Mons Aranearum* are confused. This story cannot be traced to any incident recorded in the Arthurian *corpus* and the nearest parallel to it is found in *Yder*, a romance written in France between 1210 and 1225, in which Ider killed two giants in different circumstances. For our purposes, we can note the presence at Glastonbury before 1247 of an Arthurian story different from anything now known.

The story of Ider ends with the statement that Arthur made a foundation at Glastonbury for eighty monks and gave the place possessions and ornaments. Here the interpolator of William is probably merely following Caradoc's statement that Arthur and Meluas gave 'benefits to Glastonbury' and Gerald who calls Arthur a *patronus* of Glastonbury and a *largitor et sublevator magnificus*.

So much then for the interpolator of William of Malmesbury. Adam of Damerham's account of the exhumation we have already considered and he has nothing else to record of Arthur save that *inclitus Arthurus* appears as a benefactor to Glastonbury in an undoubtedly manipulated charter of Henry II. It is with John of Glastonbury in the fourteenth century that we can see the further evolution of the legend of Arthur. First two genealogies connected with Arthur are given. Arthur is shown to have been descended from the nephew of Joseph of Arimathea and Gawaine from Arthur's brother-in-law. These genealogies are taken from the *Estoire del San Graal* and are followed by much Arthurian matter, all of which can be traced back to Geoffrey of Monmouth and Caradoc's life of St Gildas which has been slightly re-edited. Then comes an account of Arthur's victories taken from 'Nennius' and the story of Ider and the giants to which we have already referred.

So far all is fairly plain sailing. But next we have a lengthy tale describing a vision accorded to Arthur at a monastery of virgins – the chapel right adventurous – on Wirrall Hill. We can follow this story back through an English poem of *c*. 1340 called *Libeaus Desconus*, in which Glastonbury is the setting, then through an earlier French romance called *Le Bel Inconnu* to *Perlesvaus*, which gives us another version of the same story. *Perlesvaus* which was written between 1191 and 1212 claims to be based upon a Glastonbury book, and it is clear that Avalon is so described as certainly to mean Glastonbury. Thus we are beginning to see the identification of spots near Glastonbury with places mentioned in the Arthurian legend. The *Libeaus Desconus* described Pomparlés and was written about 1340; it is interesting to find the earliest mention of Street Bridge as *Pons periculosus* in 1344.

John continues with a curious piece of legendary matter said by him to have been taken from the *Gesta incliti regis Arthuri*. This is in two sections. The first refers to a quest made by Lancelot and his friends of the round table and the explaining by a hermit of the mystery of a spring which will change in scent and colour until a great lion is bound. The other section says that in the quest the vessel called the Holy Grail, nearly at the beginning of the book, will be found where the White Knight expounds the mystery of a wonderful shield. Incidents similar to the first are recorded in *Perlesvaus* and to the second are found in the *Estoire del Saint Graal*, but not 'nearly at the beginning of the book'. Of the *Estoire* we should note that it is closely connected with Robert de Boron's *Joseph d'Arimathie* of between 1191 and 1212 in which a certain Peter is told to go to the 'vaus d'Avaron' to await the coming of the son of Alain, the nephew of Joseph of Arimathea. With regard to *Perlesvaus* which clearly identifies Avalon with Glastonbury and refers also to Caer Wydr or the fortress of glass, we have a common factor which we have already noticed in Chrétien de Troyes' *Erec* which describes Maheloas as lord of the *isle de voirre*, thus going back to Caradoc's Melwas and his *urbs vitrea*.

The story of Joseph of Arimathea, which is closely bound up with the domestic traditions of Glastonbury in regard to her origins, will not take us so long to examine, even if there is much that remains obscure. We can sum up quite briefly what William of Malmesbury himself has to say about the origins of Glastonbury. According to William the wattle-church was the most ancient in the land, it was built by missionaries sent by Pope Eleutherius in AD 166 and some say that it was built by the actual disciples of Christ. There is of course no mention of Joseph of Arimathea. For some of these statements we need look no further than to Freculf of Lisieux and the Anglo-Saxon Chronicle. The only important point is the tradition founded, William says, upon written evidence of good credit, that 'the church of Glastonbury did none other man's hands make, but the actual disciples of Christ built it'. In this connexion there is an important passage in the life of St Dunstan written by 'B' about the year 1000, a life certainly known to William. 'B' says that 'the first neophytes of the Catholic law found . . . an ancient church, built, it is said, by no human skill, but prepared by God for man's salvation, which afterwards the maker of the heavens himself by many stories of miracles and many mysteries of virtues showed that he himself had consecrated it to himself and to the holy Mary, mother of God'. Here we should notice that the ancient church was not built by, but was discovered by the first neophytes of the Catholic law; indeed, the church was not built by human hands at all. It is not clear how far this is meant to be rhetorical, for we have echoes of Hebrews IX II (Vulgate) *tabernaculum non manufactum, id est, non huius creationis* and Revelations XXI 2 *Jerusalem novam descendentem, a Deo paratam*. Further the 'maker of the heavens' is usually applied to the Father, as in the Nicene Creed, and not to Christ and we should surely not stress the technical meaning of 'consecrate', but rather take the passage to mean that, as a result of the portents experienced, the early Christian converts were later convinced that the ancient church was especially hallowed by God for his own honour and that of his mother, as it were a tabernacle of God prepared in heaven. In this sense 'B's remarks are perfectly sensible: the early Christian converts found an ancient church and believed it to have been prepared by God for them. But it is easy to see how 'the first neophytes of the Catholic law' could become 'the disciples of Christ' and how these disciples could become not the discoverers but the makers of the church.

This is practically all that William of Malmesbury had to say of the earliest origins of Glastonbury. His interpolator has more to add. The disciples of St Philip now number eleven 'of whom, it is said, St Philip put at the head his dearest friend Joseph of Arimathea who buried the Lord'. We may note that this is the only reference that is made to Joseph. Pagan kings give the disciples portions of land, hence Glastonbury Twelve Hides. These holy men are told by the archangel Gabriel to build a church in honour of the Blessed Virgin. Here the interpolator quotes his sources.

The first of these is the Charter of St Patrick. This fantastic forgery, composed before 1247, mentioned the disciples of St Philip and St James and the admonition of the archangel, but does not mention Joseph of Arimathea. The second source is *unus historiographus Britonum* as found at Bury St Edmunds and St Augustine's Canterbury. The quotation given is very similar to the one from the Life of St Dunstan we have already mentioned. The third source is un-named writings of the ancients.

This is literally all that we know of the sources of the early thirteenth-century tradition of the coming of St Joseph of Arimathea, a tradition, as we have seen, still very vague and indefinite. How are we to account for the saint's presence?[4] There are perhaps two possibilities to be considered. The first of these is some form of the Arthurian legend that brought Joseph to Glastonbury. With the early history of the Grail legend we cannot concern ourselves, but it is quite possible to trace the growth of the Celtic notion of the mystic cauldron of Annwfn, the christianisation of this magic cup of healing, first into the dish and then into the sacred cup, of the Last Supper, and the parallel identification of Annwfn with Avalon and of Avalon with Glastonbury. We can then conceive of a story, apparently known at Glastonbury and probably lying behind the late twelfth-century de Boron's *Joseph d'Arimathie* and its amplification in the *Estoire del Saint Graal*, which brought Joseph the Grail-bearer to Glastonbury. But the medieval Glastonbury writers merely use this story to bring Joseph himself to Glastonbury; they never asserted that he brought the Grail.

That is one line of approach, we may now suggest another. One of the vexed questions of hagiology is the story of the growth of the cult of St Mary Magdalen. There is first the process by which the martyrs Maria and Martha become identified with the sisters of Bethany and the confusion between Mary of Bethany and Mary Magdalen. Then there are the parallel cults of Mary Magdalen, Martha and Lazarus in Provence and in Burgundy. At the moment it is impossible to say at what date Joseph of Arimathea is added to this group of emigrants from the Holy Land. But the fact remains that the cult of Lazarus has been traced back to the tenth century at Autun

---

[4] See V. M. Lagorio, 'The Evolving Legend of St Joseph of Glastonbury', *Speculum* 46 (1971), 209–31.

and, more recently still, it has been shown that Avalon was before Autun in the cult of Lazarus. But equally at Glastonbury we find evidence of an early cult of Lazarus. His festival occurs in a contemporary addition to the tenth-century Leofric missal and in a twelfth-century Glastonbury *collectarium*. This festival is unknown in any other English Kalendars of these dates. Is it possible that here we come somewhere near to a clue to the introduction of the cult of Joseph of Arimathea at Glastonbury, is it possible that legends connecting him with Avallon in Burgundy were transferred by a natural confusion to the isle of Avalon? At the moment this can be no more than a query, for no reference to an early cult of St Joseph at Avallon has yet been found. But it is interesting in this connexion to note that the *Estoire del Saint Graal* was written in Burgundy, that St Mary Magdalen is mentioned in an eleventh-century Glastonbury kalendar at Cambridge, that the hermitage mentioned in the Glastonbury version of *Perlesvaus* was dedicated to her and that Abbot Michael of Amesbury in the mid-thirteenth century dedicated also to her his new alms-houses. But all this is nothing more than a shadow of a clue.

The interpolator of William also has more precisions to add to William's story of the origins of Glastonbury. Phaganus and Deruvianus are named among the missionaries sent by Eleutherius, names doubtless derived by way of Geoffrey of Monmouth and Gerald of Wales from a forged letter of Pope Honorius II.

Most of what John of Glastonbury has to tell us about Joseph of Arimathea has exhaustively been examined by Armitage Robinson and, apart from the so-called prophecy of Melkin, its sources are not very obscure. The early history of Joseph is taken from *apocryphal* literature, particularly from the Gospel of Nicodemus and the *Transitus Mariae*, from Petrus Riga's *Aurora*, and from the Arthurian legends which we have already discussed. Nor does what John of Glastonbury has to say about Joseph appear to be very startling: all that is added to these sources is that the saint brought with him to Glastonbury cruets containing the blood and sweat of Christ and that he was buried at an unknown spot in the monks' cemetery. For the last two statements, which appear first in John, we have to turn to the prophecy of Melkin which he quotes in full.[5]

Leland saw the original text of this prophecy and described it as an *exemplarium vetustatis* and it is certainly couched in a style that is antique, obscure and ungrammatical. Its general sense, however, is clear: Avalon has always been known as the burial-place of pagans. Buried there is Abbadare powerful in Saphat, who sleeps there with 104,000 among whom was Joseph from across the sea who lies *in linea bifurcata* against the south

[5] See J. P. Carley, 'Melkin the Bard and Esoteric Tradition at Glastonbury Abbey', *The Downside Review* 99 (1981), 1–17.

corner of the wattle-church built by the thirteen inhabitants of the place. Joseph has with him in his coffin two silver cruets filled with the blood and sweat of the prophet Jesus. The whole of this is couched in terms which defy exact translation and any interpretation of it abounds with difficulties of every kind. Dr Margaret Murray has made an ingenious plea for its Coptic origin; others hold that it stems from Arabian astro-mythology, while Armitage Robinson seems to imply that it was a fourteenth-century forgery. Certainly it could be of oriental origin and ancient in date. It could be ancient but have been interpolated by the hand of a fourteenth-century discoverer – perhaps the John Blome who in 1345 secured permission to search for the body of St Joseph at Glastonbury 'because it is said in certain ancient writings that the body was there buried'. It could be a *tour-de-force* of monastic forgery. It is either the earliest, or the latest, link in the chain that connects Joseph of Arimathea with Glastonbury. It is either of great, or of almost no, significance and, like the King Of Hearts, we can only murmur uncertainly 'important, unimportant; unimportant, important'.

Whatever the origin of Melkin, it is clear that Glastonbury accepted the prophecy with gratitude, though she never pretended to have understood it. William of Worcester in the fifteenth century quotes a Glastonbury collect begging God to reveal the burial place of St Joseph and we know from William Good that this uncertainty prevailed to the very end.

It is on this note of uncertainty that we must end. It would be pleasant to be able to believe that the later traditions were but belated discoveries of earlier truths, but, if evidence is to retain any meaning and historical analysis any validity, we must conclude that we know nothing that can warrant our making such an assertion. If anything is clear in this tangled story, it is that William of Malmesbury had heard nothing of these later claims. But to assert the opposite view-point – that perhaps of Armitage Robinson, that the Glastonbury legends were for the most part a deliberate piece of concoction by unscrupulous inventors bent upon according a fictitious pre-eminence to Glastonbury – that is, perhaps, equally naive. If our investigation has shown anything, it has shown something far more complex. Ancient traditions, new traditions, Welsh, Breton and possibly Burgundian traditions, forged evidence, interpolated evidence, genuinely misunderstood evidence and, finally, fact – fact known and fact but half remembered – all these have played their part in an attempt to make intelligible both to itself and to others the history of a place reaching back far beyond certain record.

And there we must leave it. We have made some tentative equations which, if valid, do something to solve the questions that present themselves so urgently to the enquirer. And it may be that just as we cannot advance far in mathematical calculation without introducing irrationals into our equations, so, perhaps, these historical surds may in time become the solvents of truth. And it is therefore at levels deeper than those with which the historian may presume to deal – levels where poetry and symbol achieve a validity of their own – that we may still hear the hooves of Arthur as he rides from Camelot, and the wearied footfalls of the Decurion bringing from Palestine the Holy Grail.

V

MAGNA TABULA: THE GLASTONBURY TABLETS
(Part 1)

Jeanne Krochalis

Preface[1]

The Glastonbury Tablets are a large, hollow wooden box, about 3 feet by 1½ feet, with two hinged wooden leaves inside. On the parchment pasted over the inside front and back and the leaves is written the history of the abbey from its purported foundation by Joseph of Arimathia in AD 63 to the refurbishings of 1382 under Abbot John Chinnock (1375–1420). Arthur, the Holy Grail, the lost chapels of Phaganus and Deruvianus, of King Ine and of St David, the community of Patrick, the Celtic saints, Saxon kings and Anglian relics, all figure prominently in the nearly six hundred lines of text.[2] On the last leaf are over eighty indulgences granted by bishops with sees ranging from Laodicea *in partis infidelibus* to the local bishop of Bath and Wells. The fifteenth-century pilgrim who could read Latin by the candlelight available in the abbey would be thoroughly informed about what Glastonbury considered its authentic history, and the spiritual benefits he or she could gain from being there.

Some, of course, were sceptical. The compiler of the *Nova legenda*

---

[1] I would like to thank James P. Carley, Robert W. Frank, Jr, Michael Lapidge, Felicity Riddy and Michael Robson, OFM, for help of various kinds. Much of the research was done at the University Library, Cambridge, and much of the writing on computers at Clare Hall, Cambridge, whose staff were particularly helpful. Colin Harris and his assistants in the reading room trundled the *Magna Tabula* out for repeated inspections. I would also like to thank the staff in Duke Humfrey's Library and the New Library, Bodleian Library, Oxford, in the British Library, London, and at Upholland College.

[2] The thorn tree is not mentioned in any text until the early sixteenth century. See R. F. Treharne, *The Glastonbury Legends* (London, 1975), p. 123. For a possible surviving crown of thorns relic now at Stanbrook Abbey, see J. P. Carley, *Glastonbury Abbey, The Holy House at the Head of the Moors Adventurous* (Woodbridge, 1988), p. 130.

Angliæ adds to his sober life of Patrick the account of the Irish saint's thirty-year stay at Glastonbury, and also the Glastonbury stories of St David. At the end, before going on to the still more remarkable account of Patrick's Purgatory, he adds:

> Ego uero in prescriptis et dubiis, et in sequentibus nonnullis, auctoritatem discutiendi et difinendi mihi non presumo, sed tamquam relator simplex, que in diversis libris et locis cum laboribus et difficultate sedulus indignator reperire potui, ardua peritus ventilanda relinquens sine invidia, communico.³

(Indeed, I do not presume for myself the authority of discussing and defining what has been written before, both in dubious cases and in some of the following material, but [I regard myself] as a simple teller of things which I, diligent and unworthy, was able to gather from diverse books and places with labours and difficulty; relinquishing to the skilled without envy the arduous task of explaining.)

The compiler of the Glastonbury tablets was himself a *relator simplex* of no mean skill. He did not merely copy and condense the Glastonbury traditions known at the close of the fourteenth century; from diverse books and places (chiefly, but by no means exclusively, the chronicles of William of Malmesbury and John of Glastonbury) and from his own knowledge of the abbey and its relics, he gathered a sense of what Glastonbury meant to convey to the literate visitor who came to view its church and surroundings. In this two-part article I have attempted to track his sources, and to look at what his selections from them reveal about the abbey's attitude to the Arthurian myth, to British history, and to the cults of certain saints. The two parts have four sections. **Part I: 1. Tablets.** Because the *Magna Tabula* is in an unusual format, I begin with a discussion of the uses of tablets in medieval churches and an overview of the contents of the Glastonbury tablets. **2. Physical Description.** Because there is no thorough catalogue description of the *Magna Tabula* in print, a detailed examination of the object itself is included, ending with a list of contents of the forty-one separate items which are on the six tablets.⁴ **3. Edition.** The edition of the

---

3 *Nova Legenda Angliæ*, ed. C. Horstmann, 2 vols. (Oxford, 1901), II, 293. This compilation used to be ascribed to John Capgrave, under whose name Wynkyn de Worde printed his edition in 1516; recent scholarship has questioned the attribution, and it is here treated as anonymous.
4 A number of scholars have described it briefly, and there is a half-page description available in the Bodleian Library, Oxford, in the typescript catalogue of Medieval Manuscripts kept in Duke Humfrey's Library. Published commentaries have tended to concentrate on particular passages, and to assume that most of the material came from William of Malmesbury or John of Glastonbury. This is truer of Tablets 1–4 than of Tablets 5 and 6, though even in the first four, the sources are more varied.

Latin text, with its textual notes, follows. **Part II** will be published in *Arthurian Literature XVI*, and will contain: **4. Glossary.** Each king, saint, and place poses different problems, and many are cited in several different places on the tablets. In order to focus discussions of figures such as Arthur, Patrick, David, King Edgar, or Ynyswitrin, I have prepared a glossary of names, which is organized alphabetically; the bishops and archbishops who gave indulgences on Tablet 6 are alphabetized by their sees at the conclusion of the Glossary.

1. Tablets

a. Tablets in Churches

Tablets may strike us as unusual, but they were popular in English churches in the later Middle Ages. They were too big and heavy to be stolen or borrowed. Like the Bibles chained in Elizabethan churches, they served as permanent reference works, always available for consultation. That they contain texts, without any pictures, implies a literate audience. The *Magna Tabula*, and the two other surviving examples, are unillustrated. The monks themselves would of course have been literate, though the abbey's numerous lay brothers would not necessarily have known how to read. The church itself was filled with other images, including stained glass, statues, wall paintings, altar frontals. A few crosses and an image of the Virgin on display in the church are mentioned on the tablets. It seems likely that, by the late fourteenth century, most visitors would at least have been accompanied by someone literate. Many would have been clerics themselves. Among the lay groups, it is remarkable how often pilgrim narratives and miracle stories mention groups accompanied by a chaplain. The abbey itself could also have provided a guide and reader.[5] For those guides, the tablets would have served as useful reference texts.[6]

---

[5] At the other extreme from the tablets, Oxford, Bodleian Library, Laud Misc. 750 is a small belt book, made of leaves which were folded in four, then hung from a tongue on to a belt loop. Most volumes in this shape are calendars, almanacs, or practical scientific texts, such as treatises on urine, which it would be useful for a doctor to be able to carry about. This book was written at Glastonbury in the thirteenth century. Though only a part survives, it contained a brief chronology from Adam, and a version of William of Malmesbury's *De antiquitate*. One purpose it could have served would be to provide a portable text for guides showing visitors about the abbey. For a brief description with plate, see A. G. Watson, *Catalogue of Dated and Datable Manuscripts c. 435–1600 in Oxford Libraries*, 2 vols. (Oxford, 1984), I, 98, and II, no. 118.

[6] Canon Purvis, following F. Harrison, suggested that the York tablets were made for the York Vicars Choral who, by a statute of 1294, had to pass an examination in the histories of the Minster and of the world, as a condition of admission, but this connection has been dismissed by Dobson. J. S. Purvis, 'The Tables of the York Vicars Choral', *Yorkshire*

York Minster has the only other surviving English tablets, which are triptychs, now kept in the Minster Library. There are two of them. Both are bigger overall than the *Magna Tabula*. The first measures 56 inches in height, and 35½ inches in width closed, with two side panels of 16¾ inches. The second is 45½ inches tall, and 27½ inches across closed, with two side panels of 13¾ inches; it is a little shorter than the *Magna Tabula*, but wider. We can probably assume that the other examples were of roughly comparable size. The York tablets contain local and universal history.[7] The life and miracles of St William were in another tablet at York, kept near his altar, which is now lost.[8]

There were other tablets which do not survive.[9] We know about those at the cathedrals of Durham, Lichfield, Lincoln, Ripon[10] and Winchester. These last were still in the cathedral in the early seventeenth century.[11] The

Archaeological Journal 41 (1966), 741–8. B. Dobson, 'The Later Middle Ages, 1215–1500', in *A History of York Minster*, ed. G. E. Aylmer and R. Cant (Oxford, 1979), p. 108, n. 227.

7   Purvis, 'The Tables of the York Vicars Choral', pp. 747–8. The York history is printed in *The Historians of the Church of York, and its Archbishops*, ed. J. Raine, 3 vols., RS 77 (London, 1886), II, 446–463. They were made under Archbishop Arundel (1388–97), and so are contemporary with the Glastonbury tablets. Manuscripts include London, British Library, Cotton Titus A.xix (Kirkstall), Cotton Cleopatra C.iv (written in a northern hand), and Harley 1808 (also northern). The manuscripts seem to have been copied from the tablets. The world history set has not been printed, but was used by John de Foxton in 1408, and collated by J. B. Friedman in *John de Foxton's Liber cosmographiae (1408), an Edition and Codicological Study*, ed. J. B. Friedman (Leiden, 1988). See also J. B. Friedman, 'John Siferwas and the Mythological Illustrations in the Liber Cosmographie of John de Foxton', *Speculum* 58 (1983), 391–418. For the tablets dealing with St William, see Raine, *Historians of the Church of York*, II, xxxi.

8   Tablets with the Passion of St George, discussed in G. Gerould, 'The Legend of St Wulfhad and St Ruffin at Stone Priory', *PMLA* 32 (1917), 323–37, and again in Gerould, ' "Tables" in Medieval Churches', *Speculum* 1 (1926), 439–40, are pictures alone, without any text. They were described as a 'tabula lignea stans super parvum altare in parte boreali, ex opposito summo altari, cum platis et imaginibus cupreis deauratis, continens passionem S. Georgii' (quoted from Sir William Dugdale, *Monasticon Anglicanum*, 6 vols. [London, 1846], VI, 1364 in Gerould, ' "Tables" in Medieval Churches', p. 439). Plates and images of copper gilt sound rather like an icon. For similar items elsewhere in the royal circle, see J. Stratford, *The Bedford Inventories: The Worldly Goods of John Duke of Bedford, Regent of France (1389–1435)* (London, 1993), item B 112, pp. 199 and 307–8, citing the Windsor altar-piece from M. F. Bond, *The Inventories of St George's Chapel, Windsor Castle, 1384–1667* (Windsor, 1947), p. 96.

9   The fullest list, with very brief discussion, is in A. Gransden, *Historical Writing in England, II, c. 1307 to the Early Sixteenth Century* (Ithaca, NY, 1982), p. 495; it contains everything except York, Ripon, Winchester, St Peter upon Cornhill, Bawburgh, Seaford and the continental examples.

10 For Ripon, see Raine, *Historians of the Church of York*, II, pp. xxix and 467–75.

11 J. Ussher, *Britannicarum ecclesiarum antiquitates* (London, 1687), pp. 29, 67 and 73. The first edition was printed in Dublin in 1639, which provides a *terminus ante quem* for

churches of St Peter upon Cornhill and St Paul's, both in London, also had tablets, as did the church of Bawburgh in Norfolk.[12] Five other monastic sites have left records of tablets: Bury St Edmunds, Stone Priory in Staffordshire, Worksop in Nottinghamshire, Christ Church, Canterbury and St John the Baptist, Colchester.[13] The geographical spread suggests that there were probably many more examples which were casualties of the Reformation.

They were not only an English fashion; Arnold noted that a similar tablet had existed 'for ages' in the Santa Casa at Loreto,[14] and Ussher discusses the tablet at Zurich, which had information about the continental travels of King Lucius.[15] The guide to Rome in London, British Library, Cotton Titus A.xix mentions that *in muro sancti basilii fuit magna tabula infixa ubi fuit scripta amicitia facta inter romanos et Judeos tempore Jude Machabei* (fol. 12v). The holes in the back of the Glastonbury tablets suggest that they too were fixed to the wall in some fashion (see section 2, Physical Description, below).

---

the tablets Ussher actually saw. According to the Winchester tablets, King Lucius was buried at Gloucester Cathedral (p. 73), which is not part of the Glastonbury tradition.

[12] N. Denholm-Young, 'The Birth of a Chronicle', *Bodleian Quarterly Record* 7 (1933), 326 and n. 5, 237–8, cited in Gransden, *Historical Writing, II*, 495. For Durham, see also W. A. Pantin, 'Some Medieval English Treatises on the Origins of Monasticism', in *Medieval Studies Presented to Rose Graham*, ed. V. Ruffer and A. J. Taylor (Oxford, 1950), pp. 200–201. For St Paul's and St Peter upon Cornhill in London, see Ussher, *Antiquitates*, pp. 32, 36 and 73. Both sets seem to have been there when Ussher was researching. For St Paul's, see also F. Riddy, 'Glastonbury, Joseph of Arimathea and the Grail' in *The Archaeology and History of Glastonbury Abbey*, ed. L. Abrams and J. P. Carley (Woodbridge, 1991), pp. 317–31 (p. 326). Those at St Peter are mentioned in John Stow, *The Survey of London* (London, 1912), pp. 174 and 423. The text on the tablets at St Peter may have been related to the chronicle on fols. 237ra-242rb (to 1108) or the chronicle from 1140 BC to AD 1385 which follows it on fols. 242v–243rb in London, British Library, Royal 13.D.i, an historical miscellany from St Peter upon Cornhill. The manuscript also contains Geoffrey of Monmouth. According to J. Crick, the script is 'strongly reminiscent' of Cambridge University Library Dd.1.17, which may be a Glastonbury book. Could St Peter upon Cornhill also have taken the idea of tablets from those on display as early as 1385 at Glastonbury? See J. Crick, *The Historia Regum Britannie of Geoffrey of Monmouth, III: A Summary Catalogue of the Manuscripts* (Cambridge, 1989), no. 111, pp. 181–3 (p. 182). For Bawburgh, see R. M. Wilson, *The Lost Literature of Medieval England* (London, 1952) p. 95, citing *Proceedings of the Norfolk and Norwich Archaeological Society* 19, 250.

[13] For Bury St Edmunds, see *Memorials of St Edmund's Abbey*, ed. T. Arnold, RS 96 (London, 1890), I, 84. Stone and Worksop are cited by Gerould, ' "Tables" in Medieval Churches', 439–40. Stone is discussed more fully in Gerould, 'The Legend of St Wulfhad and St Ruffin', 323–37 (pp. 332–7). Those at Canterbury and Colchester are in Pantin. All are mentioned by Gransden, *Historical Writing, II*, 495.

[14] *Memorials of St Edmund's Abbey*, p. 84n.

[15] Ussher, *Antiquitates*, p. 71.

For some sites, very little is known about the contents of the tablets. At Bury St Edmunds, we know from Herman's account that the tablets, in place by the 1190s, told how a multitude of the faithful had built a church for Edmund in Beodric which was repaired in the time of Canute, and has lasted.[16] We do not know whether the text was verse or prose. At Lichfield, the tablet 'contained the story of the cathedral's foundation, a list of the bishops of Lichfield, and a list of the kings of Mercia, on folding boards'.[17] At St Paul's the tablets began with the second-century mission of Phaganus and Deruvianus to unspecified English places, and went on to record that the church itself was first founded by Archbishop Mellitus under King Ethelbert of Kent.[18] The *tabula* at Winchester related the history of the cathedral from its foundation by Phaganus and Duvianus (a common variant) in AD 169, five years after the date of their foundation at Glastonbury as recorded on the *Magna Tabula*. St Peter upon Cornhill claimed a foundation date of AD 179, by King Lucius; it was the first church in London, and the seat of the archbishopric until the arrival of Augustine at Canterbury.[19] We do not know how far forward these tablets brought the histories they recount, or whether they contained any other texts.[20] At Durham, the emphasis of the tablets was on monastic rather than local history. By the time of Prior John Wessington (1416–46), there were tablets describing monastic saints, and another set of tablets hanging opposite the altar of Sts Jerome and Benedict. Texts survive for the second set.[21]

In some other cases, texts which were on tablets survive in other copies. The York Miracles of St William survive in a manuscript of the seventeenth-century antiquarian Roger Dodsworth, copied 'Out of a Table in the Revestry in the Cathedral Church of York'.[22] William was archbishop from 1153–54. The text includes a forty-day indulgence from Pope Nicholas IV (1288–92), after the 1283 translation of his body to the new shrine behind the high altar. At his translation, the bishops present granted indulgences amounting to 444 days in all; the bishops are not named individually as all eighty-eight are on the *Magna Tabula*, but their cumulative indulgence was

---

[16] *Memorials of St Edmund's Abbey*, pp. 84–5.
[17] A. Gransden, *Historical Writing*, II, 495. The folding boards sound rather like the York triptychs. These tablets were destroyed in 1643 by Parliamentarians. See H. E. Savage, *The Lichfield Chronicles* (Lichfield, 1915), pp. 8–10, cited in Gransden.
[18] Ussher, *Antiquitates*, pp. 32 and 36.
[19] Ussher, *Antiquitates*, p. 36.
[20] For a possible date of *c*. 1385 at St Peter upon Cornhill, see the sources cited in n. 12 above.
[21] Pantin, 'Some Medieval English Treatises', 200–201; the texts are in Durham Cathedral Library, B. III. 30, fols. 31–4 and fols. 46–54.
[22] Oxford, Bodleian Library, Dodsworth 125, fol. 131, printed in Raine, *The Historians of the Church of York*, II, 531–43.

reported on the tablets.[23] The text includes miracles dated 1318 and 1319, so the tablets cannot be earlier than the first quarter of the fourteenth century. In 1422–23 the Ros family of Helmsley Castle gave the great St William window which is still in the north aisle, with scenes of his miracles.[24] Perhaps tablets kept at the shrine inspired the donors. But anyone who has ever stood perplexed before a window filled with panels depicting the miracles of a saint can appreciate how useful a guide such tablets could have been once the window was in place.

At Ripon, tablets were begun by John de Allhallowgate, who flourished from 1344 to 1365, and continued by his successor. Their composite verse text, giving a history of Ripon and York from St Wilfrid to the late fourteenth century, is preserved in two manuscripts. An English account of St Lewinna, martyred *c.* 685 by Saxon invaders, was on the walls of her church at 'Seevorhd', probably Seaford, Sussex, until her relics were translated to St Winnoc, Bergues, in 1078.[25]

At Stone priory there were three sets of tables, probably made in the 1420s.[26] One, kept on the Epistle side of the choir, told about the seventh-century founding saints, Wulfhad and Ruffin, in 382 lines of verse.[27] On the right side of the choir was a tablet with the names of the lords who came over with William the Conqueror, and another, of 162 verse lines, about the foundation of the priory by St Armamild, its subsequent history as a Saxon double house, and its Norman re-foundation as a house of Augustinian canons.[28] In Bawburgh Church, Norfolk, was a triptych with an English life of St Wulfstan, in seventy-five rhyme royal stanzas, plus an eight-line envoi (525 + 8 = 533 lines). The text survives in Lambeth Palace Library 935, no. 8.[29] At Worksop, the tablets were composed *c.* 1410, by 'one Pigot' as a guide to the tombs in twenty-nine rhyme royal stanzas, with some Latin

---

[23] Raine, *The Historians of the Church of York*, II, 541.

[24] K. M. Longley and J. Ingamells, *The Beautifullest Church: York Minster 1472–1972: A Tribute from York Minster Library and York City Art Gallery*, Exhibition Catalogue (York, 1972), p. 8.

[25] For the Ripon text, see Oxford, Bodleian Library, Rawlinson 446 and London, British Library, Cotton Cleopatra C.iv. It is printed by Raine, *The Historians of the Church of York*, II, 464–75. For his discussion of date and authorship, see p. xxix. An account of the transfer of St Lewinna, by Drogo, survives in Paris, Bibliothèque Nationale, lat. 5296, p. 243 (ref. as given in Wilson), cited in Wilson, *Lost Literature* (London, 1952), p. 94. See also D. Farmer, *The Oxford Dictionary of Saints*, 3rd edn (Oxford, 1992), who says the relics were transferred from Bergues near Dunkirk to either Seaford or Alfriston. AASS Jul. v (1727), 608–27.

[26] Gerould, 'The Legend of St Wulfhad and St Ruffin', 331.

[27] Edited, from the surviving copy in London, British Library, Cotton Nero C.xii (c. 15), in G. H. Gerould, *Saints' Legends* (New York, 1916), pp. 273–5.

[28] Text in Dugdale, who says it hung there until the Dissolution. See Gerould, 'The Legend of St Wulfhad and St Ruffin', 325, citing Dugdale, *Monasticon*, VI, 230–1.

[29] Wilson, *Lost Literature*, p. 95.

insertions.[30] At Christ Church, Canterbury, the treatise on Benedictine writers by William Gillingham (c. 1367–1409) was painted on tablets and hung on a column on the north side of the choir.[31] This is reminiscent of the Durham tablets. And at Colchester, tablets were put up in 1526 containing a chronicle from the Creation to 1382, a treatise on the origins of monasticism, and notes on the construction of certain monasteries, beginning with Glastonbury in AD 164, and ending with Leystone in 1363. The dates in the texts suggest that they may have replaced tablets originally put up in the late fourteenth century.[32]

Except for Bury St Edmunds and Seaford, which are oddly early, all these examples fall within the time frame of the *Magna Tabula*. So do the two surviving York tablets. The first contains extracts from chronicles and documents relating to York on the left panel; a 512-line poem on the history of York, from its legendary foundation to the time of Archbishop Thomas Arundel (1388–97); the right panel has documents asserting York's primacy over the churches of Scotland, Orkney and the Isles. The second triptych has material relating to the history of England in the left and centre panels, and a history of the world on the right.[33]

The Glastonbury *Magna Tabula* thus fits the pattern indicated by the other tablets. Almost all the surviving tablet texts are primarily accounts of the foundations, local history and documents which would be useful in disputes about ecclesiastical precedence and authority. The texts range from about 200 to about 600 verse lines, or comparable amounts of prose. Books can be borrowed and not returned, or even go temporarily astray; individual indulgences and charters can easily be mislaid. A wooden box, 3 or 4 feet high, could function as an institution's permanent reference collection, to be consulted on site only. The surviving examples are written in large, clear script, with few abbreviations, so they can be read easily. They could be deciphered by schoolboys with moderate Latin and reading skills, and may well have been used in teaching. They probably served two other purposes as well: informing the visitors, as I have already suggested, and recording the institution's own important records and dealings with the outside world. The contents of the Glastonbury *Magna Tabula* will indicate what image of itself Glastonbury intended to convey in the years around 1400.

---

[30] Dugdale, *Monasticon*, VI, 122–4, cited in Gerould, 'The Legend of St Wulfhad and St Ruffin', 336. This gives 203 verse lines, plus the prose, an amount of text which would fit on two of the leaves of the *Magna Tabula*.

[31] Pantin, 'Some Medieval English Treatises', 208, citing J. Leland, *Commentarii de scriptoribus Britannicis*, ed. A. Hall, 2 vols. (Oxford, 1709), 213. The treatise does not survive.

[32] Pantin, 'Some Medieval English Treatises', 207–8. The manuscript copy which survives is Oxford, Bodleian Library, Gough Essex 1.

[33] Purvis, 'The Tables of the York Vicars Choral', 736–48.

The Glastonbury *Magna Tabula*: Oxford, Bodleian Library, Lat. hist. a. 2, page 1.
The prophecy of Melkin, the descent of Ygerne and Arthur from Joseph of Arimathia, and the descent of Galahad from King Peter of Orkney. By permission of the Bodleian Library, Oxford.

b. The Glastonbury Tablets: Overview

i. The Texts: Early History

At both York and Winchester, the *tabulæ* contained information about the foundation of the old cathedral by Phaganus and Deruvianus, as well as its subsequent history. They also appear at St Paul's, and the king who summoned them, Lucius, appears at St Peter upon Cornhill. Bede recounts that, in the second century, King Lucius sent to Pope Eleutherius for missionaries but does not name the missionaries. Geoffrey calls them Faganus and Duvianus and his identification gained wide acceptance.[34] They turn up in the Glastonbury tradition by the thirteenth century.[35] Later in the Middle Ages, several churches seem to have seized upon these missionaries as proof of their own early foundations. Antonia Gransden has noted their use at Winchester by Thomas Rudborne in the fifteenth century, though they are not mentioned in the thirteenth-century account of the foundation and early history of the minster.[36] But Ussher also cites a Winchester *libellus* written 1,265 years after the foundation by Phaganus and Duvianus in AD 169, that is, in 1334.[37] And they appear as *Sancti ffuganus collega suus damianus* on the Ripon Tables compiled in the late fourteenth century.[38] Glastonbury may have been the first to take them up, but by the late fourteenth century their reputation as founders was widespread. Both Winchester and York had tablets on display telling all their visitors exactly how ancient their foundations were. No wonder that the

---

[34] The most inventive use of Faganus and Duvianus is probably that of the Cambridge Carmelite Nicholas Cantelupe, who claimed that they converted three thousand philosophers at Cambridge. Cantelupe did not stop there; he gave the charter of King Arthur to the university, which was confirmed and delivered by Arthur's nephew, Gawain. Quotations, including the text of the charter, are in Ussher, *Antiquitates*, p. 69; Arthur's charter of AD 529, p. 268. Printed in T. Hearne, *Thomæ Sprotti Chronica* (Oxford, 1719), pp. 262–80, from the copy in Cambridge, Gonville and Caius, 249/277, and two others. See Crick, *HRB Manuscripts*, no. 29, pp. 45–9.

[35] Bede, *Historia ecclesiastica*, ed. B. Colgrave and R. A. B. Mynors (Oxford, 1969), I, ch. 4. For Geoffrey's sources for the names – perhaps from early Welsh church dedications in the Llandaff area – see J. S. P. Tatlock, *The Legendary History of Britain: Geoffrey of Monmouth's Historia Regum Britanniæ and its Early Vernacular Versions* (Berkeley, 1950), pp. 230–4. Tatlock assumes the whole of ch. 22 is William's work, whereas Scott assumes the bulk of it, including the Phaganus and Duvianus section, is the work of a later reviser; see *The Early History of Glastonbury: An Edition, Translation and Study of William of Malmesbury's* De Antiquitate Glastonie Ecclesie, ed. J. Scott (Woodbridge, 1981), p. 187.

[36] See A. Gransden, 'Antiquarian Studies in Fifteenth-Century England', *Antiquaries' Journal* 60 (1980), 75–97 (p. 78). Rudborne lists no founder earlier than Ine for Glastonbury.

[37] Ussher, *Antiquitates*, p. 67.

[38] Raine, *The Historians of the Church of York*, II, 465, line 63.

Glastonbury tradition stresses that it was here the two missionaries stayed. Moreover, Glastonbury alone could put them in second place, after the first foundation by Joseph of Arimathia. Joseph and his descendants, down to Arthur, occupy the first tablet; Phagan and Deruvian come at the top of the second tablet. If the back of the box was nailed to the wall, the second tablet would probably be the first thing a reader saw on opening it; then, if he or she had been to York or Winchester, or had even read Bede, he or she would want to know what could possibly come before the missionaries of Eleutherius. And there, in a text from the apocryphal *Gospel of Nicodemus*, was Joseph. Britain is not mentioned in the New Testament among the destinations of the first missionaries, but the *Gospel of Nicodemus* was regarded as nearly as authoritative. And John of Glastonbury had grafted on to it an acccount of Joseph's companions, Nascien and his son Celidoine, drawn from French Grail romances of the thirteenth century. The compiler of the *Magna Tabula* has gone back to one of these and added Celidoine's marriage and acquisition of the kingdom of North Wales. This would no doubt have been of interest to Welsh pilgrims who visited Glastonbury, bringing their ancestors into the Grail tradition.

The first tablet ends with the prophecy of Melkin, and a group of short texts which prepare for King Arthur.[39] This is the one place which seriously disarranges the historical order; Arthur's coming is still four centuries away. Nevertheless, putting him here emphasizes his position as the culminating point of a Christian tradition which went back to apostolic times. It also suggests that he must have been one of the chief attractions for visitors. Those not interested in history might still know his romantic adventures, and those of his followers, Lancelot, Gawain and Galahad. Their ancestry, too would be known, at least vaguely. The organization and most of the material came from John of Glastonbury's chronicle, Chapters 20 and 21, where it also concludes the account of Joseph of Arimathia. John took the material from genealogies in the Vulgate Grail romances, where, as Jane Burns has pointed out, two sorts of lineage are continually important, the lineage of bloodline and that of spiritual influence.[40] Both are evident in the Arthurian genealogies. In the first, Arthur himself is descended from Joseph; in the second, his nephew Galahad is descended from Joseph's companion Peter of Orkney. John, or perhaps an earlier Glastonbury source, has added a Glastonbury twist. Nowhere else is Arthur descended from the Fisher Kings through his mother Ygerne.[41] The quotation about Joseph from Peter Riga's *Aurora* is ingeniously placed between the prophecy of Melkin,

---

[39] The prophecy has been examined in detail in J. P. Carley, 'Melkin the Bard and the Esoteric Tradition at Glastonbury Abbey', *The Downside Review* 99 (1981), 1–17.
[40] E. J. Burns, *Arthurian Fictions* (Columbus, Ohio, 1985), p. 46.
[41] *The Chronicle of Glastonbury Abbey: An Edition, Translation and Study of John of*

ostensibly from the pre-Christian British tradition, and the genealogies. The *Aurora* was one of the most popular adaptations of the Bible and formed part of every monastic library. Its presence gives added authority to the information around it, the sources of which are another, and decidedly less certain, tradition.

Both William of Malmesbury and John of Glastonbury give texts of a number of charters in their chronicles, and documents appear on both the surviving York Tablets. The only document preserved on the *Magna Tabula*, however, is the Charter of St Patrick, which is given in full on Tablets 2 and 3. It is an addition in William of Malmesbury's text, crafted most probably in the thirteenth century. It is probably included because it fills the time gap between the apostolic period of Joseph of Arimathia and St Philip and the second-century mission which Bede recounts, and is the only record to do that. It establishes that the Glastonbury tradition is not only ancient but also continuous. At York and in London there were drastic breaks in continuity before Pope Gregory sent Augustine and Theodore. York could only claim continuity from the sixth century.

The Charter of St Patrick also establishes the connection between Glastonbury and Ireland, which seems, in view of the large number of Irish bishops who gave indulgences, to have been important in the twelfth and thirteenth centuries. Irish pilgrim trade may have been still active in the fourteenth and fifteenth centuries. We have no records from the Glastonbury guest house, nor any lists of visitors to the abbey, to enlighten us.

ii. The Texts: Saints and Kings

The Charter of St Patrick carries the reader over to the next opening, Tablets 3 and 4. Most of the rest of this space is occupied by the stories of the saints and kings who visited, lived, and in some cases died, at Glastonbury, and of the saints whose relics were there, from Patrick in the fifth century to King Edmund Ironside, the last of the Saxon line replaced by Canute in the early eleventh century.

The relics mentioned here were mostly acquired in the Saxon period, and include many English, Irish and a few Welsh saints. Irish saints include Patrick, Columba, Brigid, Benignus and the locally martyred Indract. Claims to Columba and Brigid became decidedly problematic after the discovery of their relics at Down in the late twelfth century, and indeed the *Magna Tabula* is cautious on Tablet 3 about what relics Glastonbury has. But their long and close associations with the abbey are stressed, and on Tablet 4 Patrick is given as one of the three archbishops buried at Glaston-

Glastonbury's 'Cronica sive Antiquitates Glastoniensis Ecclesie', ed. J. P. Carley (Woodbridge, 1985), pp. 279–80. See notes to chs. 20 and 21.

bury.⁴² Benignus, who was a follower of Patrick and his successor as abbot at Glastonbury, had died at Meare nearby. In the late eleventh century his body had been moved to Glastonbury, and his cult was still of local importance. Indract too appears at Glastonbury as a follower of Patrick. He was a king's son and a pilgrim who sought out Patrick's establishment on pilgrimage to Rome, only to meet his death there. Patrick's and Brigid's relics at Glastonbury might be open to question, but Benignus and Indract reinforced their spiritual presence there. Irishmen travelling to England would be likely to land at Bristol; Glastonbury was nearby, and would make an appropriate stop. I shall discuss the Irish connection further below, in relation to indulgences, a surprising number of which come from Irish sees. This may account for the brief mention of the Irish missionaries Furseus, Ultanus and Idanus among the saints; most of their work was in Gaul, but their cults were celebrated in Ireland as well. Furthermore, Canterbury, the rival establishment for the relics of Dunstan, had a head-relic of St Furseus.⁴³ Glastonbury's claim to Ultanus and Idanus could be seen as one more instance of the competition with Canterbury.

Welsh saints are few in number but important. They are David, Wenta, Iltuyd and Gildas. David is featured prominently in the Glastonbury traditions, from William of Malmesbury to the tablets. David was formally canonized by Pope Calixtus II (1118–24) in 1120, and St David's was recognized as a pilgrimage site, which offered English and Welsh pilgrims a viable alternative to longer continental journeys.⁴⁴ Two pilgrimages to St David's were equivalent to one to Rome, and three to a pilgrimage to Jerusalem.⁴⁵ The privilege granted to Glastonbury by Pope Calixtus in 1123, which is included by William of Malmesbury, allowed Glastonbury to keep whatever had been granted to it by *apostolici*, archbishops, bishops, kings and other magnates.⁴⁶ It may have been sought at least partly to keep pilgrims coming to Glastonbury rather than – or, for some pilgrims, en route to – the newly-important shrine in Wales. The tablets, after all, noted that

---

⁴² See Carley, *Chronicle*, p. 66, for John of Glastonbury's doubts.
⁴³ Farmer, *Saints*.
⁴⁴ Tatlock, *Legendary History*, p. 246.
⁴⁵ E. G. Bowen, *Devi Sant/Saint David* (Cardiff, 1983), p. 91. This is the same Calixtus who made Compostela an archbishopric, and encouraged pilgrimage to St James. This bull is not in U. Robert, *Bullaire du Pape Calixte II 1119–1124: Essai de Restitution* (Paris, 1891), though see no. 406, a confirmation of royal and other privileges to St David's, pp. 208–9, dated 25 May 1123.
⁴⁶ Scott, *The Early History*, pp. 162–4. He translates *apostolicis* as 'apostles', and regards it as interpolated, but surely it means apostolic vicars, i.e. popes and papal legates. W. W. Newell regards the bull as 'ungenuine' ('William of Malmesbury on the Antiquity of Glastonbury', *PMLA* 18 [1903], 459–512 [pp. 501–2]), but gives no grounds; it is also in *The Great Chartulary of Glastonbury*, ed. A. Watkin, 3 vols., Somerset Record Society 59, 63, 64 (1947–56), I, 169, omitting *apostolicis*. Its inclusion in the Chartulary indicates

David had come to consecrate the church of St Mary, only to be replaced by Christ himself. The abbey claimed David's relics and had his sapphire altar, which had been rediscovered and adorned by Abbot Henry of Blois (1126–71). The other Welsh saints all cluster around David. St Wenta, David's aunt, is listed first and so was presumably the most prominently displayed in the reliquary of the virgins. In some versions of his life, Iltuyd was David's mentor and tutor. He also taught the historian, Gildas, whom a Glastonbury tradition insisted was buried here. The presence of Gildas, like that of Bede discussed below, marked Glastonbury as the repository of the early history of Britain in the most literal way. Here were the bodies of its two greatest historians. Gildas preserved the last of the British tradition; Bede recorded the triumph of Christianity and the formation of the English nation.

Bede brings us to the third major group of saints, the Northumbrians. These northern saints were clearly important: they are repeated on Tablet 6 after being listed on Tablet 4.[47] Besides Bede, they include Aidan, bishop of Lindisfarne (died 651), Paulinus (died 644), and a good list of the early abbots of Wearmouth; Benedict Biscop (died 690); Benedict's deputies while he was in Rome, Sefrid and Esterwine (died 686); Ceolfrid (690–716); and Hubert or Hwætbert (c. 716–47). Boisil (died c. 661), prior of Melrose and praised by Bede, was also included.

The fourth major group is from or connected with Whitby: Hild (died 680); her companion Begu; and Eanfled (born 626), wife of King Oswy of Northumbria and a nun at Whitby.

Both these latter groups of relics are described on the tablets as the gift of the ecclesiastic Ticca who came from the north, fleeing the Danes and bringing relics with him. He remained, became an abbot at Glastonbury, died and was buried in the abbey. The list of his relics should place him in the eighth century, but he is a problematic figure.[48] William of Malmesbury, or an interpolator, dates him to 754, too early for a Danish invasion in the north. He has been associated with the abbot of an unidentified monastery who signs a charter of King Æthelbald of Mercia in 757 (Cotton Charters VIIII. 3).[49] In my opinion, he is probably ultimately based on the (apocry-

---

that it was regarded as authentic at Glastonbury. It is also in Robert, *Bullaire du Pape Calixte II*, no. 404, pp. 205–6, also omitting *apostolicis*. See Scott, p. 210, nn. 175–6.

[47] The reason for the repetition is unclear. At Compostela, one could get a list of relics and indulgences to take away. The shorter list at the top of Tablet 6, and the sum of indulgences in red at the bottom, would fit nicely on a vellum sheet, such as is described by Hieronymus Münzer and William Wey, and recorded by Purchas his Pilgrim as being displayed in the cathedral. See J. Krochalis, '1494: Hieronymus Münzer, Compostela and the *Codex Calixtinus*', in *Pilgrimage to Compostela: A Book of Essays*, ed. L. Davidson and M. Dunn (New York, 1996), pp. 69–96 (p. 95, n. 81).

[48] See Scott, *The Early History*, p. 194, n. 55, and the Glossary.

phal) Archbishop Tadiacus of York, who fled his see in the collapse of the country after the death of Arthur, taking with him the bodies of various saints. He is found in Geoffrey of Monmouth, and also in the History of York which appears on the York Tables, and in several other manuscripts.[50] William or a later Glastonbury historian presumably knew a variant version of the story, perhaps one not closely dated, and tried to place a fleeing northern ecclesiastic in a plausible sequence of events.

The existence of a long poem on the life, death and Glastonbury connections of St Hild indicates that her cult was still alive at Glastonbury in the fifteenth century.[51] Hers were among the relics which we know were at Glastonbury earlier; they may have been, as John of Glastonbury claims, among the gifts of Edmund the Elder, though they came from Ticca, according to the tablets.[52]

That Glastonbury continued to claim relics such as those of Bede, whose tomb had been at Durham for centuries, does seem somewhat surprising. Perhaps they could do so because northern pilgrims were few. Only one bishop of Durham and one of York among the givers of indulgences come from north of the Trent, and both had probably previously held preferments in the diocese of Bath and Wells. But Glastonbury also claimed Paulinus, usually considered to be buried at Rochester, and, of course, Archbishop Dunstan of Canterbury. Paulinus was important because he covered and roofed the old wattle church, in effect rebuilding it. This too may well arise from an early tradition which got muddled; in Rhigyfarch's *Life of St David*, Glastonbury is among the twelve churches built by his tutor Paulinus.[53] Bede's Paulinus, though he has no known connection with Glastonbury, also built churches. What would be easier than to attribute a particular church to the wrong Paulinus?

---

[49] S. Foot, 'Glastonbury's Early Abbots', in *The Archaeology and History of Glastonbury Abbey*, ed. Abrams and Carley, pp. 163–90.
[50] Raine, *The Historians of the Church of York*, II, 451, lines 154–5.
[51] A. G. Rigg, 'An Edition of a Fifteenth-Century Commonplace Book: Trinity College Cambridge, MS O. 9. 38', 2 vols. (unpublished D.Phil. dissertation, Oxford, 1966), II, pp. 414–33. The poem is summarized, with a few quotations, in Rigg, *A History of Anglo-Latin Literature 1066–1422* (Cambridge, 1992), pp. 22–4, which is the twelfth-century section of the volume, though he notes that 'It could, in fact, have been composed anytime between the death of William the Conqueror in 1087 and the middle of the fifteenth century, the date of the manuscript.' (p. 22).
[52] Carley, *Chronicle*, pp. 18–20. Edmund's gifts included the relics of St Oswald and most of the other relics assigned here to Ticca: Aidan, Ceolfrid, Boisil and Bede; Benedict Biscop, Hesterwine, Sigfried and Herebert, abbots of Wearmouth; Hild, Hebba and Begu. In the tablets, he does not even appear among the relic donors, though he is listed among the kings buried there. For Glastonbury sending relics of Hild to Whitby in the late twelfth century, see Part 2, 4. Glossary.
[53] *Rhigyfarch, Life of St David*, ed. J. W. James (Cardiff, 1967), p. 33.

Dunstan was an important part of the Glastonbury tradition. He had been abbot there before becoming archbishop of Canterbury, and although the Canterbury monks claimed that they had his body, Glastonbury knew that monks from the abbey who knew Dunstan personally had rescued it from Danish invasions, and that the abbey had had it ever since. The account of the translation is the last saintly story on Tablet 3; five short miracles follow. They refer to three crosses and two images of the Virgin which could be found in the church, and they make a bridge to the relics in reliquaries which begin Tablet 4.

From the twelve disciples sent by Philip in AD 63 to Dunstan, this tablet repeats the names we have already encountered. But there are additions, which lead into the lists of kings, *duces*, archbishops and bishops which follow. Those not mentioned already include Edith, Edmund, Eanfled and the Saxon kings buried there: Ine, Edgar, Edmund the Elder and Edmund Ironside. The four *duces* on Tablet 4 all have Saxon names and were prominent in royal administration. These give Glastonbury an important place in the great Saxon tradition.

If the relics of St Ursula and her mother Daria were indeed the gift of Abbot Henry of Blois, then Glastonbury was still actively acquiring relics associated with early British history in the twelfth century. Though the centre of Ursula's cult was Cologne, she was a fourth-century British princess, martyred for her refusal to sleep with a Hunnish prince. Her story is in Geoffrey of Monmouth (*Historia regum Britanniae*, Bk V, 15–16), and her cult was known among the Cologne merchants in London in the twelfth century but it was not widespread in England.[54] Henry must have thought her appropriate for Glastonbury.

The few Roman martyrs were largely relics brought by Saxon kings. There are a handful of French saints, mostly from the Merovingian and Carolingian missionary period. Of these a number, like Queen Bathildis who began life as a Saxon slave, have English connections, or like Furseus, Idanus and Ultanus, were originally Irish. Gertrude of Nivelles was connected with Furseus and his companions.

But even here there has been selection. For instance, while many of the saints brought by King Edgar are included, Valerius, Abdon and Sennen, Poppa, archbishop of Troyes, Germinianus, Conan and Salvius are not. Valerius, Abdon and Sennen are early Roman martyrs; the others are French. Possibly French saints were little regarded because Glastonbury was on the wrong side of England to attract many French pilgrims.

Relics mentioned in William of Malmesbury's account and not included here may have been lost in the fire of 1184, though St Cecilia turns up in

---

[54] Tatlock, *Legendary History*, pp. 236–40. Farmer, *Saints*, says there were only two ancient churches dedicated to her, though there is a window in Holy Trinity Church, York.

John of Glastonbury's list. St Neot, trained by Dunstan at Glastonbury, was not included, perhaps because his later career was in Cornwall, where he died.[55] But why not mention the relics of recent English saints, such as Becket or Edmund Rich? Why not mention the considerable number of relics of Christ and the Virgin Mary obtained from the Holy Land? It looks as if there is a deliberate focus on relics not available elsewhere south of the Trent. Hailes in Gloucestershire had the blood of Christ; many places had bits of the sponge and cross, and chunks of the hill of Calvary.[56] A handful of early martyrs might be seen as reinforcing the antiquity of the place – especially if they were royal gifts – but what made Glastonbury unique was its Celtic and Saxon heritage. That was what would attract visitors. The tablets, after all, went up when Chaucer was writing about Constance and King Alla of Northumbria, and using the name of the early British king Arviragus in the Franklin's Tale and the Arthurian adventure of the knight and the loathly lady for the wife of Bath. Ancient Britain may have been fashionable at the close of the fourteenth century.

For a place that had never been a double house and had no nearby nunnery, there is also a strong interest in women saints: seventeen women to thirty-six men, including Patrick but not Phaganus and Deruvianus. Many were royal, including Bathildis, Edith, Hilda, Ebba, Eanfled. The Welsh Wenta too had royal blood. In the early period, a number of donors to Glastonbury had been women. The one relic donor actually mentioned on the tablets was a woman, Alswitha, who acquired the important relics of St David. The Saxon pyramids included women's names; Guinevere accompanies Arthur. We have no means of knowing how many pilgrims were women, including women who controlled money, like Margery Kempe.[57]

The list of kings on Tablet 4 begins where the genealogies left off at the end of Tablet 1, with Arthur. The genealogies traced his descent from Joseph of Arimathia, the noble centurion who had buried Christ. Here the saints and kings from the British past root Arthur himself as a Christian king in Glastonbury. Where else could a sixth-century British king be buried? At

---

[55] William of Ramsay wrote his Life in the early thirteenth century. John Whitaker, *The Life of St Neot, The Oldest of All the Brothers to King Alfred* (London, 1809). This edition is described by Rigg, *Anglo-Latin Literature*, p. 365, n. 70, as 'an incredibly slipshod transcription' of the manuscript, Oxford, Magdalen College 53; see also his discussion of the life, p. 177.
[56] For typical collections of relics from the Holy Land, and Glastonbury's acquisitions, see D. Bethell, 'The Making of a Twelfth-Century Relic Collection', in *Studies in Church History* 8, ed. G. J. Cummins and D. Baker (Cambridge, 1962), pp. 61–72.
[57] Margery Kempe apparently did not go to Glastonbury while waiting for a ship at Bristol, but she remarks that other pilgrims came and went, seeking other ports. She did go to the Holy Blood at Hailes. See *The Book of Margery Kempe*, ed. W. Butler-Bowden (New York, 1944), pp. 93–5.

Glastonbury, he rested among his predecessors, contemporaries and successors. Here we have the account of the discovery of his tomb and that of his wife Guinevere in the late twelfth century. It is a vivid narrative and one of the few bits of tablet text which is not copied or condensed from one specific source. The information, of course, is familiar – the curtained dig, the beauty of Guinevere's hair, which crumbles at the touch of a monkish hand – but the compiler gives his own version.

After Arthur come other Saxon kings: Centwine, Edgar, Edmund Ironside. Then come the archbishops and bishops buried in the abbey. Here, as at Worksop, the tablets serve as a guide to tombs and markers in the church. This is followed by short notes about the names of Glastonbury, Avalon, and Iniswitrin, names doubtless familiar to visitors, then as now, from Arthurian romance rather than from history. Then the reader would need to turn the tablet over for the final opening.

What is remarkable to the modern reader, and perhaps would have struck the more knowledgable among the medieval visitors, is the conservatism and narrow geographical orientation of the history presented on the *Magna Tabula*. The Saxon past and the Celtic connection dominate. The most recent king buried in the abbey, and celebrated as a patron, is Edmund Ironside who died in 1016. There is no effort shown on these tablets to attract Norman patronage, there are no lordly burials, no recent royal privileges. Glastonbury's troubles with its Norman abbots and bishops of Bath and Wells have been well documented, but by the fourteenth century kings were again visitors and patrons. None of this is mentioned on the tablets, however. Neither Henry II's interest nor Edward I's visit are cited in the accounts of Arthur's tomb, nor is the visit of Edward III and Queen Philippa for three days in 1331.[58] The focus is all on Arthur and the Saxon kings, not on more recent monarchs. As the text of Tablet 4 affirms: 'isti in ueritate reges. et alii plures Britonum et Anglorum Principes: ibidem requiescunt' (These were, in truth, the kings and the other princes of the British and the English; they lie here). The three archbishops, Patrick of Ireland, David of Wales and Dunstan of Canterbury, unify the British realms in religious power. Arthur and the kings unify the royal and political heritage.

iii. The Texts: Miracles

---

[58] For Edward I's visit and its motives, see J. C. Parsons, 'The Second Exhumation of King Arthur's Remains at Glastonbury, 19 April 1278', *Arthurian Literature* 12 (1993), 173–7. For Edward III, see Watkin, *The Great Chartulary* I, pp. lxxiv–lxxv and 194–5, and Carley, *Glastonbury Abbey*, p. 43. In 1284, Edward I and Queen Eleanor went on pilgrimage to St David's. They were there on Sunday, on the eve of the feast of St Katherine (25 November). See the *Annales Ecclesie Menevensis* in *Anglia Sacra* II, 651.

The third tablet ends with five short miracle stories, tied to crosses and statues which were on display in the church, richly ornamented objects of spiritual power before which the pilgrim could pause in prayer. The chronological range seems deliberate. The venerable cross before which Aylsi failed to bow, and so met his fate after the great fire of 1184, invokes the power of ancient holy objects. Its presence might also remind monks, both visitors and those of the house, not to be similarly cavalier in their treatment of the relics they viewed or lived among. So did the cross which bled from its arrow wounds. Another cross had humbled King Edward at the behest of Dunstan. A statue of the Virgin had miraculously survived the great fire, and the account by the fourteenth-century scholar, Edmund Stourton, of the statue of the Virgin which answered when the *Salve Regina* was recited, was a reminder that miracles could still happen to the devout. These brief stories reaffirm the long tradition of spiritual effectiveness, and imply that it still operated at Glastonbury.

It is notable that none of these miracle stories relates to cures. No one born blind or deaf or dumb or crippled is healed; no madness is cured. True, the Danish soldiers who are blinded have their sight restored (Tablet 5, Text 33), but their blindness is a punishment divinely inflicted for their sin and it is lifted when they repent. Tales of cures were available; John of Glastonbury records a miracle of Ticca, and miracles which occurred at the tomb of Benignus are in the *Nova legenda Angliæ*. In the absence of a shrine book, it is difficult to be sure how to interpret this. Nevertheless, the evidence of the *Magna Tabula* suggests that Glastonbury encouraged the sort of pilgrim who came, as people went to Rome or Jerusalem, simply because the site was holy ground. The story of Glasteing and his sow near the end of Tablet 4 makes it clear that from its very foundation the place was magical. The tablet concludes with a brief passage on the holiness of the cemetery, showing the continuity of its power in Christian times.

These sections lead logically into Tablet 5, where the holy ground is gone over again, with stories of vengeance on those who profaned it, like the abbot's cook and Arnulphus. The story of the sultan who wants a piece of the holy earth follows. This tale takes a Glastonbury tenant abroad as a crusading knight, and proves that even a pagan in a far-off land has heard of Glastonbury and can recognize the sanctity of its very earth. The encounter of a Glastonbury monk with the monk of St Denis, which comes next, proves that even the oldest foundation in France had acknowledged the antiquity of Glastonbury for several centuries. The monk's affirmation leads logically into the mention of the earliest churches, King Ine's silver chapel and the two ancient pyramids which contained the oldest known burials at Glastonbury. We do not know what remains of the pyramids a visitor would have seen in the later Middle Ages but even the ruins would be impressive, and the tablet's account, unchanged from William of Malmesbury's twelfth-century report, would tell him what had been visible. Presumably at least traces of the lettering could still be made out.

When the tablets were open, 5 and 6 would be seen at once, so a brief list of saints comes again at the top of Tablet 6, to remind the visitor of the reason for the long list of indulgences which follows. Then comes the description of the most recent major work of construction at the abbey, Abbot John Chinnock's restoration of the chapel of St Michael in 1382. This would bring the reader to the present day, when he or she could gain numerous indulgences just by being on pilgrimage to this sacred place. The sheer magnitude of the list was bound to be impressive. English and foreign visitors might even find a local bishop somewhere in the two columns. The tablets from St William's altar at York listed 444 days of indulgences; those here gave 64 years and 197 days.

iv. The Texts: Indulgences

The bulk of the indulgences date from the late twelfth and thirteenth centuries, and none is provably after *c.* 1325. The most recent definitely identifiable bishops are also the most local: John de Dronkesford, bishop of Bath and Wells (1309–29), and John de Eglescliffe, bishop of Llandaff (1323–47). Most of the bishops are English, Irish or south Italian. The English bishoprics include Bath and Wells, Canterbury, Coventry and Lichfield, Durham, Ely, Exeter, Hereford, London, Norwich, Winchester, Worcester and York. The most frequent benefactors are the southern bishoprics: Bath and Wells, Exeter and Canterbury. The others, granting one or two indulgences, suggest a specific occasion or connection rather than regular contact. The only bishop of York to grant a Glastonbury indulgence, for instance, was probably Walter Giffard, who was raised partly in Wiltshire and was translated to York from Bath and Wells. One indulgence each from Norwich, Coventry and Lichfield, Rochester and Durham, suggests specific occasions which further researches in episcopal history might succeed in tracing. Meetings of Parliament (Glastonbury was a mitred abbey), business in London or at court, and synods could probably explain all so far untraced contacts with English bishops. Evidence for some connections is in the Glossary which forms Part 2 of this article.

The only Scottish bishop is Gilbert of Dunkeld; it may be worth noting that the synod of Bristol was held near Glastonbury in 1216, when he was bishop. The Welsh bishops come from St David's and Llandaff, whose territory included Glastonbury lands and whose bishops occasionally acted as suffragans for the bishops of Bath and Wells.

The number of Irish bishops is in some ways surprising. Glastonbury had a few Irish properties, acquired at the time of the Norman Conquest of Ireland in 1171: the village of Kilcomman, with a priory in honour of Philip,

James and St Cumine; the village of Ardaneer, with a priory of Ocymild.[59] But these went to the bishop of Bath and Wells in the settlement of 1203.[60] They cannot explain the large number of Irish bishops who granted indulgences for visiting the site. While many Irish bishops acted as suffragans in English dioceses, the number of indulgences is greater than the number of suffragans. The fourteen bishoprics cover the southern part of the country pretty thoroughly; most come from the southern archdioceses of Dublin and Cashel. Only Armagh is a northern see. The others are Annaghdown, Cashel, Cloyne, Cork, Dublin, Kildare, Killaloe, Leiglin and Kildare, Limerick, Lismore, Meath, Ossory, and Waterford.

Bristol was the most convenient port for any southern Irishman travelling to England or the continent, and Glastonbury was a holy site nearby. Visits from Irish pilgrims in the twelfth and thirteenth centuries seem a logical inference. But, as Roger Stalley has recently demonstrated, the first two Norman archbishops of Dublin rebuilt their cathedral using new building at Glastonbury and Wells as very close models. John Comyn had administered the finances of Glastonbury for two years before becoming a bishop and so must have known the area and its resources, and his successor, Henry of London, carried on the tradition. The stone and the stonemasons for Christ Church, Dublin, came from Somerset, and the West Country was the dominant architectural influence in southern Ireland for a generation.[61] This may have helped create an interest in Glastonbury as a place of pilgrimage.

The other large group of bishops is Italian. Acquino in the centre and Amelia in Umbria could be visited by Glastonbury monks en route to Rome. But of the seven Italian indulgences, five come from south Italian sees: Bovo (south of Bari); Bitonto (north of Bari); Larino (halfway between Naples and Rome on the west side); Monopoli, on the coast halfway between Brindisi and Bari; Tarentino in the arch of the boot. These belonged to the Norman kingdom of Sicily, which had ties with England. One can cluster these Italian bishoprics around the date 1297–98. All except Larino have a candidate who fits at that point, and Larino's bishop did other collective indulgences at the papal curia. At a council, they could have encountered emissaries from Glastonbury, but no council met between Lyons in 1274 and Vienne in 1309, and no Glastonbury journey to Sicily is mentioned in the surviving abbey records. Nevertheless, a collective indul-

---

[59] Carley, *Chronicle*, p. 170. On p. 38, John of Glastonbury points out that no one had given land to Glastonbury since the Norman Conquest in 1066, and this was still true after 1300. Presumably the brief tenure of Irish lands had dropped out of Glastonbury tradition.
[60] Charter no. 126; summary, Watkin, *The Great Chartulary*, I, p. xliii; text, p. 178.
[61] R. Stalley, 'Irish Gothic and English Fashion', in *The English in Medieval Ireland: Proceedings of the First Joint Meeting of the Royal Irish Academy and the British Academy*, ed. J. Lydon (Dublin, 1982).

gence gained by some Glastonbury emissary to the Papal court is the most likely explanation.

Some of the holders of exotic sees, especially those *in partis infidelibus* who could not reside in their bishoprics, also worked at the curia, and turn up in collective indulgences. Matthew of Veglia, Cyprian of Bova, Perronus of Larino and Romanus of Croja come in this category. A few holders seem to have been Englishmen, or acted as suffragans in English bishoprics. Augustine of Nottingham, who was bishop of Laodicea in Cyrea, fits both categories; William of Ragensis was a suffragan in Norwich, and Bernard of Ragusa ended up as bishop of Carlisle. In some ways the bishop list is less exotic than it seems.

But if not exotic, it is still impressive. Eighty-eight ecclesiastics, including three popes (if one includes Eleutherius), two papal legates, and over eighty archbishops and bishops, granted indulgences to pilgrims to Glastonbury. The effect is of a vast collective indulgence, suitable for a church of international and historic importance. Their place on the last tablet would remind the visitor to stop to pray as well as gaze, to gain his 64 years and 197 days. And if it reminded him to make an offering, so much the better. We do not know the average donations received under Abbot Chinnock, but in 31 Henry VIII (1540), the sacristan netted £311 12s 6d, largely from oblations and offerings in the old church. That was slightly more than half the income allotted to the cellarer to feed and clothe the monks, and see to the decoration of the church.[62]

v. The Texts: The Compiler(s)

Who put the *Magna Tabula* together? The general inspiration is likely to have come from Abbot Chinnock himself. The English delegation pressed the Glastonbury claim to primacy at the Council of Pisa in 1409; it was argued again at the Council of Constance in 1417, when Chinnock was head of the English delegation. The tablets were a public proclamation of the abbey's history, and they stated that Joseph and his companions came to Glastonbury in AD 63. The date was given twice, as fifteen years after the Assumption of the Virgin in Text 1, and as sixty-three years from the birth of Christ and fifteen years after the Assumption in Text 8. Valerie Lagorio has pointed out that, at both international councils, the date was put earlier, shortly after the Passion, to make Glastonbury earlier than the French

---

[62] C. T. Flower, 'Obedientars' Accounts of Glastonbury and other Religious Houses', *Transactions of the St Paul's Ecclesiological Society* 7 (1911), 50–62. For accounting purposes, the sacristan, chamberlain, hostler, refectorer, pittener, almoner, precentor, infirmarer and the medar and gardener, who supplied mead as well as produce, came under the cellarer's budget line.

foundation of St Denis, or than the presence of St James at Compostela.⁶³ Those claims we urged by other English ecclesiastics, though not Chinnock himself. At the Council of Siena in 1424 the English clerics used Glastonbury's date of AD 63. On the tablets (Text 35), Glastonbury only claims to be as early as St Denis; the monk of St Denis tells Geoffrey that each foundation is the oldest in its own country, but he adds that Glastonbury is holier. The story is an old one; it is set in the time of Abbot Henry of Blois, and occurs in thirteenth-century expanded versions of William of Malmesbury's chronicle. Its presence on the tablets, however, suggests an awareness of the issue of primacy which accords with Chinnock.

The tablets may have been Chinnock's idea, and would certainly have needed his encouragement. (The carpenter who constructed the *Magna Tabula* itself would have been a lay brother or outside paid workman.) It seems likely that Chinnock would have delegated the details of the actual texts to an abbey historian, aided if necessary by a good scribe. We have several named scribes from the period of John Chinnock's abbacy, but only one, John Merylynch, shows any interest in history.⁶⁴ His is not the scribal hand of the tablets – his own is distinctive, and easily recognizable – but he may have been involved in their compilation.

Five manuscripts which Merylynch used or wrote survive. Oxford, Bodleian Library, Laud Lat. 4 contains an early fifteenth-century copy of John of Salisbury's *Policraticus*.⁶⁵ London, British Library, Harley 641 contains the chronicle of Martinus Polonus and Harley 651 a *Provinciale*

---

⁶³ V. M. Lagorio, 'The Evolving Legend of St Joseph at Glastonbury', *Speculum* 46 (1971), 211–31 (pp. 220–3). The fullest subsequent discussion of the primacy of Glastonbury is in J. P. Carley, 'A Grave Event: Henry V, Glastonbury Abbey, and Joseph of Arimathea's Bones', in *Culture and the King: The Social Implications of the Arthurian Legend*, ed. M. B. Shichtman and J. P. Carley (Albany, NY, 1994), pp. 129–49 (pp. 131–2).

⁶⁴ John Taunton's name occurs in the Glastonbury psalter with calendar, Upholland 98 (now London, British Library, Additional 64952), which is written in a formal textura hand, not that of the tablets. There is no plate in F. Wormald, 'The Liturgical Calendar of Glastonbury Abbey', *Festschrift Bernhard Bischoff zu seinen 65. Geburtstag*, ed. J. Autenrieth and F. Brunholzl (Stuttgart, 1971), pp. 32–40, but I examined it at Upholland, Lancs., some years ago. Ker suggests that Taunton might have been the scribe. We know nothing else about him. N. R. Ker, *Medieval Libraries of Great Britain: A List of Surviving Books*, 2nd edn (London, 1964), p. 264. Oxford, Oriel College 15 was written by Nicholas Fawkes in 1389. The text is Robert Holcot, and Watson suggests he may have been resident in Oxford at the time. Plate in A. G. Watson, *Catalogue of Dated and Datable Manuscripts c. 435–1600 in Oxford Libraries* (Oxford, 1984). See also J. P. Carley, 'An Annotated Edition of the List of Sixty-three Monks who Entered Glastonbury Abbey during the Abbacy of Walter de Monington', *The Downside Review* 95 (1977), 306–15. The Geoffrey of Monmouth manuscript from the 1380s mentioned under Script below is not certainly a Glastonbury book, so I have not included it here.

⁶⁵ See Watson, *Catalogue of Dated and Datable Manuscripts in Oxford Libraries*, I, no. 581, p. 95, with plate in II, no. 254.

episcopatum. Oxford, Queen's College 304 is an historical miscellany, containing the chronicles of Peter of Ickham, Nicholas Trivet, and Adam of Murimouth continued to 1380, genealogies of the kings of England, a list of the abbots of Glastonbury ending with John Chinnock and a history of the bishops of Wells.[66] It begins with a treatise on the origins of monasticism, and seems to have been compiled between 1401 and 1420.[67] In 1411, Merylynch also wrote the *tabula* to a now fragmentary manuscript of William of Malmesbury's *De antiquitate* which belongs to Dr Simon Keynes.[68] He had the kind of interests our compiler needed, and at least one of the right texts. He must have studied William of Malmesbury carefully in order to write his table for the manuscript. The chronicle of Martinus Polonus indicates an interest in papal history; John of Salisbury's *Policraticus* implies an interest in political theory with an historical bent. If Merylynch was not responsible for the selection and presentation of the material on the tablets, he is at any rate representative of the interest in monastic and local history at Glastonbury under Abbot Chinnock.

vi. Conclusion: The Use and Survival of the Tablets

The tablets were a way of making even the casual visitor aware of the importance of the Glastonbury traditions. At Glastonbury itself, the sense of the past was still vivid on the eve of the Reformation. Many of the monks in 1538–39 took their names in religion from those of familiar saints and holy men: Richard Bede, John Ceolffryde, Nicholas Urban, Thomas Appolliner, Henry Ine, Robert Gylde, Richard Beyll (for Boisil?), John Aydan, Martin Indract, John Arthur, John Grimethy, Robert Ider, John Deryvuan, John Phagan, William Dunstan, William Kentwyn, Thomas Athelstan, John Aldelme, William Joseph, John Neott, William Athelwolde, John Elphege, John Powlyn, Richard Ultan, Simon Edgar, Roger Wulffryde, G. Britwolde, John Oswolde, John Pantaleon, John Alrude, Anstitili Alwyn.[69] Most of these names were probably not widespread among hagiographers and historians of the later Middle Ages, though Joseph, Arthur, and the Grail

---

[66] There is a plate in Carley, *Glastonbury Abbey*, p. 155, showing the immediate ancestry of Arthur, and information about SS Brigid and David.

[67] Pantin, 'Some English Treatises', 189–215 (pp. 196–8).

[68] *J. Merylynch de perquisito suo* occurs in both Harley manuscripts and in Queen's College 304; Laud Lat. 4 was *perquisitus et scriptus per J. Merylynch*; the William of Malmesbury *tabula* was *editum per J Merylynch*. See N. R. Ker, *Medieval Libraries of Great Britain*, p. 264 and pp. 90–1. On the change of ownership from Sir Geoffrey Keynes to Dr Simon Keynes, see A. G. Watson, ed., *Medieval Libraries of Great Britain: A List of Surviving Books, ed. N. R. Ker, Supplement to the Second Edition* (London, 1987), p. 38.

[69] Aelred Watkin, 'Glastonbury, 1538–9 as Shown by its Account Rolls', *The Downside Review* 67 (1949), 437.

had a flourishing life in romances. The Glastonbury Patrick, Brigid, Indract and Benignus were little-known by the late fourteenth century, and their cults needed to be made available again. Only a garbled version of the life of Indract, mixed with that of Benignus, is in John of Tynemouth's vast *Historia Aurea* in Oxford, Bodleian Library, Bodley 240, from the first half of the fourteenth century. We know that Bishop Grandisson of Exeter borrowed Cambridge, Trinity College R.5.36, the history of the abbey, in 1411, but we do not know what he made of it.[70] But by the time of London, British Library, Cotton Tiberius E.i, which includes John of Bridlington (canonized 1401), Glastonbury material was available, and so made an appearance in the *Nova Legenda Angliæ* printed by Wynkyn de Worde.[71] The Tiberius scribe clearly had reservations. The enterprising scribe of Cotton Titus A.xix, from the Yorkshire Cistercian house of Kirkstall, working sometime in the 1470s or 1480s, copied parts of the tablets themselves, as well as the brass tablet on the earlier churches and part of the liturgy of St Benignus, but made no comment.[72] A later user of the manuscript, however, noted alongside the account of Arthur: 'Ego henricus non concedo'. An early sixteenth-century hand was even more sceptical: 'Hoc est valde mirus'.

What happened to the *Magna Tabula* at the dissolution is not known, but somehow it survived. It must have been on display or at least available when the commissioners came, for the word *papa* has been scraped out in a number of places.[73] Sometime between 1603 and 1639 Archbishop Ussher saw it in the collection of Lord William Howard at Naworth Castle.[74] Ussher made thorough use of the *Magna Tabula*, which he treated as an independent historical authority. He also had seen Cambridge, Trinity College R.5.33 and Oxford, Bodleian Library, Laud Misc. 750, both British Library manu-

---

[70] The inscription recording the loan is on fol. 1v. Seeing the *Magna Tabula* may have made him eager to know more about the history of the abbey.

[71] *Nova Legenda Angliæ*. These observations result from my own examinations of both Bodley 240, which has never been printed in its entirety, and Cotton Tiberius E 1, which was used by Horstmann.

[72] For the tablet, see J. Goodall, 'The Glastonbury Abbey Memorial Plate Reconsidered', *The Antiquaries' Journal* 66 (1986), 364–7.

[73] It has been scraped out three times on each of Tablets 2, 4 and 6.

[74] Ussher, *Antiquitates*, p. 9. The first edition of this book appeared in Dublin in 1639; Lord William Howard did not take possession of Naworth until 1603. Ussher mentions Howard's library in a letter to Camden dated 30 October 1606, but there is no correspondence with Howard and no surviving letter mentions a visit to Naworth. We know that Ussher was in England in 1609, 1613, April 1615, Autumn 1619, November 1623 – August 1626, 1628 and 1631. There may have been other visits before the publication of the *Antiquitates*. See C. R. Erlington and J. H. Todd, *The Works of Archbishop James Ussher*, 17 vols. (Dublin, 1847–64), I, 34, 50, 64, 92, 131 and 205; XVI, 7.

scripts of William of Malmesbury's chronicle as well as the relic list in London, British Library, Cotton Titus D.vii and at least one manuscript of John of Glastonbury's chronicle. References to his quotations from the *Magna Tabula* are included in the contents list which concludes the physical description below. I have not collated his quotations, but he had clearly studied the texts carefully.

Thomas Pennant saw the *Magna Tabula* at Naworth in 1773:

> ... a vast case, three feet high, which opens into three leaves, having six pages pasted in; being an account of S. Joseph of Arimathaea and his twelve disciples, who founded Glastonbury.[75]

The *Magna Tabula* was still at Naworth when Bennett saw it in 1888. It seems to have remained in the family until the twentieth century. According to an unpublished letter in the files at the Bodleian Library, Oxford, from Julian Brown, dated 5 March 1962, Lord Morpeth thought that his father, Lord Carlisle, had sold the tablets before 1939. The *Magna Tabula* was bought by the Bodleian Library at Sotheby's sale on 28 October 1947, lot 524.

2. Physical Description

i. Dimensions and Appearance

The *Magna Tabula*, closed, is a wooden box 48 inches in height and 21¼ inches in width. The width of the front is made up of one board 19 inches long, with a much smaller board, 2¼ inches wide, glued to it. The back is a single board. It is 1¼ inches thick. The boards are scratched and gouged, though not deeply, in a number of places, and there is some cracking on the left half of the back board. On the front, there are four hand-hammered nails at the upper and lower left corners, in a pattern of three across the top, quite close together, and one below the leftmost nail. The pattern is repeated at the bottom, but in addition there are several wooden pegs, which are almost invisible to the casual eye. On the back board, there are similar patterns of four hand-hammered nail heads on the outer corners, top and bottom, and similar wooden pegs. There are, in addition, six holes, in two rows of three, at the top centre, and similar holes, in two rows of four, at the centre of the bottom. This suggests that the back was fixed to prongs of some kind for support. The box has never been dated; it looks now exactly as it did in the

---

[75] Pennant, *Tour to Alston Moor in 1773* (London, 1801), pp. 174–5, quoted in J. A. Bennett, 'A Glastonbury Relic', *Proceedings of the Somersetshire Archaeological & Natural History Society* n.s. 14 (1888), 117–22.

photographs which accompany Bennett's 1888 article.[76] It is possible, however, that the boards, especially the front board, have been repaired since the fifteenth century. The two inner boards are covered with parchment, but the Bodley catalogue (unprinted) has added 'modern' above the line in describing them.

There are two large hinges at the top and bottom of the boards, which are clearly older than the three smaller hinges in the centre of the inner leaves. To the untutored eye, they could be original, though the smaller hinges look post-medieval. There is no record at the Bodleian Library of the box being examined by a medieval archaeologist.

The inner boards are pasted over completely with parchment. On each side of each board, and on the front and back pastedowns, two parchment leaves have been used. All are 17½ inches wide, but the lengths of the skins vary.

Leaf	Top (inches)	Bottom (inches)	Written Space, ac. x down (inches)
1	28½	12³/₈	16–16½ x 37¼
2	28¼	12½	16–16½ x 38¾
3	28¼	12½	16–16½ x 38½
4	27½	12¾	16–16½ x 38
5	27⁵/₈	12	16–16½ x 38⅓
6	28	12½	16–16½ x 39⁵/₈

The parchment was written on after being glued to the boards; on Leaf 6, ascenders and the initial capital letter go across the glue in *Glastoniensis*. On Leaf 4, there is a split, at the bottom of the top parchment, 5³/₈ inches from the left margin. This must have occurred after writing. The parchments have been pasted to the boards, but there is also a dark blue tape around all the edges, with small white dots painted to look like nail-holes on it. This is coming unglued in places and does not look medieval.

The parchment looks worn and smudged, as though it had been examined by candle or rushlight. On Leaf 3, from line 16 down the rest of the page, the red ink has run and there are small smudges of what look like white paint – perhaps from the nail-hole decorative programme – on all the leaves.

---

[76] One photograph also appears in J. Armitage Robinson, *Two Glastonbury Legends* (Cambridge, 1926), plate iv. A photograph of Tablets 5 and 6 appears in Carley, *Glastonbury Abbey*, p. 140.

ii. Script

The *Magna Tabula* is written in a rather rounded textura hand of the late fourteenth or early fifteenth century. It is not a hand which can be identified elsewhere in the surviving Glastonbury manuscripts of the same period.[77] There are 94–101 long lines of text per leaf. The body of the letter forms is ³/₁₆ inches and the ascenders and descenders are rather short, about ¼ inch. Lower case **a** is a closed, rectangular form, with the cross-bar slanting up to the right, or, occasionally, a more 8-shape, with a hairline upper bow. The bow of **e** slants up to the right as well. Though the bow of lower case **d**, and the upper bow of **g**, are sometimes lozenge-shaped, broken strokes are used sparingly, and straight or curved minim strokes contribute to the overall impression of a rounded script. **i** and **y** are usually dotted, with a hairline slanting up to the right. The **et** sign is the tyronian nota, with a hairline approach stroke, and a cross-bar slanted up to the right. Capital letters resemble the lower-case forms. Abbreviations are used sparingly. Even bitings of rounded letters, such as **-do**, **-bo**, are not consistently used. Although the hand is not strikingly calligraphic, the scribe has written carefully, and the result would have been easy to read when the tablets were reasonably new.

iii. Decoration

There are borders on all the pages, some worn, and in places covered with the nineteenth-century tape. The borders are blue and red scrollwork; there are stylized animal heads in line-fillers on Leaves 5 and 6; those on Leaf 6 are larger.

There are blue initials flourished with red, from two to four lines high, with long capital **I** extending, in a triangle, to eight or nine lines. Occasionally, a capital letter in the brown text ink is flourished in red. The flourishing is typically English, with four leaves coming out from a central stem, or a branching stem with leaves or stylized flowers, sometimes with three-bulb finials. There is occasionally a netting pattern in the background. The rubrics are in red, with the first letter blue, not generally flourished. Within

---

[77] For instance, the large historical miscellany, including Geoffrey of Monmouth, which may be from Glastonbury, and is now Cambridge, University Library, Dd.1.17. The Glastonbury attribution rests largely on the presence of the text of Gildas; see Crick, *HRB Manuscripts*, no. 40, pp. 67–71. For other manuscripts, see Compiler above. The other Glastonbury copy of Geoffrey, Oxford, Bodleian Library, Bodley 622, is rather earlier than the tablets, and the large miscellany edited by A. G. Rigg, Cambridge, Trinity College O.9.38, cannot be earlier than 1438. For Bodley 622, see Crick, *HRB Manuscripts*, no. 137, pp. 24–35, and J. P. Carley and J. Crick, 'Constructing Albion's Past: An Annotated Edition of *De Origine Gigantum*', *Arthurian Literature* 13 (1995), 41–114 (p. 71).

paragraphs, new sentences have capital letters, sometimes in red, unflourished, and sometimes in the text ink. When names are capitalized, there is sometimes a line of red through the first initial.

iv. Date

The hand of the tablets can be dated generally to the late fourteenth or early fifteenth century, but it is hard to be more precise when dealing with formal display hands, which were by nature conservative and used fewer abbreviations than book or document hands. The same is true for the decoration. There is some historical help. The tablets must have been compiled after 1382, since they mention the rebuilding of the chapel of St Michael in that year, and the relics which were in it (Text 40). It seems logical to assume that the date, which is the only modern one on the tablets, was included so specifically because it celebrated a recent event. John Chinnock, who is named as responsible for the work, was abbot of Glastonbury from 1375 until 1420. His abbacy confirms the palæographical evidence for dating.

As I have already mentioned, Chinnock was involved in several international councils at which the English delegates argued for the primacy of Glastonbury over St Denis or Compostela. It is tempting to suggest that the Council of Pisa in 1409, or Chinnock's presence as head of the English delegation at the Council of Constance in 1417, provided the impetus for making the tablets. No such connection is made on the tablets themselves, however, and the lack of indulgences from bishops at any of them might argue that the tablets should be dated before 1409, since we might expect Chinnock to have brought new indulgences back with him to the abbey. The councils, in short, are not decisive in dating the tablets precisely, though a date before 1417 is perhaps likelier than 1417–20.

Even the date of 1382 may not provide an exact *terminus a quo*. Was the chapel actually finished in 1382? London, British Library, Additional 15142 is a Glastonbury accounts roll for the twenty-eighth year of John Chinnock's abbacy, that is, 1403.[78] If St Michael's chapel was the same as the abbot's chapel, it as well as the latrine ('capella et latrine domini') was receiving the attentions of a tiler who got nine pence for two days' work. In the same year, lathes, lathe-nails, and stones ('libere petre per capellam, xiijd'), and coping-stones ('tabliamentis') and paving-stones were purchased, these to go 'super pivonem ejusdem capelle'; it took the mason

---

[78] This document is a roll, containing the rents for Kington and the treasury accounts compiled and balanced by Thomas Cook, treasurer. Income from land, wheat, and miscellaneous sources came to £127 8s 5d, and expenses were about half of that: £66 10s 1d. The abbey was clearly comfortably off, and well able to afford the outside workmen who appear in the account.

three days' work, for which he got twelve pence. The cleanup ('in aria ciusdem capella de novo niterendi') cost another eight pence. It is possible that after twenty years some tiles needed to be replaced; fourteen pence might not have bought enough stones for the whole chapel. In the same year a tree-trunk 14 feet long and 2 feet wide was cut up into two planks and fourteen *tabulae*. The size of the resultant boards is not given, but the cost was 11s 10d. Could they have been for making one or more *magnæ tabulæ* for the chapel?

In the same year, the 'porthia ante ostrium aule' got two posts, with one light and two 'antici'; for this operation, four new hinge-hooks ('gingi'), two hinges ('vertivelli'), one 'stapull' and 'cl*eis*' were bought, at a total cost of nine pence. If the boards had gone to making tablets, we might expect the hinges for them to have been entered in the abbot's accounts.[79] And in the same year, a new staircase or ladder ('scala') of twenty-two steps ('gradibus') was made, though the material is not specified, and it could have been of stone, not wood. The accounts are tantalizing, but certainly not conclusive. It seems safer to date the tablets 1382–1420.

3. Edition

i. Texts and Notes to Text

When the Reverend J. A. Bennett wrote up his inspection of the Glastonbury Tablets in 1888 at Naworth Castle, he remarked that the texts were all in Hearne's editions of the chronicles of John of Glastonbury and Adam of Damerham, so there was no need to print them.[80] He was only partly right. There are forty-one sections of text, and the relationship of each section to its sources and analogues varies enormously. Some sections, such as the Charter of St Patrick, agree word for word with John's text. Others, such as the accounts of St Benignus and St Brigid on Tablet 3, Texts 12 and 13, are clearly related to John's, but far from identical. Some sections of the *Magna Tabula* clearly have a version of William of Malmesbury's *De antiquitate ecclesie Glastonie* at hand, though not necessarily that reproduced in Adam of Damerham. The first text of Tablet 2, Text 8, about the disciples of St Philip at Glastonbury, comes directly from a version of William of Glastonbury's *De antiquitate*; it is not in John's chronicle. Sometimes, as in the section on Ticca, Text 19, only the presence of both texts on the compiler's

---

[79] For a door of the period at Glastonbury, see Carley, *Glastonbury Abbey*, p. 60.
[80] J. A. Bennett, 'A Glastonbury Relic', *Proceedings of the Somersetshire Archaeological & Natural History Society* n.s. 14 (1888), frontispiece and 117–22. Bennett also consulted the transcript of the Rev. T. Lees, Vicar of Wreay, Carlisle, but does not seem to have looked at any medieval manuscript sources.

writing-table explains the text of the tablets. For some sections, including some Arthurian material, the closest surviving comparable text is found in the late fifteenth-century Cotton Titus A.xix, whose scribe must have worked directly from the tablets, or with no more than one intervening copy. The account of Patrick's successor St Benignus (Text 12), and Text 15 on St David, are close to, though not identical with, material in Cotton Titus A.xix. And, while most of the Grail and Arthurian material comes from John of Glastonbury, material at the end of the account of Josephus (Text 1), about Nascien's son Celidoine's marriage to the daughter of the king of Persia, comes directly from the *Estoire del Saint Graal*. The information in the account of the rediscovery of Arthur's grave on Tablet 5 (Text 27) is found in several sources, but the wording does not match any of them. The same is true of Text 26, the list of relics at Glastonbury found on Tablet 4, and the similar Text 39 at the top of Tablet 6.

The texts of the *Magna Tabula* edited below have been collated with all possible sources, but the shifting relationships between them and other manuscripts create editorial problems. One cannot simply compare the texts word by word. Even when using the chronicles of William of Malmesbury and John of Glastonbury closely, the compiler of the tablets had constrictions of space and sometimes a different context for the information, so that first and last sentences of chapters, which frequently serve as transitions in William's or John's texts, either do not appear on the tablets, or are considerably altered. Many sections are not precise copies; in the shorter texts, the two chronicles often provide a source for information and phrasing, rather than for specific words. Changes in sources and analogues often occur from one paragraph to the next, and sometimes even within a paragraph. For this reason, a statement about comparable material in other sources is given in the first footnote to every section.[81]

In order to show where a given reading comes from, and when the basic source changes, I have noted the source of a reading before the reading itself.

In collating William of Malmesbury's and John of Glastonbury's texts, I have included readings found in all the manuscripts of both chronicles, in order to try and identify the closest surviving manuscript to our compiler's exemplar. For the expanded *De antiquitate*, based on William of Malmesbury, the answer is clear; the text is very close to Scott's base manuscript, Trinity College R.5.33 (mid-thirteenth-century), though, if the compiler used that actual manuscript, he ignored even its thirteenth-century glosses. It is improbable that as careful and eclectic a reader as the compiler shows

---

[81] All related manuscripts are also listed in the Contents section of the manuscript description. I have not collated the extracts from Ussher's *Antiquitates*, but they are listed, with page references, in the table of contents in the description of the manuscript.

himself to be would have ignored all of them. It seems more likely that he used a copy made before the glosses were added.[82] For John of Glastonbury, the problem is compounded by the fact that the only extant fourteenth-century manuscript is itself incomplete.

In the notes, reference is also made to the various manuscripts cited by both Scott and Carley in their textual notes. As can be seen from the list below, however, Scott and Carley use the sigla C, T and B to refer to different manuscripts. In order to minimize confusion for the reader, I have put the edition being cited first, then the base reading of that edition if it differs from the text of the tablets, then the siglum for the manuscript and its variant. A reference to William of Malmesbury or John of Glastonbury, in the form Wm: *Sed* or JG: *Sed* means that the reading *Sed* is found in the text as printed in Scott's edition of William, on the page cited in the first note for this section, and that there are no variants. A reference such as Wm: *ut* T means that Scott's manuscript T has a reading different from his base text which is relevant here, often because it agrees with the text of the tablets.[83] References to Scott and Carley, followed by a page number, are to their notes and introductory material. Chapter and line numbers are included where a text begins in the middle of a chapter. As neither edition has line numbers on the page, this seemed a more helpful way of targeting a text than giving only a page number.

In general, one can conclude from studying the variants that there must have been texts of both William of Malmesbury and John of Glastonbury at Glastonbury Abbey around 1400 which do not now survive. As I have already said, the compiler of the *Magna Tabula* used something very close to Scott's T, Trinity College R.5.33, for his *De antiquitate* material, but without many of the marginal and interlinear additions it would have had by the time the *Magna Tabula* was assembled. See, for instance, the variants in Text 9, the account of Phaganus and Deruvianus. Small interlinear additions in T do not appear on the tablets. It is, of course, possible that the scribe of the tablets had Trinity R.5.33 itself, and ignored the corrections and additions.[84] On the whole, however, it seems likelier that he had a copy

---

[82] In this context, it may be worth remarking that the now-fragmentary Keynes manuscript had a table of contents supplied by John Merylynch, whose possible connection with the *Magna Tabula* is discussed above. See n. 67.

[83] The use of *Wm* begs the questions of what was in William of Malmesbury's original text, and what is a later addition, matters not always absolutely clear. The version of William available in the time of Abbot John Chinnock is likely in any case to have been interpolated, but William would no doubt have been considered as the author by the compiler of the tablets. Where there is a problem about when information became part of the Glastonbury tradition which affects a reading, there is a comment in the textual notes. The problems arising from conflicting traditions, especially about relics, are discussed in Part 2, 4. Glossary, under the relevant name.

made from its pre-correction state. As all the corrections were made by the latest in the mid-fourteenth century, the copy was most probably made before *c.* 1350.

This copy is unlikely to have been Adam of Damerham's manuscript, London, British Library, Additional 22934, Scott's M (*c.* 1313), since the larger additions found in M are never included on the tablets and, where M's reading diverges, the tablets do not follow it. See, for instance, the incorporation of *ut fertur* into the text of M about the apostolic church at Glastonbury in Text 9.14, or the inserted phrases at 8.30 and 9.3. Similarly, Oxford, Bodleian Library, Laud Misc. 750 (second half of the thirteenth century) had many additions to its text, of which the compiler of the tablets shows no knowledge. At 5.86–87, for example, there are seven variant readings in L, none of which appears on the tablets. Scott's C (London, British Library, Cotton Cleopatra C.x) is fifteenth-century and only occasionally relevant.

For John of Glastonbury, the situation is less clear, but the *Magna Tabula* text is closer to Carley's base manuscript, Cambridge, Trinity College R.5.16 (T), than to any of the other surviving manuscripts. For John, the extant surviving manuscripts, apart from T, are, in fact, later in date than the tablets, but we have no way of knowing how many other copies might have been available at Glastonbury. Small variations, including the spellings of proper nouns, are frequent; many have been collated to see if any close relationship emerged. The collation has revealed that no surviving manuscript of John of Glastonbury's chronicle is as close to the text of the tablets as Trinity R.5.33 is to the text of William of Malmesbury. All the manuscripts include Abbot Chinnock's adornment of the image of the Virgin in Text 24, omitted, perhaps for lack of space, near the end of the tablet. A (Oxford, Bodleian Library, Ashmole 790) shows many other small omissions, and P (Princeton University Library, Garrett 153) has numerous small variations, in both cases, probably too many to have arisen in one stage of copying from T. A sampling of their readings is included, to indicate the patterns of variation which occur.

We do not know how many manuscripts of either author were at Glas-

---

[84] The passage about Lancelot and Gawain found on Tablet 1, 2.1–9, is added in the margin of Scott's MS T after rather than before the account of the disciples of Philip (Tablet 2, Text 8). It could be argued that its place on the tablets would be later if the compiler had been using T, but he must, in any case, have taken the other Arthurian information on Tablet 1 from another source, or sources. No surviving source has all six short passages: this section, the prophecy of Melkin, the verses from the *Aurora*, the verses from a chronicle, and the two genealogies. Clearly the compiler wanted Arthur featured on Tablet 1. In Scott's MS T, the prophecy of Melkin is on the front flyleaf, in a later hand.

tonbury in the late fourteenth and early fifteenth centuries. The last complete library catalogue was compiled in the 1240s; after that, we have only lists of donations.[85] If there were several manuscripts of William of Malmesbury and of John of Glastonbury available, it would be risky to conclude that the compiler of the tablets always used the same manuscript of each.

ii. Editions Cited

The main editions used are those of Scott for William of Malmesbury with interpolations, and of Carley for John of Glastonbury.

Adami de Domerham, Historia de rebus gestis Glastoniensibus, e codice ms. perantiquum, in bibliotheca collegii S. Trinitatis Cantabrigiae, 2 vols., ed. T. Hearne (Oxford, 1727). This is Scott's H, not collated.
Barber, R., 'Was Mordred Buried at Glastonbury? An Arthurian Tradition at Glastonbury in the Middle Ages', *Arthurian Literature* 4 (1984), 37–69. This article, while not an edition, contains an itemization of the Arthurian quire of Cotton Titus A.xix. 'Barber, no.' refers to the item number of a Titus text in Barber's list.
The Chronicle of Glastonbury Abbey: An Edition, Translation and Study of John of Glastonbury's Cronica sive Antiquitates Glastoniensis Ecclesie, ed. J. P. Carley, trans. D. Townsend (Woodbridge, 1985).
The Early History of Glastonbury by William of Malmesbury: An Edition, Translation and Study of William of Malmesbury's De Antiquitate Glastonie Ecclesie, ed. and trans. J. Scott (Woodbridge, 1981).
Johannis, confratris & monachi glastoniensis, Chronica, sive, Historia de rebus glastoniensibus, ed. T. Hearne, 2 vols. (Oxford, 1726).
Evangelia Apocrypha, ed. K. Tischendorf (Leipzig, 1853; 2nd ed. Leipzig, 1876).
The Gospel of Nicodemus, ed. H. C. Kim (Toronto, 1973).
Ussher, J., *Britannicarum ecclesiarum antiquitates* (London, 1687).

iii. Manuscripts Cited

Oxford, Bodleian Library, Lat. hist. a. 2 (B), Magna Tabula. Scott's B; Carley's Magna Tabula.
Cambridge, Trinity College R.5.16 (711). Carley's base manuscript, C.
Cambridge, Trinity College R.5.33 (724). Scott's base manuscript, T.
London, British Library, Additional 22934. Scott's M.
London, British Library, Cotton Cleopatra C.iv. Scott's C.

---

[85] For Glastonbury's medieval catalogues and book lists, see *English Benedictine Libraries: The Shorter Catalogues*, ed. R. Sharpe, J. P. Carley, R. M. Thomson and A. G. Watson (London, 1996), pp. 157–245. I am grateful to James Carley for letting me see a copy of his list in advance of publication. The older edition is T. Williams, *Somerset Medieval Libraries* (Bristol, 1897), in which he reprints the list from Hearne's edition of JG.

London, British Library, Cotton Tiberius A.v. Carley's T.
London, British Library, Cotton Titus A.xix. Cited here as Titus A.xix.
London, British Library, Cotton Titus D.vii. Carley's Titus.
London, British Library, Cotton Vespasian D.xxii. Carley's V.
Oxford, Bodleian Library, Ashmole 790. Carley's A.
Oxford, Bodleian Library, Bodley 854. Carley's B.
Oxford, Bodleian Library, Bodley 957. Carley's B[1].
Oxford, Bodleian Library, Laud Misc. 750. Scott's L.
Princeton, Princeton University, Robert Garrett 153. Carley's P.

iv. Editorial Conventions

Manuscript spelling has been preserved, including the use of u for both u and v; v occurs occasionally initially, usually as an upper case letter. J, as distinct from i, is not used; upper case i has a long form only in flourished capitals in the left margin. I and J have, however, been separated in the Glossary. Names of people and places are only infrequently capitalized in the manuscript; capital letters have been used for proper names throughout this edition, for ease of reading. Headings are in red, and initial capitals of sections and occasionally of paragraphs within sections, are in blue flourished with red. These appear in **boldface**.

Abbreviations are few and conventional; they have been expanded silently. The scribe's usual forms *ihu' xps*, *xipanus* have been expanded *Ihesus Christus* and *Christianus*. His usual form, frequently written out, is *Glastonia-æ*, but *Glastoniens-ensis* also occurs. Where *Glaston'* appears, I have expanded it as *Glastonia* when appropriate. Some words have variable spelling: *historiographus* and *historiagraphus* both appear. A few spellings which are exceptionally odd (e.g. *Eadditha*) are followed by [*sic*].

The scribe ordinarily uses only two marks of punctuation: a full stop, at the ends of clauses and sentences, in lists, and around numbers; and a *punctus flexus*, which is a more major stop and usually coincides with a modern sentence boundary or with the modern colon, as at the start of an itemized list. I have transcribed it with a colon. There is also an occasional question mark. Scholars are becoming more aware that the punctuation used by medieval scribes writing prose, though different from modern conventions, does usually represent a comprehensible system. The scribe of the tablets indicates paragraphs and major and minor divisions between clauses. These marks do not always correspond to modern sentence divisions, but do separate the text into readable units. In view of the growing interest in medieval punctuation as a feature of scribal style, I have preserved it here.

The manuscript is worn and difficult to read in places. Where I have had to guess at a reading, usually from the source or analogous text, the reading is in angle brackets <>. Emendations of the scribe's few errors are underlined in the text and discussed in the footnotes.

v. Contents and Sources

Tablet 1

1. 1–116   Incipit tractatus de sancto Ioseph ab Arimathia extractus de libro quodam quem invenit Theodisius imperator in Ierusalem <in pretorio> Pilati

Based on the Late Latin version of the apocryphal *Gospel of Nicodemus* or *Acts of Pilate*, but much condensed, and beginning where Joseph of Arimathia enters the action. For the most convenient edition, see *The Gospel of Nicodemus*; the text here is occasionally closer to the D version in Tischendorf, *Evangelia Apocrypha*. Not included in William of Malmesbury's text or the expanded *De Antiquitate*, but in John of Glastonbury, pp. 46–50, and Titus A.xix, fols. 18–19 (Barber, no. 5), with some variation at the end, indicating independent use of the *Estoire del Saint Graal*. See *The Vulgate Version of Arthurian Romance*, ed. O. Sommers, 7 vols. (Washington, 1908–12), I. Part of this section is quoted in Ussher, *Antiquitates*, p. 9.

2. 1–13.   Hec scriptura reperitur in gestis incliti Regis Arthuri.

John of Glastonbury, ch. 20, lines 11–end, p. 52. Not in William of Malmesbury, but in a marginal note in Trinity R.5.33, printed by Scott, p. 46, and, according to Carley, *Chronicle*, p. 279 note 75, also partly in Additional 22934; also in Titus A.xix, fol. 19 (Barber, no. 6). The first episode is from the Vulgate *Lancelot*, 455, 464–8. The second is from the *Queste del Saint Graal*, 24–7 and the *Estoire*, 285.

3. 1–15.   Ista scriptura inuenitur in libro Melkini: qui fuit ante Merlinum.

John of Glastonbury, p. 54; Titus A.xix, fol. 19–19v (Barber, no. 6). Not in William of Malmesbury or the expanded *De antiquitate*, but in Titus D.vii, fol. 29v, Cotton Cleopatra C.x, fol. 98, and Arundel 220, fol. 274. See J. P. Carley, 'Melkin the Bard and Esoteric Tradition at Glastonbury Abbey', *The Downside Review* 99 (1981), 1–17. Part of this is quoted in Ussher, *Antiquitates*, p. 12.

4. 1–10.   Versus de sancto Ioseph de Aurora que et biblia uersi(fi)cata dicitur.

John of Glastonbury, p. 54; Titus A.xix, fol. 19v (Barber, no. 6). Not in William of Malmesbury. From Peter of Riga, *Aurora Petri Rigæ biblia versificata*, ed. P. Beichner, 2 vols. (South Bend, 1965). The passage here comes from *Evangeliarum*, II, 531–2, lines 2807–8; 2813–16; 2819–20. For an expanded version placing Joseph at Glastonbury, found in a Glastonbury Abbey manuscript, BL Cotton Cleopatra C.x, see Carley, *Chronicle*, p. 280, n. 82.

5. 1–6. Item versus reperti in quibusdam cronicis ubi agitur de rege Arvirago.
John of Glastonbury, p. 50; Titus A.xix, fol. 19v (part of Barber, no. 6), immediately under the verses from the *Aurora*. Not in William of Malmesbury or the verse epitome of Geoffrey of Monmouth by John Bevers but, like no. 27 (the epitaph of Arthur), it is added in the margin of a copy of the chronicle attributed to John Stafford in Titus A.xix, with two additional lines. It comes after line 195: *Arviragus semper serviret lite remota*, just before his death in line 196. It may have been composed at Glastonbury to fit that chronicle, which also has coupled rhyme. For Stafford, see J. Hammer, 'Une version métrique de l'*Historia Regum Britanniæ* de Geoffroi de Monmouth', *Latomus* 2 (1938), 131–51. The chronicle, without these marginal additions, is also in Harley 1808, Harley 2386, Cotton Claudius D.vii and Bodleian Library, Digby 186. Quoted in Ussher, *Antiquitates*, p. 8.

6. 1–7. Hec scriptura testatur quod Rex Arthurus de stirpe Ioseph descendit.
John of Glastonbury, p. 54, immediately following the verses from the *Aurora*, and repeated on p. 72, except for the final phrase. Also in Titus A.xix, fol. 19v (Barber, no. 6).

7. 1–5. Item de eodem.
John of Glastonbury, p. 54; Titus A.xix, fol. 19r (Barber, no. 6).

Tablet 2

8. 1–59 Incipit quomodo duodecim discipuli sanctorum Philippi et Iacobi apostolorum primo ecclesiam in Glastonia fundauerunt.
William of Malmesbury, pp. 42–6; Titus A.xix, fols. 19v–20r (Barber, no. 7). Not in John of Glastonbury, who phrases similar information differently.

9. 1–45. Quomodo Sanctus Phaganus et Deruuianus Britannos ad fidem conuerterunt et ad insulam Auallonie uenerunt
William of Malmesbury, pp. 46–50; John of Glastonbury, pp. 56–8; not in Titus A.xix. Part of this section is quoted in Ussher, *Antiquitates*, pp. 55–6.

10. 1–13. De Sancto Patricio
Close to the last half of William of Malmesbury, ch. 8, p. 54. Information such as dates from John of Glastonbury, ch. 23, p. 58, which was added in

Scott's base manuscript, Trinity R.5.33 in the fourteenth century; Scott, pp. 188–9. Not in Titus A.xix.

Tablet 3 (begins 11.54)
11. 1–91. Carta Sancti Patricii
William of Malmesbury, pp. 54–60; also in John of Glastonbury, pp. 60–4, but this text is closer to William. See especially the notes to the collation from 3.11 on, where William and John diverge for several sentences. The text cannot have been composed before the late twelfth century, and so was not known to William of Malmesbury. See Scott, *The Early History*, p. 191, note 35. Not in Titus A.xix. It was used for the Anglo-Norman version of the early fourteenth century; see Robin Flower, under Brigid in the Glossary below.

12. 1–5. De Sancto Benigno
William of Malmesbury, p. 62. John of Glastonbury has more extensive materials on St Benignus, including the flowering staff, in chs. 29 and 30, but there are no close verbal parallels until the concluding sentence of ch. 30, p. 70. The version in Titus A.xix, fol. 20v (Barber, no. 9), which includes a hymn and prayer from his liturgy, is different again. But Titus includes a somewhat condensed version of 3.00–00 on fol. 21v, after the account of St Patrick.

13. 1–12. De Sancta Brigida
Brigid: William of Malmesbury, p. 60, and John of Glastonbury, p. 66, contain most of the same information, but the wording here is not identical with either. Not in Titus A.xix, though Brigid, Columkilla, Indract, Vincent and Gildas are all mentioned, in that order, on fol. 21v, after St Benignus and before St David.
Indract: William of Malmesbury, ch. 12, p. 60, and ch. 20, p. 68, with some phrasing not identical with either. Much of the same information is in John of Glastonbury, ch. 5, pp. 16–18. Indract is mentioned in Titus A.xix, in the list of saints on fol. 23. See also Ussher, *Antiquitates*, pp. 46–7.

14. 1–10. De sanctis Kolumkilla et Gilda
William of Malmesbury, p. 62. *De Sancto Columkilla*; for Gildas, William, p. 54. John of Glastonbury, p. 74, is a much fuller account. Gildas is not mentioned in Titus A.xix, except in the list of saints on fol. 23.

15. 1–19. De Sancto Dauid
William of Malmesbury, pp. 62–4; John of Glastonbury, p. 86, and Titus A.xix, fols. 20–20v (Barber no. 8), all tell the story of David coming to consecrate the church at Glastonbury, but all three versions are different.

Titus A.xix, however, includes this version in an account of the saints buried at Glastonbury on fol. 21v. William of Malmesbury, pp. 80–2, *De altare sancti Dauid quod dicitur uulgo saphirus*, recounts David's adventures in the Holy Land, and the gifts of the patriarch of Jerusalem, which included the altar stone, but does not mention its angelic provenance.

16. 1–6. De reliquis Sancti David.
William of Malmesbury, ch. 16, lines 7–11, p. 64; John of Glastonbury, p. 130. Scott does not consider this to be William's work. The text is closer to William than John. Titus A.xix, fol. 23r is closest to the text here.

17. 1–6. De reliquis a Guelia Glastonie translatus.
William of Malmesbury, p. 64; John of Glastonbury, p. 130. Not in Titus A.xix.

18. 1–6. De Sancto Paulino.
William of Malmesbury, pp. 66–8, and John of Glastonbury, p. 51, both record the visit of Paulinus and his building restoration, but the language is not close for the first half; John is close for the second half. Not in Titus A.xix. Part of this is quoted in Ussher, *Antiquitates*, p. 60.

19. 1–19. De Sancto Ticca
William of Malmesbury, p. 68, including some readings which agree with Scott's manuscript T, but lacking Ticca's epitaph. John of Glastonbury, pp. 107–8, with different relics, but including the epitaph. Titus A.xix., fol. 21v, has a shortened version, including the relics, but not the epitaph.

20. 1–18. De translatione Sancti Dunstani a Cantuaris ad Glastoniam.
William of Malmesbury, pp. 72–4; John of Glastonbury, pp.142–4, but neither is verbally close enough to collate. Titus A.xix, fol. 22v (Barber, no. 11). Cotton Cleopatra C.iv, fols. 62r–63r has a similar version.

21. 1–10. De ueuerabili cruce que quondam locuta est
William of Malmesbury, p. 78; John of Glastonbury, pp. 42–4; Titus A.xix, fol. 22v (Barber, no. 12).

22. 1–12. De alia cruce de qua cecidit diadema.
William of Malmesbury, pp. 78–80; John of Glastonbury, p. 44; Titus A.xix, fol. 22v (Barber, no. 13).

23. 1–5. De cruce uulnerata
William of Malmesbury, p. 80; John of Glastonbury, p. 44 ; Titus A.xix, fol. 22v (Barber, no. 13).

24. 1–6. De quadam ymagine beate Marie.
William of Malmesbury, p. 80; John of Glastonbury, p. 44; Titus A.xix, fols. 22v–23 (Barber, no. 14).

25. 1–7. De ymagine antiquioris capelle
John of Glastonbury, p. 44; Titus A.xix, fol. 23 (Barber, no. 15). This account is closer to Titus.

Tablet 4

26. 1–78. De sanctis ibidem requiescentibus
This section seems to be based on the same information as William of Malmesbury, p. 70, which is also found in John of Glastonbury, pp. 16–18, with fuller information from other chapters. Philip and James, Phaganus and Deruvianus, and Patrick are also discussed in William, p. 86, on the abbots and founders, but the language is not the same.
26.46–49: John of Glastonbury, p. 51, records the visit of Paulinus while still bishop of Rochester in 625. From *muros* to *perdurauit*, the passage is the same; it is also the same on Tablet 3.57–59.
26.53–61: William of Malmesbury, p. 68, Northumbrian Saints.
Part of this is quoted in Ussher, *Antiquitates*, p. 33 (Phaganus and Deruvianus); cf. p. 56.

27. 1–48. De rege Arthuro et de aliis regibus. ibidem requiescentibus
The same information, though not word for word, is in John of Glastonbury, pp. 180–1, based on Adam of Damerham.
The epitaph of Arthur, and names of the following kings, are in Titus A.xix, fol. 22r, in the account of famous burials at Glastonbury. The epitaph is also on fol. 109r, in the margin. See also M. P. Brown and J. P. Carley, 'A Fifteenth-Century Revision of the Glastonbury Epitaph to King Arthur', *Arthurian Literature* 12 (1993), 179–91.
27.28–32: John of Glastonbury, p. 30. Part of this is quoted in Ussher, *Antiquitates*, p. 59 (Centwine); for Arthur, see pp. 61–2.

28. 1–4. De archiepiscopis
There is no specific list of archbishops buried at Glastonbury in either William of Malmesbury or John of Glastonbury, but the burials are all mentioned in both sources. Titus A.xix, fol. 22, does not list archbishops or bishops; it goes directly to the *duces*. The names are in Ussher, *Antiquitates*, p. 59.

29. 1–16. De episcopis
William of Malmesbury, p. 84; John of Glastonbury, p. 30. A reference, with the text of Hedda, is in Ussher, *Antiquitates*, p. 59.

30. 1–7. De ducibus
William of Malmesbury, ch. 31, p. 84: last sentence of the chapter. John of Glastonbury, p. 30; Titus A.xix, fol. 22r.

31. 1–9. De Glasteing et de fratribus suis
William of Malmesbury, p. 52, first sentence omitted; chapter headed: *Quomodo multitudo popularis primitus Glastoniam inhabitauerit.* Also in John of Glastonbury, ch. 2, line 7, p. 10, but the wording is closer to William. Not in Titus A.xix.

32. 1–11. De diversis nominibus eiusdem insule
William of Malmesbury, p. 52; John of Glastonbury, p. 11, has the same information, but different wording, before the account of Glasteing and his brothers.

Tablet 5

33. 1–68. De dignitate et sanctitate ecclesie beate marie glastonie ac eiusdem sancti cimiterii
William of Malmesbury, p. 66. Heading: *De sanctitate et dignitate Glastoniensis ecclesie.* The beginning is not in John of Glastonbury. Titus A.xix, fol. 22r, has a condensed version.
5.11: John of Glastonbury, ch. 13, p. 32, line 5.

34. 1–38. Quando quidam Soldanus misit pro quadam porcione huius sancti cimiterii
John of Glastonbury, pp. 32–4. Titus A.xix, fols. 22v–23r, has a much condensed version, which does not name Rainaldus.

35. 1–20. Quomodo monachus quidam de Sancto Dionisio de Glastonia referebat
William of Malmesbury, p. 50; John of Glastonbury, p. 10, with variant phrasing in the first few lines. Not in Titus A.xix. The version here is very close to William.

36. 1–12. De fundationibus ecclesiarum in insula Auallonie
William of Malmesbury, p. 94; John of Glastonbury, p. 95, with numerous differences; Titus A.xix, fol. 23r, lines 13–23; Barber, no. 16. The version here is closest to Titus.

37. 1–16. De capella argentea quam ibidem fecit Ina cum suis uasis
William of Malmesbury, p. 96; Titus A.xix, fol. 23r, lines 23–end. Not on Barber's list. The version here is closest to Titus.

38. 1–21. De duabus piramidibus
William, p. 84, with heading; John of Glastonbury, p. 30, right after the list of kings, bishops and *duces* buried at Glastonbury. Not in Titus A.xix.

Tablet 6

39. 1–37. Nomina sanctorum in ecclesia Glastoniensi requiescentium sub breuitate collecta
The material here is collected from elsewhere on the tablets. Information on the early founders comes from the accounts on Tablets 1 and 2; the list resembles that on Tablet 4. There is no comparable list in William of Malmesbury or John of Glastonbury, though the concluding sentence is taken from the first sentence of John's ch. 6, p. 20. Nor is the list in Cotton Cleopatra C.iv comparable. See the individual references for Tablet 4, and Part 2, 4. Glossary.

40. 1–19. De capella sanctorum Michaelis et Ioseph et sanctorum in cimiterio requiescentium.
This paragraph is printed by Bennett, 1888, and in J. P. Carley, 'A Grave Event: Henry V, Glastonbury Abbey and Joseph of Arimathea's Bones', in *Culture and the King: The Social Implications of the Arthurian Legend*, ed. M. B. Shichtman and J. P. Carley (Albany, NY, 1994), n. 10, p. 142, with modernized punctuation. It is also found in Titus A.xix, fols. 21v–22r, as part of the history of the abbey; other bits of this section in Titus are on Tablet 3.

41. 1–136. Indulgentie morum pontificum legatorum archiepiscoporum episcoporum Glastoniensis concessa
Unpublished; some overlap with the list in Hearne, *Johannis Confratris et Monachi Glastoniensis Chronica sive Historia de Rebus Glastoniensibus*, 2 vols. (Oxford, 1727), II, appendix.

TEXT

Tablet 1

1. Incipit tractatus de sancto Ioseph ab Arimathia[1] extractus de libro quodam quem invenit Theodisius imperator in ierusalem <in pretorio>[2] Pilati

Quoniam dubia sepe legentem fallunt. certa dubiis ablatis atque ex antiquis
5 hystoriagraphorum[3] dictis probata[4] de antiquitate Glastoniensis ecclesie quedam subinferemus.[5] Crucifixo[6] Domino et completis omnibus que de eo fuerant prophetata: accessit Ioseph ab Arimathia ille nobilis decurio ad Pilatum[7] et peciit corpus Ihesu. et acceptum inuoluit syndone et posuit eum in monumento in quo nondum quisquam positus fuerat.[8] Uidentes[9] autem
10 Iudei quia corpus Ihesu sepelierat Ioseph: querebant apprehendere eum simul[10] cum Nichodemo necnon et[11] aliis qui aduocati eius fuerunt coram Pilato. omnibus autem se occultantibus: hii duo memorati Ioseph uidelicet et Nichodemus ostenderunt se illis dicentes <u>Quare contristati estis</u>[12] aduersum nos quia sepeliuimus corpus Ihesu. Non bene egistis aduersus iustum.
15 neque recogitastis quanta beneficia erga nos[13] operatus est. sed crucifixistis eum et. lancea uulnerastis. Audientes Iudei sermones istos. apprehenderunt

---

[1] JG, Ch. 18, p. 46: *ab Arimathia* omitted T. This section is found only in JG; William and the *De antiquitate* tradition do not include Joseph of Arimathia. It is also in London, British Library, Cotton Titus A.xix, fols. 18–19. The Arthurian section of Titus has been described by Richard Barber, 'Was Mordred Buried at Glastonbury?', 37–69. For readers interested in the legend, I have included references to the chapters in Kim's and Tischendorf's editions.

[2] The MS is very worn and difficult to read in the first few lines; the text in angle brackets is conjectural, consistent with what is legible of the letter forms. Tischendorf reads: *pretorio Pontii Pilati*

[3] Titus: *historiographorum*

[4] JG: *prolicta; probata* P; Titus *probata*

[5] Titus: *subinferamus*

[6] Kim 11.3; Tischendorf 11.2.

[7] JG: *Pilatum, ut euangelice prodit historia,*

[8] Both Kim and Tischendorf make the point that the tomb was Joseph's own: *monumentum suum.*

[9] JG: *Audientes autem Iudei quod Ioseph corpus Ihesu sepelierat.* Titus: *Audientes;* Kim, Tischendorf 12.1.

[10] JG: *simul* omitted.

[11] Titus: *cum*

[12] MS: This phrase is underlined.

[13] Titus: *nos* omitted, but a caret; *vos* added in margin.

Ioseph et incluserunt eum in cubiculo ubi non erat fenestra, et signauerunt ostium super cla\v/em Annas et Cayphas et custodes posuerunt qui eum[14] custodirent. Nichodemum uero liberum dimiserunt quia ipse solus Iospeh
20 uidelicet. corpus Ihesu peciit. ac principalis incentor fuerat sepulture eius. Et[15] post hec congregatis omnibus per diem sabbati cum sacerdotibus et leuitis cogitauerunt qua morte occiderent Ioseph. Et congregatione facta: iusserunt[16] principes Anne et Cayphe ut presenteretur[17] Ioseph. Et aperientes signa ostii: non inuenerunt eum: Missis[18] autem undique exploratoribus
25 inuentus est Ioseph in ciuitate sua Arimathia. Hec[19] audientes principes sacerdotum et omnis populus Iudeorum[20] gauisi sunt et glorificauerunt Deum Israel. quia inuentus est Ioseph quem incluserant in cubiculo. Et facientes congregationem magnam: dixerunt principes sacerdotum. Quo ordine possumus adducere ad nos Ioseph et loqui cum eo: Et tollentes
30 thomum carte: scripserunt ad Ioseph dicentes. Pax tecum et omnibus qui tecum sunt. Scimus quia peccauimus in Deum et in te. Dignare ergo uenire ad patres[21] tuos et[22] ad filios tuos. quia admirati sumus nimis de assumptione tua. Scimus enim quia malignum[23] consilium cogitauimus aduersum te: et Dominus[24] liberauit te de maligno consilio nostro. Pax tibi Domine Ioseph
35 honorabilis ab omni plebe. Et[25] elegerunt septem uiros amicos Ioseph. Et dixerunt ad eos. Dum[26] peruenitis ad Ioseph salutate eum in pace: dantes ei[27] epistolam. Et peruenientes uiri ad eum: salutauerunt[28] eum pacifice. dederuntque[29] illi libellum epistole. Cum autem[30] legisset Ioseph epistolam:[31] dixit Benedictus Dominus Deus meus[32] qui liberasti Israel ut non

---

[14] JG: *custodirent eum.*
[15] JG: *Et* omitted. Kim, Tischendorf 12.2. In both these texts, a great deal more space is devoted to the search for Jesus, the Jews' questionings and the testimony of Nicodemus. Joseph is found in Kim, 15.1.
[16] Kim 12.2; Tischendorf 14.3.
[17] JG: *presentarent*; Titus: *presentaretur*
[18] Kim 15.1; Tischendorf 15.2.
[19] Kim 15.2 here agrees almost exactly for several sentences.
[20] Kim: *Iudeorum* omitted.
[21] JG: *partes* A.
[22] JG, p. 46: *et . . . tuos* omitted T.
[23] Titus: *consilium malignum*
[24] Kim: *Dominus suscepit te et ipse Dominus*
[25] Kim, Tischendorf 15.3.
[26] Kim: *Cum*
[27] Kim: *ei* omitted.
[28] Kim: *salutantes*
[29] Kim: *et dederunt ei*
[30] Kim: *autem* omitted.
[31] Kim: *epistolam* omitted.
[32] Kim: *meus* omitted.

40 effunderet sanguinem meum. Benedictus Deus[33] qui protexisti me sub alis tuis.[34] Et osculatus est Ioseph uiros qui[35] uenerant ad se: et suscepit eos in domum suam.

Alia[36] autem die ascendit super asinum suum et ambulauit cum illis. et uenit in Ierusalim. Et cum audisssent omnes Iudei occurrerunt ei obuiam
45 dicentes **Pax** in introitu tuo[37] pater. Quibus respondens Ioseph dixit **Pax** uobis omnibus sit. Et osculati sunt eum omnes: et[38] suscepit eum Nichodemus in domum suum. Fecitque ei conuiuium. Alia[39] autem die conuenientibus in unum Iudeis:[40] dixerunt ad Ioseph Annas et Cayphas **Da** confessionem Deo Israel et manifesta nobis omnia que interrogatus fueris.
50 Quia ergo contestati fuimus de eo quod sepelisti corpus Ihesu: et inclusimus te in cubiculo propter diem sabbati. Postera die querentes te non inuenimus.[41] et admirati sumus nimis. et pauor nos comprehendit usque nunc cum te suscepimus iam[42] presente te coram Deo manifesta nobis quid de te actum sit. Respondens[43] autem Ioseph: dixit[44] **Q**uando me reduxistis[45] in
55 die[46] Parasceve ad uesperum dum starem ad orationem die sabbati media nocte suspensa est domus in qua eram a quatuor angelis et uidi Ihesum sicut fulgorem lucis. et pre timore cecidi in terram. et tenens manum meam eleuauit me de terra. rosaque perfudit me, et extergens faciem meam:[47] osculatus est me: et dixit michi Noli timere Ioseph respice in me et uide
60 quia ego sum. Et respexi et dixi. Rabboni Helyas Et dixit michi Non sum Helyas sed ego sum Ihesus: cuius corpus sepelisti. Et dixi ad eum. Ostende michi monumentum ubi posui te. et tenens manum meum deduxit[48] me in locum ubi sepeliui eum et ostendit michi syndonem. et fatiale in quo caput eius[49] inuolui. Tunc cognoui quia Ihesu est[50] et adoraui eum et dixi Benedic-
65 tus qui uenit in nomine Domini. Et tenens manum meam duxit me in

---

[33] JG, p. 48: *Deus meus*; *meus* omitted P.
[34] Titus: *tuis* omitted.
[35] Kim: *qui . . . se* omitted.
[36] Kim: 15.4. From here on, the number of small verbal differences increases, though the narrative is basically the same.
[37] JG, p. 48: *tuo* omitted A.
[38] Tischendorf 15.4.
[39] Kim: 15.5.
[40] JG: *convenientes in vnum Iudei.*
[41] JG: *inuenius* P.
[42] JG: *et*
[43] Kim 15.6.
[44] Tischendorf 15.6.
[45] JG, Titus: *reclusistis*
[46] JG: *diem*
[47] Titus: *meum et*
[48] JG: *deduxit* T; *et duxit* A; *et deduxit* P.
[49] Titus: *suum*
[50] JG: *est* P2, A, T; omittted P.

Arimathiam in domum meam et dixit michi. Pax tibi: usque ad quadragesimum diem non exeas de domo tua. ego autem uadam ad discipulos meos.[51] Et hiis dictis disparuit. Post hos[52] denique quadraginta dies. fidei feruore animatus sepedictus uidelicet Ioseph ab[53] Armiathia de[54] quo restat sermo beati Philippi apostoli discipulatui se contulit[55] atque eius salubri doctrina affluentuer refertus et ab ipso cum filio suo[56] Iosephe baptizatus est[57] Postea uero[58] a beato Iohanne apostolo ipso[59] predicationi Ephesorum insudante. beate perpetueque uirginis Marie paranymphus delegatus est eiusdem quoque[60] gloriose uirginis uenerande assumptioni[61] cum beato Philippo ceterisque discipulis interfuit atque ea que de Domino Ihesu Christo atque[62] eius gloriosa[63] genetrice Maria audierat et uiderat instanter per diuersas regiones predicans[64] ac[65] multos conuertens ac[66] baptizans: tandem .xv°. post eandem[67] gloriosam assumptionem anno cum memorato filio suo Iosephe[68] ad Sanctum Philippum in Gallias uenit.[69] Ac deinde secundum quod legitur in libro qui dicitur graal.[70] Ioseph ab Arimathia qui Dominum sepeliuit. baptizatus est[71] a beato Philippo apostolo uenit in maiorem Britanniam. sibi et semini eius promissam cum uxore. et filio Iosephe nomine. quem ipse saluator noster in ciuitate Saraz prius in epis-

---

[51] Tischendorf and Kim 15.6 end here. After this, the *Gospel of Nicodemus* is no longer a source.
[52] JG: *hec*; *denique quadraginta dies* omitted.
[53] JG: *sepedictus videlicet* omitted; *nobilis*; Titus: *de*; Ussher, p. 9 includes *Joseph . . . in episcopum consecravit*
[54] JG: *de quo restat sermo* omitted.
[55] JG: *tradidit*
[56] Titus: *suo* omitted; JG: *et* omitted.
[57] JG: *est* omitted T.
[58] Titus: *uero* omitted.
[59] JG: *dum ipse predicacioni Effesorum insudaret*
[60] JG: *quoque* omitted; Titus: *que*
[61] JG: *venerande* omitted.
[62] JG: *ac*
[63] JG: *gloriosa* omitted.
[64] JG: *predicauit*
[65] JG: *multosque*
[66] JG: *et*
[67] JG: *supradicte beate uirginis assumpcionem; eandem gloriosam* omitted.
[68] JG: *Iosephe, quem Dominus Ihesus prius in ciuitate Sarath in episcopum consecrauerat*
[69] JG diverges here. Before mentioning the Grail, John says that when the disciples dispersed, as Freculf Bk II, Ch. 4 says, Philip converted many in France. Then, wishing to spread the word of God even further, he sent twelve disciples to Britain, of whom his dearest friend Joseph was one. Joseph's baptism by Philip is not mentioned. The texts converge again at *Uenerunt autem cum eis*, line 45. The Grail version referred to seems to be the Vulgate *Estoire*. See Carley, p. 278.
[70] Titus: *graall*; gloss in lower margin in sixteenth-century hand K: *qui dicitur graall.*
[71] Titus: *est* omitted.

copum consecrauerat. Uenerunt autem cum eis.[72] sexcenti et amplius tam uiri quam femine. qui omnes uotum uouant[73] quod ab uxoribus propriis abstinerent. quousque terram[74] sibi promissam ingressi fuissent. **Quod tamen preuaricati sunt omnes preter centum quinquaginta.** qui iubente Domino mare super camisiam ipsius Iosephes transeuntes. in nocte resurrectionis Dominice: applicuerunt in mane.[75] Aliis autem penitentibus et Iosephe memorato pro eis orante: missa est nauis a Domino quam rex Salomon artificiose suo tempore fabricauerat usque ad Christi tempore duraturam. in qua die eadem ad suos socius peruenerunt. cum quodam duce Medorum nomine Natiano.[76] quem Ioseph prius baptizauerat in ciuitate Saraz cum rege ciuitatis[77] eiusdem nomine Mordrains. Cui Dominus postea in uisu apparens manus et pedes perforatus cum latere lanceato ostendit. Cui rex quasi[78] multum compatiens ita dixit. **O Domine Deus meus quis tibi[79] talia[80] inferre presumpsit?** Et Dominus: hec michi inquit fecit rex[81] Northwallie. qui seruum meum Ioseph[82] nomen meum in suis partibus predicantem. cum sociis suis carceri mancipauit. inhumanitus negans eius uictui necessaria **Tu ergo gladio tuo accinctus.** ad partes illas properare non differas: ut uindictam facias de tyranno et seruos meos soluas a uinculis. Rex autem euigilans et de uisione sibi ostensa exultans in Domino: disposita domo sua et regno iter cum exercito suo arripuit et Deo ducente ad locum perueniens regi prefato mandauit. quatinus seruos Dei liberos abire permitteret Ille uero mandato eius nullatenus adquiescens. ei cum indignatione mandauit. quatinus absque mora de terra sua exiret Quo audito rex Mordrians uenit contra eum cum suo exercitu et duce Natiano[83] superius memorato: qui ipsum in bello iusta ultione peremit Tunc rex Mordrains accedens ad carcerem[84] in quo rex ille iniquus Ioseph inclusum cum suis sociis detinebat: ipsum cum gaudio magno inde eduxit narrans ei uisionem sibi ostensam a Domino super liberatione[85] eorum. Tunc uniuersi gaudio magno repleti: immensas graciarum actiones Domino persoluebant[86] **Rex autem**

---

[72] JG: *eis – ut legitur in libro qui Sanctum Graal appellatur; cum eis* omitted T.
[73] JG: *uouerant*
[74] JG, p. 50: *terram*
[75] JG: *mare* T.
[76] Titus: *nationo*
[77] JG: *eiusdem ciuitatis cui nomen Mordrains*
[78] JG: *quasi multum* omitted A.
[79] Titus: *tibi* inserted by the scribe above the line after *talia*
[80] JG: *tale*
[81] JG: *perfidus rex*
[82] JG: *Joseph . . . meum* omitted A.
[83] Titus: *nationo*
[84] JG: *carcem* P.
[85] Titus: *liberationem*
[86] JG: ch. 18 ends here. Mordrains' gift of land is not in John of Glastonbury, or in William of Malmesbury which has no mention of Celidoine or his wife. Our compiler seems to

Mordrains dedit regnum Northwallie. Celidonio filio Natiani. data ei in uxorem filia Label regis Persarum quam idem Celidonis una cum patre eius
115 prius mirabiliter ad fidem Christianam converterat: quorum miri actus in libro predicto leguntur.

2. Hec[87] scriptura reperitur in gestis incliti Regis Arthuri.[88]

Ioseph ab Arimathia nobilem decurionem cum filio suo Iosephes dicto. et aliis pluribus in maiorem Britanniam que nunc Anglia dicta est uenisse et ibidem uitam finisse: testatur liber de[89] gestis incliti regis Arthuri, in
5 inquisitione scilicet cuiusdam illustris militis dicti Lancelotti[90] de Lac. facta per socios rotunde tabule. uidelicet ubi quidam heremita exponit Walwano misterium cuiusdam fontis: saporem et colorem crebro mutantis. ubi et scribebatur quod miraculum illud non terminaretur: donec ueniret magnus leo qui et collum magnis uinculis haberet constrictum. Item[91] in sequentibus
10 in inquisicione uasis quod ibi uocant[92] sanctum graal: idem refertur fere[93] in principio. ubi albus miles exponit Galaat filio Lanceloth[94] misterium cuiusdam mirabilis scuti quod eidem deferendum commisit quod nemo alius sine graui dispendio ne una quidam die poterat portare.[95]
[blank line]

3. Ista scriptura inuenitur in libro Melkini: qui fuit ante Merlinum.[96]

Insula Auallonis auida funere paganorum pre ceteris in orbe ad sepulturam eorum omnium sperulis prophecie uaticinantibus decorata et in futurum

---

have consulted his Grail volume separately. The sentence is in Titus A.xix, which is one indication that the tablets were the source of much of that manuscript's Glastonbury material.

[87] Wm, p. 46, from a thirteenth-century marginal addition in MS T to the end of ch. 1; JG ch. 20, line 10, p. 52. No heading in Wm; JG and Titus A.xix, fol. 19 have the heading.
[88] Carley, p. 279, n. 75, gives the source of this episode in the Vulgate *Lancelot*, 455, 464–8.
[89] JG: *de gestis* omitted P.
[90] Wm, JG: *Lanceloth*; Titus *lanceloth de Lake*
[91] Carley, p. 279, n. 75, gives the source of this episode in the *Queste*, 24–7, and the *Estoire*, 285.
[92] MS: *vocant*, with initial v.
[93] Titus: *fore*
[94] Wm, JG: *Lancelot*
[95] Marginal glosses in Titus, hand K, sixteenth-century: *misterius cuiusdam; albus miles*.
[96] JG, p. 54; not in Wm; in Ussher, p. 12. Barber, 1985, no. 6, groups this and the following short texts together. It survives separately in several other manuscripts cited by Carley: Cambridge, Trinity College R.5.33 (flyleaf in *De antiquitate*, fifteenth-century hand), British Library, Cotton Titus D.vii, fol. 29v old foliation, 32v modern foliation, as one of a series of prophecies on Britain, beginning with one by Becket; Cotton Cleopatra C.x, fol. 98; Arundel 220, fol. 274. It is also in Titus A.xix, fols. 19–19v, collated here. In Titus A.xix the verses are written successively, not in two columns. Trinity R.5.33 was collated; there were no variants. There is a variant version in Cotton Cleopatra C.iv, fols. 87v–88: *Nota quod Rex Arviragus paganus britonis post incarnacionem ihesu christi*

ornata erit altissimum laudantibus. Abbadare potens in Saphat paganorum nobilissimus. cum centum quatuor milibus dormitionem ibi accepit. Inter quos Ioseph de[97] marmore ab Aramathia nomine cepit sompnum perpetuum. Et iacet in linea bifurcata iuxta meridianum angulum oratorii cratibus preparatis super potentem adorandam uirginem supradictis sperulatis locum habitantibus tredecim.[98]

Habet enim secum Ioseph in sarcofago duo fassula alba et argentea cruore prophete Ihesu et sudore perimpleta. Cum reperietur eius sarcofagum integrum illibatum in futuris uidebitur et erit apertum toto orbi terrarum. Ex tunc nec aqua nec ros celi insulam nobilissimam habitantibus: poterit deficere. Per multum tempus ante diem iudicialem in[99] Iosaphat: erunt aperta hec. et uiuentibus declarata.[100]

4. Versus de sancto Ioseph de Aurora que et biblia uersi(fi)cata[101] dicitur.[102]

Cum sero fieret: Ioseph decurio diues
Ciuis de Ramatha: iustus honestus adest.
Clam seruus Christi:[103] fuit hic a preside corpus
Postulat ergo Ihesu: precipit ille dari
Prebet opem Nichodemus ei qui tempore noctis
Uenerat ad Ihesum: corde fatendo[104] fidem.
Hii mundum corpus: inuoluunt syndone munda.
Inque petra tumulant: qui petra nostra fuit.

---

concessit ioseph ab arimathia / insula aualonis qui britanice inswytryn uocatur. Mewynus qui ante merlinum fuit inter cetera gesta de tempore britonum in libro suo hec dicit. Ioseph ab Arimathia nobilis de curia [sic] in insula aualonie cum xi sociis suis sompnum cepit perpetuum. Et iacet in meridiano angulo linie bifurcata oratorii adorande uirginis habet enim secum duo vasculo alba et argenter cum cruore et sudore magni prophete ihesu perimpleta. Post multum tempus ante diem iudicii corpus eius integrum et illibatum reperietur et erit apertum toto orbi terrarum. Et tunc res nec pluuia deficiet habitantibus in insula nobilissima.

97 JG: *de* omitted A.
98 Titus: *tresdecim*
99 Titus: *in Josaphat* omitted.
100 JG: *Hucusque Melkinus.*
101 MS: *uersicata*; JG, Titus: *versificata*
102 In Titus the verses are written out successively, not in two columns. JG: *hic* omitted P. *Aurora*, ed. P. Beichner, II, lines 2807–8; 2813–16; 2819–20, pp. 531–2.
103 Beichner: *Christi seruus*
104 Beichner: *tenendo*

5. Item uersus reperti in quibusdam cronicis ubi agitur de rege Arvirago.[105]

Intrat Auallonam:[106] duodena caterua uirorum.
Flos Arimathia:[107] Ioseph est primus eorum.
Iosephes[108] ex Ioseph: genitus patrem comitatur.
Hiis aliisque decem ius Glastonie propriatur.

6. Hec scriptura testatur quod Rex Arthurus de stirpe Ioseph descendit.

Helains[109] nepos Ioseph genuit Iosue. Iosue genuit Aminadab. Aminadab geniut Castellors. Castellors genuit Manaal. (M)anael[110] genuit Lambord et Urlard. Lambord genuit filium qui genuit Ygernam. de[111] qua rex Uterpendragun genuit nobilem et famosum regem Arthurum. per[112] quod patet quod rex Arthurus de stirpe Ioseph descendit.

7. Item de eodem[113]

Petrus consanguineus Ioseph ab Arimathia rex Orcanie[114] genuit Erlan. Erlan genuit Melianum Melianus genuit .Arguth. Arguth genuit Edor. Edor genuit Loth qui duxit in uxorem sororem regis Arthuri. De qua genuit quatuor filios. scilicet. Walwanum. Agravayns.[115] Gwerehes. Gahieres.[116]

---

[105] JG, p. 50; Titus A.xix, immediately after the *Aurora* extract. This is one of the indications that the tablets were a direct source for Titus. Also in Ussher, p. 8. See Carley, p. 278, for their inclusion by William of Worcester, and several later antiquarians. They are also found in the margin of the John Stafford chronicle in Titus A.xix, fol. 107v, with no variants but with a heading: *Joseph de Arimathia dicit*, and two additional lines at the end: *Ad bretones iui post quam Christum sepeliui /Glastoniam ueni, bretones docui, requieri*. The last two are bracketed and marked '*Tunc duo*'.
[106] JG: *Avallioniam*
[107] JG: *Arimathie*
[108] JG: *Josephus; Josephes* P.
[109] This genealogy is in JG, ch. 21, p. 54, from which this section is taken, and repeated in ch. 32, p. 72.
[110] MS: *anael*. The large capital H for *Helains* is also in the margin of this line.
[111] JG, p. 54: *ex*
[112] JG: *per ... descendit* omitted in ch. 32, p. 72, but included in ch. 21, p. 54. It is in Titus.
[113] JG, ch. 21: no separate heading; Titus includes the phrase, though the scribe runs this together with the previous paragraph; Titus *Agrayuayns*.
[114] JG: *Organie*
[115] JG: *Agraueyns*
[116] JG: *et Geheries*; Titus: *Galieries*

Tablet 2

8. Incipit[117] **quomodo duodecim discipuli sanctorum Philippi et Iacobi apostolorum primo ecclesiam in Glastonia fundauerunt.**
[blank line]
Post dominice Resurrectionis gloriam. ascensionisque triumphum. ac spiritus paracliti de supernis missionem qui discipulorum corda temporalis pene adhuc formidine trepidentia repleuit scientiam omnium linguarum tribuendo: erant omnes credentes simul cum mulieribus et Maria matre Ihesu ut Lucas narrat euangelista et uerbum Dei disseminabatur crescebatque numerus credentium cotidie. eratque omnibus cor unum et anima una. Inuidie ergo facibus ascensi sacerdotes Iudeorum cum phariseis et scribis. concitauerunt persecutionem in ecclesia. interficiendo prothomartirem Stephanum. et fere a finibus suis omnes procul pellentes. Hac igitur persecutionis pro cella seuiente dispersi credentes. petierunt diuersa regna terrarum a Domino sibi delegata. uerbum salutis gentibus propinando. Sanctus autem Philippus ut testatur Freculfus libro secundo capitulo iiii^{or}[118] regionem Francorum adiens gracia predicandi: plures ad fidem conuertit ac baptizauit. Volens igitur uerbum Christi dilatari: duodecim ex suis discipulis[119] ad euangelizandum uerbum uite missit in Britanniam quibus ut ferunt karissimum amicum suum Ioseph ab Arimathia qui et Dominum sepeliuit prefecit. Venientes igitur in Britanniam anno ab incarnatione Domini .lxiii. ab assumptione beata Maria .xv°. fidem Christi fiducaliter predicabant. Rex autem barbarus cum sua gente tam noua audiens et[120] inconsueta: omnino predicationi eorum consentire renuebat. nec paternas traditiones commutare uolebat. Quia tamen de longe ueuerant uiteque eorum[121] exigebat modestia: quondam insulam siluis. rubis. atque paludibus circumdatam ab incolis Ynuswitrin[122] nuncupatam. in lateribus <sue> regionis ad habitandum concessit. Postea etiam alii duo reges licet pagani successiue[123] comperta eorum uite sanctimonia: unicuique eorum unam porcionem terre[124] concesserunt ac confirmauerunt. Unde et .xii. hide per eos adhuc et creditur nomen sorciuntur. Predicti itaque sancti in eodem

---

[117] William of Malmesbury (not interpolated) in Wm, pp. 42–6, with heading; Titus A.xix, fol. 19v, immediately after the preceding selection. Not in JG, but compare the end of ch. 18, p. 48, where Freculf is mentioned. Barber, no. 7. Wm: *Glastoniensis*
[118] Wm, Titus: *iiii*^{to} *(quarto)*
[119] Wm: *eligit* inserted above the line, T; *eligit et* M.
[120] Titus: *et inconsueta* omitted.
[121] MS: There is a change of ink from black to brown, but the same scribe continues.
[122] Wm: *ynsuuitrim*; Titus: *ynswsitrin*
[123] Wm: *successiue* omitted here; inserted before *unicuique*.
[124] Wm: *unam hidam* inserted above the line; text M, L.

deserto conuersantes: post pusillum temporis uisione archangeli Gabrielis admoniti sunt: ecclesiam in honore sancte Dei genitricis et uirginis Marie in loco celitus eis demonstrato construere. Qui diuinis preceptis non segniter obedientes secundum quod eis fuerat ostensum quadam capellam inferius
35 per circuitum uirgis torquatis muros perficientes consumauerunt. In anno post passionem Domini xxxi⁰ post assumptionem gloriose uirginis .xv⁰. ex deformi quidem scemate sed Dei multipliciter adornatam uirtute. Et cum hec in hac regione prima fuerit ampliori eam dignitate Dei filius insigniuit ipsam uidelicet in honore sue matris dedicando. Duodecim igitur sancti
40 sepius memorati in eodem loco Deo et beate uirgini deuota exhibentes obsequia: uigiliis ieiuniis et orationibus uacantes eiusdem uirginis auxilio ac uisione ut credi. pium est in omnibus necessitatibus refocillabantur. Hec autem ita se habere: tum ex carta beati Patricii tum ex scriptis seniorum cognoscimus. Quorum unus Britonum hystoriographus prout apud sanctum
45 Edmundum itemque apud sanctum Augustinum Anglorum apostolum uidimus: ita exorsus est. Est in confinio occidentalis Britannie quedam regalis insula antiquo uocabulo Glastonia nuncupata. latis locorum dimensa sinibus. piscosis aquis stagneisque circumdata fluminibus et plurimis humane indigentie apta usibus atque sacris quod maximum est dedicata
50 muneribus. In ea siquidem Anglorum primi catholice legis neophite antiquam[125] Deo dictante reppereriunt ecclesiam. nulla hominum arte ut ferunt constructam: Immo humane saluti a Deo paratam quam postmodum ipse celorum fabricator multis miraculorum gestis multisque uirtutum misteriis sibi sancteque Dei genitrici Marie se consecrasse demonstrauit. Sed de hiis
55 postea. nunc ad incepta redeamus. Sancti igitur memorati. in eadem heremo sic degentes: effluentibus multis annorum curriculis carnis ergastulo sunt educti. idemque locus cepit esse ferarum latibulum: qui prius fuerat habitatio sanctorum donec placuit beate uirgini suum oratorium redire ad memoriam fidelium.[126]

9. **Quomodo sanctus**[127] **Phaganus et Deruuianus Britannos ad fidem conuerterunt et in insulam Auallonie uenerunt.**[128]
Tradunt bone credulitatis annales quod Lucius rex Britannorum ad Eleutherium xiii⁰ loco post beatum Petrum <papam>[129] miserit oratum: ut

---

[125] Titus: *antequam*
[126] Wm: *fidelium. Quod quomodo euenerit iam prosequamur.* The passage about Lancelot and Gawain found on Tablet 1, lines 62–9, comes here in Wm's T, in the lower margin.
[127] Wm: *sancti*
[128] Wm: ch. 2, pp. 46–50, including heading; Scott considers only the last paragraph of the chapter, not on the tablets, to be authentic William of Malmesbury. JG, pp. 56–8.
[129] Wm: *papam* added interlineally in a thirteenth-century hand; in the text in M.

Britannie tenebras luce Christiane predicationis illustraret.[130] Uenerunt ergo Eleutherio mittente predicatores Britanniam duo uiri sanctissimi Phaganus uidelicet atque Deruuianus. prout Carta Sancti Patricii gestaque Britonnorum testantur. Hii igitur uerbum uite ewangelizantes: Regem cum suo populo sacro fonte abluerunt Anno domini .C.lxvi. Hinc predicando et baptizando Britannie partes peragrantes; in insulam Auallonie more Moysi legislatoris interiora deserti penetrantes sunt ingressi. Vbi antiquam Deo dictante[131] repperunt[132] ecclesiam manibus discipulorum Christi constructam:[133] et humane saluti a Deo paratam quam postmodum ipse celorum fabricator multis miraculorum gestis multisque uirtutum misteriis: sibi sancteque Dei genetrici Marie se consecrase demonstrauit.[134] Fluxerunt autem ab aduentu discipulorum Sancti Philippi in Britanniam usque aduentum sanctorum memoratorum .C. iii. anni. Igitur predicti sanctus[135] Phaganus et Deruuianus oratorio illo sic reperto: ineffabili sunt referti gaudio ibidem in Dei laudibus moram protrahentes diuturnam per nouem uidelicet annos: Locum etiam diligenter perscrutantes: figuram nostre redemptionis alia\s/que figura\s/[136] manifesta\s/[137] reppererunt quibus bene cognouerunt quod Christiani prius locum inhabitauerant. postea celesti perpendentes[138] oraculo quod Dominus ipsum locum pre ceteris Britannie specialiter elegerit: ad nomen gloriose[139] genetricis sue ibidem inuocandum.[140] Omnem etiam narrationem in antiquis scriptis inuenerunt. qualiter sanctis apostolis per uniuersum orbem dispersis: Sanctus Philippus apostolus cum multitudine discipulorum, in Franciam ueniens. duodecim ex ipsis in Britanniam misit ad predicandum. Qui predictam capellam angelica docti reuelatione construxerunt. quam postmodum filius altissimi in honorem sue matris dedicauit. Ipsisque .xii. tres reges licet pagani .xii. porciones terre dederunt ad eorum sustentationem. Insuper gesta eorum scripta inuenerunt.

---

[130] Wm, John of Glastonbury: ten lines of text comparing Lucius to Æthelbert, king of Kent, inserted before *Venerunt.*

[131] JG: *duce*

[132] MS: *ctante repperunt* written over erasure, in the hand of the scribe; Wm, JG: *reppererunt*

[133] TCC 724 (Wm's T) has a note in the margin, in a thirteenth-century hand, but not that of the scribe: *ut ferunt.* This note of scepticism could well have been deliberately omitted by the compiler of the tablets, had he seen it. It occurs in the text in Wm's M. Ussher, p. 8, using a text of John as well as the tablets, reads *et ferunt.*

[134] Wm: L, M: *Et hoc factum est tempore predicti regis Lucii qui primus Britannie regis catholice fidei et sancti baptismatis sacramenta simul cum sua gente suscepit anno Dominice incarnacionis CLXVI*to.

[135] Wm, JG: *sancti*

[136] Wm, JG: *aliaque signa manifesta*

[137] MS: The 's's are added in black ink, I think by a different scribe.

[138] JG: *per prudentes* A.

[139] JG: *gloriose Dei; Dei* omitted P.

[140] Wm: M and L insert: *et auxilium de eadem uirgine pre cunctis necesssitatibus impetrandum.*

ideoque locum ipsum pre ceteris dilexerunt. Qui etiam in memoriam primorum .xii. ex suis sociis .xii. elegerunt. et in prefata insula Rege Lucio consentiente habitare fecerunt. Qui postea in diuersis locis sicut anachorite
35 manserunt ibidem. in eisdem uidelicet locis: in quibus primi duodecim primitus[141] habitauerant. In uetustam tamen ecclesiam ad diuina obsequia deuocius complenda crebro conuenerunt.[142] Et sicut tres reges pagani dictam insulam[143] cum adiacentiis suis .xii. primis Christi discipulis dudum concesserant: ita predicti Phaganus et Deruuianus. istis duodecim sociis et
40 aliis in posterum secuturis. ab eodem rege Lucio eandem confirmari impetrabant. Sic autem multi aliis succedentes. semper tamen in numero duodenario per multa annorum curricula usque ad aduentum Sancti Patricii Hyberniensium apostoli in memorata insula permanserunt. huic etiam ecclesie sic reperte aliud addiderunt sancti neophite opere lapides oratoris.
45 quod Christo sanctisque apostolis Petro et Paulo dedicauerunt.[144]

10. De Sancto Patricio[145]

Anno dominice incarnationis. cccc.xxv. Sanctus Patricius ordinatus a Celestino <papa> in Hyberniam missus est. Item anno incarnacionis .cccc.xxxiii. Hybernia insula conuertitur ad fidem Christi predicante Sancto
5 Patricio cum multis: mirabilibus. Ille igitur munus sibi inuictum grauiter exsecutus et in extremis diebus suis in patriam suam reuertens. silicet[146] Britanniam. metropolitani pallii celsitudinem[147] spernens. Et salutationes[148] in foro respuens. super altare suum Cornubiam appulit. Quod usque hodie apud incolas magne uenerationi est.[149] propter sanctitudinem et utilitatem.
10 et[150] propter infirmorum salutem. Et[151] inde Glastoniam ueniens:[152] ibique

---

141 JG, p. 58: *prinitus* P.
142 Wm: *cotidie* interlinear gloss T, text L, M.
143 JG: *insuluam* T.
144 Wm, JG: *oratorium*. After *dedicauerunt* Wm has eight lines citing documents at Bury St Edmunds stating that the church at Glastonbury was built by disciples sent by Philip, and reiterating that according to Freculf, Philip had preached to the Gauls. Chapter 3, which follows, is the conversation between the monk of St Denis and the monk of Glastonbury found below text no. 35 and in JG, p. 9. JG has eight different lines about the oratory in honour of St Michael built on Glastonbury Tor by Phaganus and Deruvianus, and its thirty years of indulgence.
145 Wm, ch. 8, p. 54, but the text is different at the beginning. JG, p. 58, is about Patrick's youth. The date 425 for Patrick's going into Ireland, and 433 for his going to Glastonbury, are on p. 60, but the phrasing here is much closer to Wm, so I have not collated JG. Wm: *Carta Sancti Patricii episcopi*.
146 MS: written out in full; a common medieval spelling.
147 Here the text begins to agree closely with Wm, ch. 8, line 8, p. 54.
148 Wm: *salutationesque*
149 Wm: *est tum*
150 Wm: *tum*
151 Wm: *Et* omitted.
152 Here the texts diverge again; Wm says Patrick gathered together the twelve hermits,

monachus et primus abbas loci illius factus ut scriptum est. Hic primus: fratres illic in diuersis locis sicut anachorite habitantes pariter congregauit. Et eos monastice uiuere instruxit sicut sequens scriptum quod in[153] tempore suo scribere[154] fecit: manifestius declarabit.

11. Carta Sancti Patricii[155]

[blank line]

In nomine Domini nostri Ihesu Christi. Ego Patricius humilis seruunculus Dei. Anno incarnationis eiusdem. cccc.xxv.[156] in Hiberniam a sanctissimo
5 papa Celestino[157] legatus Dei gracia Ybernicos ad uiam ueritatis conuerti. Et cum eos in fide catholica solidassem: Tandem in Britanniam sum reuersus. Ac ut credo duce Deo qui uita est et uia incidi in insulam Ynsgutrim[158] in qua inueni locum sanctum[159] ac uetustum. a Deo electum et sanctificatum in honore intemerate uirginis Dei genitricis Marie. ibique[160]
10 quosdam fratres rudimentis catholice fidei inbutos et pie conuersationis. qui successerunt discipulis sanctorum Phagani et Deruuiani, quorum nomina pro uite meritis ueraciter credo scripta in celis. Et quia in memoria eterna erunt iusti, cum eosdem fratres tenere dilexissem: eorum nomina scripto meo redigere decreui.[161] Que sunt. Brumbun.[162] Hyrcgaan. Brenwal. Wen-
15 creth. Bamtonmeweng. Adelwlred. Lowor.[163] Wellias. Breden. Swelwes.

---

taught them the cenobitic life, and became their abbot. The texts converge again at 10.13, *sicut*.
[153] Wm: *idem*
[154] Wm: *scribere fecit* omitted; *conscripsit*
[155] Wm, ch. 9, pp. 54–60, heading: *Carta Sancti Patricii episcopi*. JG, pp. 60–4, heading as here.
[156] Wm: *CCCCXXX*, but corrected from a probable earlier *CCCCXXV*; see p. 54, note k. Wm: There is a thirteenth-century marginal gloss, T: *et eodem anno uel precedente misit idem papa ad predicandum ibidem uirum nomine Palladium, Britannicum genere. Sed idem cito repatriauit sine ullo effectu.*
[157] MS: *papa celestino* written in a sixteenth-century hand over an erasure.
[158] Wm: *Ynsgytrin*; JG: *Ynswitryn*
[159] JG: *sanctum* omitted A.
[160] JG: *ibique repperi*
[161] Wm, JG: *uolui*
[162] Wm: *Brumbam, Hyregaan*; the others agree with the tablets. In Wm's MS T, the final mimim of *Brumbam* has been expuncted, giving *Brumban*, as here. *Lothor* is spelled with -th. JG: *Brumban, Hiregaan, Bremwal, Wencreth, Banttomeweng, Adelwolderd, Loyor, Wellias, Breden, Swelwes, Hinloernus et alius Hyn*. Cotton Cleopatra C.iv, fol. 79v, has a list of *Nomina sanctorum inuenitur apud Glastynob'. Joseph Josephes filius suus episcopus. Bruban. Hyregaan. Brenwolde. Bantommeweng. Athelfred. Lethor. Wellies. Breden. Welewes. hynloernius et alius hyn. phaganus episcopus deruuanus episcopus.*
[163] MS: The medial letter in this name is either a thorn or a wynn, copied in a more pointed shape than the scribe's p, or y; in any case, y is usually dotted. Wynns occur also in *Esterwine*.

Hinloernius, et alius Hin. Hii cum essent nobilibus. orti natalibus: nobilitatem suam fidei operibus ornare cupientes. heremiticam uitam ducere elegerunt. Et quoniam inueni eos humiles ac quietos. elegi potius cum illis abiectus esse. magis quam in regalibus curiis habitare. sed quia omnium nostrum erat cor unum. et anima una. elegimus simul omnes habitare. Comedere et bibere pariter: et in eadem domo dormire. Sicque me licet inuitum sibi pretulerunt. Non enim dignus eram soluere corigias calciamentorum eorum.[164] Et cum uitam monasticam ita duceremus: iuxta normam probabilium patrum: ostenderunt michi prefati fratres scripta sanctorum Phagani et Deruuiani, in quibus continebatur quod .xii. discipuli sanctorum Philippi et Iacobi ipsam uetustam ecclesiam construxerunt[165] in honore prelibate aduocatricis nostre per doctrinamentum beati archangeli Gabrielis. insuper: et quod Dominus eandem ecclesiam celitus in honore sue matris dedicauerat. Et quod tres reges pagani. ipsis .xii. ad eorum sustenementum: duodecom portiones terre dederunt. Necnon et in scriptis recentioribus inueni quod Sancti Phaganus et Deruuianus perquisierant ab Elutherio papa qui eos miserat: .x. annos indulgentie.[166] Et ego frater Patricius a pie memore Celestino papa .xii. annos tempore meo adquisiui.[167] Post multum uero temporis assumpto mecum Wellia confratre meo per condensitatem silue cum magna difficultate concendimus cacumen montis qui eminet in eadem insula. quo cum peruenissemus: apparuit oratorium unum[168] vetustum. et fere dirrutum,[169] Habile tamen deuotioni Christiane. Et prout michi uidebatur a Deo electum. Quod cum ingressi essemus: tanta odoris suauiate replebamur: ut[170] in paradisi amenitate positos nos crederemus.[171] Egredientes igitur et in regredientes.[172] locumque diligentius perscrutantes: inuenimus uolumen unum in quo scripti erant[173] Actus apostolorum. pariter cum actibus.[174] et gestis Sanctorum Phagani et Deruuiani. ex magna parte consumptum. in cuius tamen fine uoluminis: inuenimus scripturam que[175] dicebat quod predicti Sancti[176] Phaganus et

---

[164] John 1: 27 *Ipse est qui post me venturus est, qui ante me factus est, cujus ego non sum dignus ut solvam ejus corrigiam calceamenti.* John the Baptist's words about Christ are the source for Patrick's assertion here.

[165] JG *construxerunt . . ecclesiam* omitted A, probably by eyeskip.

[166] JG: *triginta annos indulgentie*; no variants recorded. Ten years' indulgence agrees with the list on Tablet 6 (see note below); Wm has *decem*, written out in full.

[167] These are the first two indulgences listed on Tablet 6, text 41.

[168] JG: *unum oratorium*

[169] Wm: *dirrutum* P.

[170] Wm: *uti*

[171] Wm: *credrermus* T.

[172] Wm, JG: *et reingredientes*

[173] Wm: *Actus erant*, but *actus* is added above the line.

[174] Wm, JG: *actis*

[175] JG: *que; qui* A, T.

[176] JG: *Sancti* omitted.

45 Deruuianus per reuelationem Domini nostri Ihesu Christi idem oratorium edificauerant in honore Sancti Michaelis archangeli quatinus ibi ab hominibus haberet honorem: qui homines in perpetuos honores iubente Deo est introducturus. At[177] cum delectaret nos ille scriptura: nitebamur eam ad finem legere. Dicebat etenim eadem scriptura quod uenerandi Phaganus et
50 Deruuianus. moram ibi fecerunt per nouem annos. Et quod ibi etiam perquisierant triginta annorum indulgentiam: omnibus Christicolis ipsum locum[178] ab honorem beati Michaelis pia[179] uoluntate uisitantibus. Inuento igitur[180] tanto diuine bonitatis thesauro: ego et frater Wellias tribus men-

Tablet 3

<sibus ieiunauimus, oraci>onibus[181] uacantes et uigiliis: demonibusque
55 et[182] beluis multiformiter apparentibus imperantes. Quadam autem <nocte cum me sopori ded>isssem: apparuit michi Dominus Ihesus in uisu dicens Patrici serue meus. scias me elegisse locum istum <ad> honorem nomin<is> mei. et ut hic honoranter: inuocent aduitorium archangeli mei Michaelis. Et hoc tibi signum et fratribus tuis quatinus et ipsi credant.
60 Brachium tuum sinistrum arescet donec que uidisti annuntiaueris fratribus qui in cella sunt inferiori: et denuo huc redieris. Et factum est ita. Ab illo die statuimus duos fratres in perpetuum ibi nisi pastores futuri ob iustam causam aliter decreuerunt. Arnulphuo autem et Agmar[183] Hibernicis fratribus qui mecum uenerant de Hibernia. pro eo quod ad exhortationem meam
65 apud dictum humiliter oratorium manere ceperunt: presentem paginam commisi. aliam similem in archa sancte Marie retinens in monumentum posteris. Et ego Patricius[184] per consilium fratrum meorum omnibus qui siluam ex omni parte prefati montis in securi et ascia pie intentione deiecerunt. ut facilior paretur aditus Christianis. ecclesiam beate per-
70 petueque uirginis pie uisitaturis et oratorium predictum: centum dies uenie concedo.[185]

Hec autem ita ueraciter se habere: testimonio scripture uetustissime. simul cum relationibus. seniorum comprobauimus. Hic itaque sanctus

---

[177] JG: *Et*, but T reads *Ac*, and PV read *At*
[178] Wm, JG: *locum ipsum*
[179] Wm: *propria*. This indulgence is not included in the list on Tablet 6.
[180] Wm, JG: *ergo*; no variants.
[181] MS: illegible; readings here and in the next two lines supplied from Wm and JG.
[182] JG: *et* omitted.
[183] Wm, JG: *Ogmar*
[184] JG: *frater Patricius*
[185] This indulgence is listed on Tablet 6.5. Here ch. 25 of JG ends. The following sentence is not in John, but is in Wm.

supramemoratus qui est Hiberniensium[186] apostolus et in insula Auallonie
75 abbas primus. postquam predictos fratres regularibus disciplinis conuenienter informauerat. et eundem locum terris et possessionibus de dono regum ac aliorum principum competenter ditauerat: post aliquot annos[187] decursos nature cessit. et sepulturam angelo demonstrante flammaque ingenti de eodem loco cunctis uidentibus qui aderant erumpente: in uetusta ecclesia
80 ad[188] dexteram altaris promeruit. Excessit[189] ergo Patricius anno etatis suo .c.xi. incarnationis uero Domini .cccc.lxxii. qui[190] fuit annus ex quo in Hyberniam missus est .xlvii⁰. Siquidem anno Domini .ccc.lxi. in lucem uenit. Et anno Domini .cccc.xxv⁰. a Celestino <papa> in Hiberniam missus fuit. hic fuit anno etatis sue .lxiiii. et anno Domini .cccc.xxxxiii. Hibernicos
85 ad fidem Christi conuertit. Demum Britanniam reuersus: in optima conuersacione per .xxxix. annos in insula Auallonie[191] permansit. Requiuit autem in uetusta ecclesia a dextro latere altaris per multorum[192] annorum curricula .uidelicet. DCC. et .x. annos: usque ad conbustionem euiusdam ecclesie. Corpus uero suum in piramide saxea fuit collocatum iuxta altare uersus
90 austrum. quam pro ueneratione eiusdem sancti: auro[193] et argenteo postea nobiliter uestiunt domesti<co>rum <dili>gentia.[194]

12. De Sancto Benigno[195]

Anno domini .cccc.[196] lx. sanctus[197] Benignus <ue>nit[198] Glastoniam. Hic discipulus sancti[199] Patricii et successor in episcopatu eius tercius in[200] Hibernia fuit quemadmodum <eorum> gesta testantur. Hic igitur angelo
5 monente patriam pontificique dignitatem ex[201] uoto deserens. uoluntaria[202] peregrinatione suscepta <Glas>toniam Deo duce peruenit. ubi[203] et sanctum

---

[186] JG 26, p. 64, middle of the second sentence.
[187] JG: *post annos triginta nouem ab aduentu suo in insulam Auallonie decursos*
[188] Wm: *a dextra*; JG *a dextris*
[189] JG: *excessit autem hic Deo dignus anno*ᵐᵐ, *etatis*
[190] JG: *ab anno quo*
[191] JG: *Auallonis*; but compare *insulam Auallonie* ch. 2, p. 10; omitted P.
[192] JG: *multorum annorum curricula uidelicet* omitted.
[193] JG: *postea auro et argenteo*
[194] None of the material about a vision of St Patrick (ch. 27), or about the three Patricks which begins in ch. 28 of JG, is included here. Benignus comes in ch. 29, but is preceded in ch. 28 by Brigid and Columkilla.
[195] Wm, p. 62; Titus A.xix, fol. 21v, right after the account of St Patrick.
[196] Titus: *.cccc.* omitted; the scribe wrote *Sanctus Benignus* and then crossed it out.
[197] Titus: *beatus*
[198] Titus: *uenit Glastoniam. Hic* omitted.
[199] Titus: *istius sancti*
[200] Titus: *in . . . igitur* omitted.
[201] Titus: *ex uoto* omitted.
[202] Titus: *uoluntaria . . . Glastoniam* omitted; *ad hunc locum*
[203] Titus: *ubi . . . largissima et* omitted.

Patricium inuenit. Quante autem apud Deum gracie fuit multis patet uirtutum indiciis. Hoc etiam testantur eius insignia apud Ferningemere:[204] data eis precibus aqua largissima. et ex[205] eius baculo arido ingens arbor uirens et frondifera. Hic itaque post[206] immensos agones in dicta insula beato fine quieuit ac post multorum curricula annorum .i. anno Domini M°. lxxxxi°. tempore[207] Willelmi regis Rufi. Glastonia[208] honorifice translatus est.

13. De Sancta Brigida

Anno Domini incarnationis .cccc.lxxxviii. beata Brigida uenit Glastoniam. Hec autem[209] in quadam insula iuxta Glastoniam. que[210] parua Hibernia dicebatur, nunc uero pro ipsa ibi aliquantulo tempore pertendinante Brideye nominatur. relictis ibidem quibusdam insignibus suis. Uidelicet pera. monili. nola. et textrilibus armis que pro eius sanctitatis. memoria ibi ostenduntur. et adorantur. Sed utrum ibi obi<er>it uel in patriam redierit: in dubium nobis est. Indractum[211] uero sociosque suos in finibus istis martirio coronatos: et per regem Ynam ad monasterium Glastonie translatus fuisse:

---

[204] Wm: *Fernigemere*

[205] Titus: *Cuius meritis ingens arbor ex eius baculo creuit uirens atque frondifera, necnon apud Mere aqua manat largissima.*

[206] JG, ch. 30, line 15, p. 70: *post . . . quieuit*

[207] Wm: *tempore . . . Rufi* omitted; the phrase is in the concluding sentence of JG, ch. 30, p. 70.

[208] Wm, JG: *Glastoniam*

[209] JG: *Hec uero Sancta Brigida*. The date of her arrival is given in a longer sentence earlier in chapter 28, p. 66 establishing her chronological relationship to the three Patricks and Columkilla.

[210] Wm, p. 60, contains the information that Bridget came in 488, and returned to her home, leaving relics behind. The list of relics is identical. The long interpolation about the two Patricks, Brigid and Columkilla is in Scott's notes, pp. 189–91. JG: *ubi erat oratorium in honore Sancte Marie Magdalene consecratum, Bekery siue Parua Hibernia dicta, aliquantulum moram per nonnullos annos traxit et relictis.* The rest of the sentence, until *adorantur*, is the same, but John goes on to assert that she returned to Ireland, and died there, and is buried in Down. He says the chapel at Beckery is dedicated to her. Titus A.xix, fol. 21v: *Beata brigida etiam de hibernia huc venit, sicut et sanctus columkilla, sed de eorum obitu vel sepultura certum non habeatur in hoc loco.*

[211] Wm, p. 60, mentions Indract and his companions, martyred and buried at Glastonbury, but the language is not the same. Indract's burial on the right side of the altar, with his companions, and their translation by King Ine, and the pyramid at the left of the altar, are in Wm, p. 68. The burial and translation are mentioned by JG, pp. 16–18, but the pyramid is not mentioned. The full story of Indract is told by John of Glastonbury in ch. L and LI, pp. 100–4; the placement of the saint on the left of the altar, and his companions beneath the pavement, is on pp. 102–4, but the pyramid is not mentioned. See also the brief summary of Indract's martyrdom in Wm's MS L: *in libris de gestis eorum apud Glastoniam plenius habetur* (fol. 8r; Wm, p. 62). Two pyramids were excavated in 1962–63, and Radford tentatively suggested they commemorated Patrick and Indract (Carley, p. 277).

10 certissimum est corpus quidem sancti.[212] martiris Indracti in[213] piramide lapidea ad sinistram altaris in uetusta eccclesia. ceterorum in pauimento prout ut uel casus tulit. uel industria locauit.

14. De sanctis Kolumkilla et Gilda[214]

Anno ab[215] incarnatione Domini .D.iiii. Kolumkilla uenit Glastoniam.[216] quidam autem[217] a<ffir>mauit[218] hunc sanctum cursum presento uite siue ibidem consumasse sed utrum ibi[219] requiescit uel inde repatriauit[220] pro[221]
5 certo non habemus. Et[222] sicut a maioribus accepimus Sanctus Gildas n<eque in>sulsas neque infascetus historiographus[223] strenuisimi[224] regis Arthuri capellan(us).[225] cui Britanni debent si quid noticie inter ceteras gentes habent: ibidem miro[226] affectu et diuturna perendinatione inheritauit. loci sanctitudinie captus. ibique anno Dominice[227] incarnationis .D. et[228]
10 .xii. de medio factus. in uetusta ecclesia ante altare est sepultus.[229]

---

[212] Titus A.xix, fol. 21v, after St Bridget and Columkilla: *Indractum martitis socios que eius quo translatos fuisse certissimum est.*
[213] The rest of this sentence appears word for word in Wm, ch. 20, p. 68.
[214] 14.1–4 from Wm, ch. 14, p. 62, *De sancto Columkilla*, with numerous variants.
[215] Wm: *ab incarnatione* omitted.
[216] Columkilla's presence at Glastonbury is mentioned in the introduction (p. 3), and dated AD 504 in JG, p. 67, but there are no close parallels to this paragraph. Carley (n. 6, p. 271) says that according to Giraldus Cambrensis, *Topographia Hiberniae*, a book which was in the library at Glastonbury, Columkilla was buried with Brigid and Patrick the Elder at Down; the information was included in the widely read *Polychronicon* of Ranulph Higden, and is in JG, p. 67. The implication is that the compiler of the tablets consulted neither of the earlier works for this paragraph, and was here using a tradition other than John.
[217] Wm: *autem* omitted.
[218] Wm: *affirmant hunc sanctum uite sue cursum*
[219] Wm: *ibi requiescit* omitted; *sic*
[220] Wm: *repatriauerit*
[221] Wm: *pro certo non habemus* omitted; *non diffinio*
[222] Based on Wm, ch. 7, p. 54; Wm: *Nam*
[223] Wm: *historicus*
[224] Wm: *strenuissimi . . . capellanus* omitted.
[225] MS: *capellan*, with no mark of abbreviation visible.
[226] Wm: *mori . . . inheritauit* omitted; *multum annorum ibi exegit*
[227] Wm: *Domini; incarnationis* omitted.
[228] Wm: *et* omitted.
[229] In JG, p. 17, Gildas is buried near St Patrick.

15. De Sancto Dauid[230]

Anno Domini. D. lxv. Sanctus Dauid archiepiscopus Meneuencis[231] cum septem episcopis[232] suffraganeis suis Glastoniam uenit ad ecclesiam beate[233] uirginis dedicandam. Iamque paratis omnibus ad rem pertinentibus nocte in cuius crastino dedicatio fecerat apparuit ei[234] Dominus[235] dicens. Ecclesiam hanc non[236] dedices quia ego in matris mee honore et cimiterium in sepulturam seruorum meorum dedicam. Apprehensaque presulis dextera uolam manus digito perforauit et ait. Hoc[237] tibi signum eius quod dixi. Manus tua sic perforata manebit donec dixeris cras in missa. Per ipsum et cum ipso et in ipso. et illico[238] sanus eris. Surgit presul rem[239] narrat prodit signum. Videntes exhorrent[240] contrectant mirantur. Archiepiscopus[241] missam cantat plaga disparet dedicationis sententia reuocatur ne iterum homo faceret quod antefecerat Deus. Sed[242] ne tantus labor omnibus incassum uerteretur et ibi sanctis presul nichil egisse uideretur aliam ecclesiam in orientali parte eidem ecclesie contiguam fecit et dedicauit que seinte Marie se <parte *erased*> nominabatur. Ob[243] memoriam autem huius sancti miraculi dedit[244] quendam saphirum mire magnitudinis quem a patriarcha

---

[230] Wm, ch. 15, pp. 62–4, JG, p. 86, and Titus A.xix, fols. 20–20v, and 21v recount the same story; John's version has more explanatory detail, but the first two versions are roughly similar. Titus, fol. 20–20v, includes more information about David's church and its position. The wording of these first three versions is not close enough to make complete collation worthwhile, but on fol. 21v, in the account of those buried at Glastonbury, Titus has a version very close to this, and it is collated below.
[231] Titus: *Meneuencis . . . suis Glastoniam* omitted; *ad hanc eccleisam dedicandam*
[232] JG: *quorum ipse primus erat; suffraganeis* omitted.
[233] Titus: *beate uirginis* omitted.
[234] Titus: *illi*
[235] Titus: *Dominus Ihesus Christus*
[236] Titus: *ne*
[237] Titus: *Hoc . . . dixi* omitted.
[238] Titus: *tunc*. David would say the mass until the end of the consecration of the bread and wine, just before the Lord's prayer.
[239] Titus: *rem narrat* omitted.
[240] Titus: *exhorrent contrectant* omitted.
[241] Titus: *presul*
[242] JG: *Sed . . . aliam* is the same, but David's church is placed *ibidem*, not on the east side. But on p. 94, David's church is *in orientali parte uetuste ecclesie in honore beate Marie, ut pretactum est, quando ueterem ecclesiam dedicare disposuit et uacabitur ad Sanctam Mariam minorem*. Titus: *Sed . . . nominabatur* omitted. In Wm, p. 64, after David *aliam ecclesiam citato fecit et dedicauit opere*, there is an addition in Wm's L: *quam a domesticis seint Marie la petite nominabatur. Locus reuera terribilis ac metuendus est quem Deus sanctificauit et tabernaculum suum fecit*. The tablet texts show no knowledge of any other information added in L.
[243] Titus: *Et ob*
[244] Titus: *idem presul dedit huius ecclesie quendam*

Iherosolimitano per ministerium angelicum miraculose acceperat quem idem patriarcha de paradiso allatum ab angelo tulerat.[245]

16. De reliquis Sancti David.[246]

Quedam matrona nomine Alswyza[247] tempore[248] Edgari regis reliquias[249] eiusdem sancti per[250] quendam cognatum suum adquisiuit. qui tunc temporis fuit episcopus apud Rosinam Uallem quando tota terra illa ita[251] uastata
5 erat ut uix aliquis homo ibi[252] inueni<retur> nisi pauci femine et[253] etiam in raris locis et[254] eas Glastonie contulit.

17. De reliquis a Guelia Glastonie translatis.[255]

Testes sunt <Wale>nses religiosi terre illius. quod[256] ea tempestate plurima corpora sanctorum et reliquias Romam ituri secum Glastoniam detu<lerunt>. et ituriando[257] proficiscentes dimiserunt[258] ibidem Facta est[259]
5 hec translatio anno post mortem eiusdem[260] .CCCC.xx. incarnatio<nis>[261] Domince nonagentesimo .LXII.[262]

---

[245] Titus, fol. 21v, finishes here. The passage is marked by a line in the right margin, and *Nota* and *quendam saphirum* in the sixteenth-century Hand K. Wm tells of David's adventures in the Holy Land, and the presents, which included an altar *quod dicitur uulgo saphirus* in ch. 30, pp. 80–2. For the source in Rhygyfarch's *Life of David*, see Scott, p. 195, n. 64. JG does not mention the sapphire in ch. 39, p. 86, or in the discussion of Ine's church in ch. 47, but in ch. 89, p. 166, it is discovered by Abbot Henry of Blois: *Preciosum eciam saphirum a Sancto Dauid Meneuensi archiepiscopo Glastonie collatum metu guerre multo tempore absconditum, omnibus loci nesciis in quodam hostio ecclesie beate Marie repperit.* Its miraculous origin is not mentioned by either William or John. The gift of the sapphire is in Titus A.xix, fol. 20v, though not its source, which is only in the account on fol. 21v.

[246] Wm, ch. 16, line 7, p. 64; JG, p. 130; Titus A.xix, fol. 23r. JG: *quedam enim nobilis matron nomine Elfswitha*, MS C.

[247] Wm: *Aelswiza*

[248] Wm, JG: *tempore Edgari regis* omitted; *predictas reliquias adquisiuit*

[249] Wm: *predictas reliquias; eiusdem sancti* omitted.

[250] Wm: *adquisiuit per quemdam cognatum suum*

[251] JG: *ita* omitted.

[252] Wm, JG: *illic*

[253] JG: *et etiam* omitted.

[254] JG: *ut*

[255] Wm, pp. 64–6, with heading. JG: This heading is not in John, where the Welsh relics follow immediately in ch. 69, p. 130: *Nam Wallenses*. Not in Titus.

[256] Wm: *qui*; JG: *quod* omitted.

[257] JG: *ituriando proficiscentes* omitted.

[258] JG: *ibidem dimiserunt*

[259] JG: *est autem*, but T omits *autem*.

[260] JG: *eiusdem Sancti Dauid*

[261] JG: *incarnationis uero*

[262] In JG, Elswitha also gave Glastonbury relics of St Stephen (p. 130).

18. De Sancto Paulino.

Anno[263] Domini .Dc.xxv. Sanctus Paulinus. Northamhumbrorum archiepiscopus[264] Glastoniam ad perandinandum uenit. hic muros uetuste ecclesie ligneo tabulatu construere[265] fecit et extra a summo usque deorsum in terram. plumbo undique cooperire[266] fecit. Et sic illud sanctum oratorium in eadem factura usque ad combustionem eiusdem ecclesie perdurauit.

19. De Sancto Ticca[267]

Anno Dominice[268] incarnationis .Dcc.liiij. infestantibus Danis Northamhumbriam:[269] Sanctus[270] Ticca earum partium uenerabilis[271] abbas. sub obtentu pacis a borea in occidentem commigrans. cum[272] suis monachis Glastonaim[273] usque[274] peruenit. eandemque[275] ecclesiam sub[276] nomine abbatis plurimos annos rexit. Multis enim annis aquilonalis regio piratarum patuit prede: cum interim alie partes Anglie nichil suspirarent[277] hostile. attulit sane[278] secum locupletes incolatus sui obsides: reliquias scilicet[279] Sancti[280] Aidani Lindisfanensis[281] episcopi[282] corpora sanctorum Ceolfridi.

---

[263] JG: ch. 41, p. 88, sentence 2, but John omits the Danes: *Sanctus Paulinus Rofffensis presul, antea archiepiscopus Eboracensis, tercius a Iusto quem consecrauit Sanctus Augustinus, uenit Glastoniam ubi non modicum tempus perhendinans muros.* The rest is as given here. The passage is repeated on Tablet 4, text 46.45–50.

[264] In Wm, p. 66, he is archbishop of Rochester. The text is not verbally close.

[265] JG: *construi*

[266] JG: *cooperiri; fecit* omitted.

[267] Wm, p. 68: *De reliquiis a terra Northambibororum usque Glastoniam translatis. Item multo post tempore infestantibus.* JG, ch. 54, p. 104; no heading. The text is closer to Wm until the ending, where the epitaph must come from another source.

[268] JG: *Hoc tempore circiter annum Domini*

[269] Wm: *Northanimbriam*; JG: *Northanhumbriam*

[270] Wm, JG: *Sanctus* omitted. Here Titus A.xix, fol. 21v, has a condensed version of this section, beginning: *Sanctus Ticta venerabilis abbas cum monachis suis a boria sub optentu pacis ad hunc locum perueniens. Attulit secum reliquias.* Then follows the relic list as below, lines 9–14.

[271] Wm, JG: *uenerabilis* omitted.

[272] Wm, JG: *cum suis monachis* omitted; but in John, p. 18, twelve monks are mentioned as accompanying Ticca.

[273] JG: *venit Glastoniam*

[274] Wm: *concessit; usque peruenit* omitted.

[275] JG puts this after *Multis . . . hostile,* and includes the name of the abbot who succeeded Ticca: *Iste Ticta defuncto Tumberto iure abbatis Glastoniensem rexit ecclesiam.*

[276] Wm: *abbatis iure anno Dominice incarnacionis septingentesimo LIIII rexit.*

[277] Wm: *sustulerunt*; T: *susspirarent*

[278] JG: *sane namque*

[279] Titus: *scilicet* omitted.

[280] Wm: *Sancti* omitted.

[281] Wm: *Lindisfarnensis*; Titus: *episcopi atque corpora*

[282] JG here diverges, listing relics of St Idanus, the brother of St Furseus, and including relics of St Ultanus bishop, but no other northern saints. He adds the oil of the tomb of

10 Benedicti. Estrewini.[283] Sigfridi.[284] Huberti Wiorensium[285] abbatum. corpus[286] Sancti Bede presbiteri.[287] Item[288] corpus Sancte[289] Hilde abbatisse[290] monasterii quod quandam Sueneshealh[291] nunc Witebi nuncupatur. Et[292] reliquias Hebbe. Bege. Borsili. Hee igitur reliquie super altare ueteris[293] ecclesie locate: non parum Reuerentie loco adiacere. Isdem[294] porro Sanc-
15 tus[295] Ticca cum ualefecisset uite: in dextero angulo maioris ecclesie iuxta introitum uetuste: notabilem[296] accepit sepulturam ipsa[297] est et mole structure et arte celature non innobilis.[298] Testantur hii uersus circa epitaphium suum. Tumba hec mirifico: fulget fabricata decore. Desuper exsculptum: condit sub culmine Ticcam.[299]

20. De translatione Sancti Dunstani a Cantuaris ad Glastoniam.[300]

[blank line]
Anno Domini .M.xii.[301] translatus est Sanctus Dunstanus a Cantuaria ad Glastoniam qui ibidem antea fuit monachus et abbas. et postea archiepi-
5 scopus Cantuarie. Cuius reliquias uenerabilis abbas Brihedredus fecit asportare Glastoniam. iussu regis Edmundi iunioris. Eo enim tempore Cantuaria

---

St Nicholas, and relics of Giles and Germanus of Auxerre. The bodies and relics listed here are found, with some variation in order, among the gifts of King Edmund the Elder (*multas reliquias quas per terram Northanhumbrorum . . . adquisierat*) in JG, p. 122. They are also listed, not all together, on p. 18, where Aidan's body was given by Ticca, and the others by Edmund. Neither chapter mentions the old name of Whitby. On p. 122, John also includes King Sigebert's gifts of land to Ticca and the monks of Glastonbury. See Ticca and individual saints in Part 2, 4. Glossary.

283 MS: wynn, distinct from thorn, p and y; Wm, Titus: *Estrepini*
284 Wm: *Hetberti Selfridi*, but originally *Sigfridi*, with *Sel* interlined.
285 Titus: *Wigorinensium*
286 Wm: *corpus Sancti* omitted.
287 Titus: *presbiteri. Item* omitted.
288 Wm: *Hebbe, Bege. Borsili. Item*
289 Wm: *Sancte* omitted.
290 Titus diverges here: *et aliorum sanctorum reliquias. hoc abbas rexit eccciam istam pluribus annis et in eadem sepeliuit.*
291 Wm: *Streneshealh*
292 Wm: *Et . . . Borsili* omitted here; see n. 267 above.
293 Wm: *ueteris ecclesie* omitted.
294 Wm: *Idem; isdem* T; JG, p. 106, resumes with *Hic abbas cum ualefecisset*
295 Wm: *Sanctus* omitted.
296 JG: *uetuste ecclesie uenerabilem accepit*
297 Wm: *ea*; JG: *ipsa . . . suum* omitted, and *cum tali epitaphio* inserted.
298 Wm stops here; Ticca's epitaph is not given.
299 JG: *Tictan*, then *De hoc sepulcro narratur miraculum quod cum quidam aggressus esset diruere, <statim> est cecitate percussus.*
300 Wm, pp. 72–4, and JG, pp. 142–4 have the same information, more fully recounted, but the version here is not verbally close enough to suggest direct dependence. The version in Titus A.xix, however, is the same as that here.
301 Titus: *M°xii°*

funditus a Danis fuit uastata. Et non solum Cantuaria. sed etiam tota illa regio usque ad London. igne et gladio uastata fuit. Hoc tempore quando sic Cantuaria uastata fuit emisit[302] predictus abbas quatuor monachos de Glastonia qui prius fuerant cum Sancto Dunstano temporibus quibus Domino in <carne>[303] famulabatur. et ipse idem postea cum Sancto Elphego usque ad diem passionis eius conuersabantur. quorum hec <sunt> nomina. Sebricht. Echelrich. Burhsie. Aelword[304] cognomento quadrans. Isti asportauerunt reliquias Sancti Dunstani ad Glastoniam quia ipsi sepelierant eum[305] et bene sciebant certum locum ubi prius eum condiderant. Hec translatio facta est post obitum Sancti Dunstani. anno .xxiiii. in secundo annno post interfectionem Sancti Elphegi Archiepiscopi. obiit autem Sanctus Dunstanus anno ab incarnatione Domini .Dcccc.lxxx.ix.

21. De ueuerabili cruce que quondam locuta est[306]

In ecclesia Glastonie est[307] quedam crux merito uenerabilis auro. et argento cooperta que quondam locuta est immo uerius spiritus <spi>ritus[308] in ea cum quodam monacho illius loci Aylsi nomine hoc modo. Cum idem monachus per eandem crucem sicut et per altari(a) <sep>e[309] transiens nequaquam debita se reuerentia[310] inclinaret secundum regularem disciplinam: tandem quadam uice per eam transitum faciens[311] inclinauit. Crux[312] igitur in uocem quasi debitis organis formatam erumpens sic ait. Nu[313] to late Aylsi. Nu[314] to late Aylsi. Qui diuine uoce percusssus statim corruens expirauit.

---

[302] Titus: *misit*
[303] MS: illegible; space for four letters. Reading from Titus.
[304] Titus: *Aelwerde*
[305] Titus: *ipsum*
[306] Wm, p. 78; JG, pp. 42–3; Titus A.xix, fol. 22v. John includes the three crosses and the image of the Virgin in the same chapter, without sub-headings. The chapter title is: *De mirabilibus signis que Deus dedit in monasterio Glastoniensi per imagines crucifixi et sancte virginis Marie.* Wm and Titus have the heading given here. John also tells the story in ch. 72, p. 138, where he records that the cross was placed before the holy-water stoup at the monk's entrance after the fire.
[307] JG: *Est in monasterio Glastoniensi*
[308] Wm, Titus: *spiritus sanctus*; JG: *Spiritus sancti*
[309] Wm: *sepe* omitted.
[310] JG: *reuerencia se*
[311] JG: *eam transiens*
[312] JG: *Imago igitur crucifixi*
[313] JG, Titus: *Now*
[314] JG, Titus: *Now*

22. De alia cruce de qua cecidit diadema.[315]

Est etiam ibidem alia crux antiquissima que olim in refectorio stare consueuit. De hac ferunt quod cum die quadam Edgarus rex et Dunstanus[316] archiepiscopus ad mensam sederent in refectorio cogitationibus diuine uoluntati contrariis in cor Regis accendentibus[317] mirum dictu ymago dominica ligno crucis affixa toto se corpore excussit[318] ita ut motus impetu diadema eius inter regem et archiepiscopum caderet. Quid hoc portenderet[319] confessio regis[320] manifestauit. Inquisitus enim rex[321] a Sancto Dunstano quid tunc cogitaret. aut quid se acturum fore disponeret: fatebatur quod eadem hora cogitauit ut monachis ad alium locum translatis illic moniales aggergaret. Increpatus igitur reuerenter ab archiepiscopo dicente hoc diuine uoluntati contrarium. rex tale propositum reuocauit in irritum.

23. De cruce uulnerata.[322]

Est[323] ibidem tercia crux ceteris minor. populo tamen celebrior ab antiquo auro argento[324] uestita de qua olim ex percussione sagitte sanguis plurimus uirtute diuina profluxit quod qualiter euenerit. ostendunt[325] libri antiquitatum huius ecclesie.

24. De quadam ymagine beate marie.[326]

Est etiam. ibi[327] ymago[328] beate Marie quam cum ignis[329] ingens olim circumdans[330] pallas et omnia[331] altaris ornamenta consumeret.[332] ipsam

---

315 Wm, ch. 27, pp. 78–80, with heading. The heading is also in Titus.
316 JG: *Sanctus Dunstanus*
317 Wm, JG: *ascendentibus*
318 Wm: *excessit*
319 JG: *portendere* T.
320 JG: *regis continuo manifestauit*; Titus: *regis confessio*
321 JG: *rex* omitted.
322 Wm: ch. 28, p. 80, with heading. The heading is also in Titus.
323 MS: A three-line initial E serves for the initial letter on this line and on line 94 below.
324 Wm, JG, Titus: *argentoque*
325 Wm: *alias scriptum non tacebit*; JG: *alias non tacebo*; there is no mention of the ancient books.
326 Wm, ch. 29, p. 80, with the heading. The heading is also in Titus.
327 JG: *ibi etiam*; Titus: *ibi* omitted.
328 JG: *imago quedam in Sancte Dei genitricis veneracionem decenter fabricata quam.* From here to the end of the tablet, the text is heavily condensed from JG, probably to make the information fit the available space.
329 JG: *ingens olim ignis*
330 JG: *circumdaret, omnia que circa eam erant, pallas*
331 JG: *cetera*
332 JG: *combussit. Cum vero peruenisset incendium ad locum vbi erat imago illa, ipsam quasi expauescens, intactum reliquid ita ut eciam velamen candidum, dictum peplum, quod capite gestabat, odore fumi non ualeret aliquatenus obscurari. In facie . . .*

non tetigit.³³³ nec etiam peplum capiti eius appensum. In facie tamen ipsius³³⁴ pro uapore ignis uesice quasi in³³⁵ homine uiuente surgentes diuina testabantur uirtutem et per multum temporis intuentibus apparebant.³³⁶

25. De ymagine antiquioris capelle³³⁷

Existat ymago ceteris in³³⁸ antiquior Anglia³³⁹ de qua narrat Magister Edmundus Stowrtonn eiusdem loci monachus quod cum conuentus³⁴⁰ beate Marie deuotus³⁴¹ antiphonam. <u>Salue regina</u>.³⁴² decanteret ecce uidentibus multis³⁴³ ymago gloriosa³⁴⁴ ut uiuens femina se mo<uebat> puerulo: applaudens ac eum reuerenter contrectans nec ob huiusmode motibus desistebat quousque plena in choro dicta cantaretur antiphona.

Tablet 4

26. De sanctis ibidem requiescentibus³⁴⁵

Nunc de sanctis ibidem requiescentibus manifestius describemus. In eodem monasterio requiescunt .xii. discipuli Sancti <. . .>³⁴⁶ Philippi <. . . .>apostoli <. . .>sicut antea est descriptum. Hi primum oratorium in insula Auallonie construxerunt. et diu ibidem permanserant. Sed eorum

---

[333] Titus: *te*
[334] JG: *ipsium imaginis*
[335] JG: *uiui homines surgentes*
[336] JG goes on to praise the image and to mention Abbot John Chinnock's adornment of it. Carley, p. 277, n. 60, says that the information about Chinnock must be an interpolation in JG's original text. This would seem to indicate that our compiler had the original, uninterpolated version. Titus has this version.
[337] Not in Wm. JG has a longer introduction to this incident, identifying Edmund Stourton as a master of the sacred page, author of *De nominibus Ihesu et Marie*, dedicated to Pope John XXII. Titus has this version.
[338] Titus: *in* omitted.
[339] MS: *antiquior in Anglia* would be a more natural word order.
[340] JG: *conuentus Glastonie*
[341] JG: *deuotus, secundum consuetudinem antiphonam illam*
[342] MS: The words are underlined in the manuscript.
[343] JG: *secularibus in multitudine copiosa necnon monachis idipsum spectantibus, imago*
[344] JG: *virginis gloriose assistens altari in modum viuentis femine se mouebat, puerulo quem gremio tenuit applaudebat, nunc manum faciei apponens nunc alibi eundem reuerenter contrectans, nec ab huiusmodi motibus desistebat quousque plene et tractim in choro dicta percanteretur antiphona.*
[345] This section seems to be loosely based on the same information as Wm, p. 70, and JG, pp. 16–18. Phaganus, Deruvianus and Benignus are also in Wm, p. 86. The wording here is not generally the same as either Wm or John. John does not mention the indulgences on pp. 16–18, and his list of the relics is longer.
[346] MS: original parchment damaged; no text appears to be missing in any of the three erasures.

nomina: non inuenimus descripta. Multi ex paganis per eos ad fidem Christianam conuersi ac baptizati ibidem requiescunt. Quorum propter eorum multitudinem non est numerus. Illic duo Sancti Phaganus et Deruuianus multum tempus[347] perhendinauerunt. Et ab Eleutherio <papa>
10 qui eos in terram istam miserat .x. annos indulgentie omnibus sacrum locum pie uisitaturis perquisierunt. Hii uero duo sancti: regionem istam in principio ad fidem Christianam conuerterunt. sed utrum ibi requiescunt. uel inde redierunt: non inuenimus scriptum. Ibi multi ex discipulis Sanctorum Phagani et Deruuiani requiescunt. qui per ducentos sexaginta et septem
15 annos quidem \alii/ post alios usque ad aduentum Sancti Patricii in prefata insula sicut anachorite habitauerunt. Illic .xii. socii magne sanctitatis uiri requiescunt. quod Sanctus Patricius in primo aduentu suo ibidem inuenit. et eos postea congregauit ubi monastice uiuere instruxit. Horum uero nomina: in Carta Sancti Patricii reperies descripta. Ibi requiescit Sanctus
20 Patricius Hiberniensium apostolus: et in Glastonia abbas primus. per hunc autem sanctum: religio monachorum in Glastonia sumpsit exordium atque a Celestino <papa> qui cum in Hiberniam miserat omnibus ecclesiam Dei genitricis et uirginis Marie in remissione peccatorum pie uisitantibus. et de bonis sibi a Deo collatis eam honorantibus .xii. annos indulgentie acquisiuit.
25 Ille requiescit Sanctus Benignus eiusdem Sancti Patricii contubernalis et discipulis sicut antea plenius describitur. Ibi beata Brigida uirgo diu perhendinauit. set utrum ibi requiescit uel repatriauit: scriptum non munimus.[348] Illic requiescit Sanctus Indractus martir. cum septem sociis suis. Hii uero ex regali Hiberniensium progenie fuerunt. qui qualiter mar-
30 tirizati fuerunt. in eorum gestis manifeste descriptum est. Ibi in peregrinando Sanctus Columkilla uenit. et in insula illa diu perhendinauit. set utrum ibi requiescit. uel inde repatriauit. pro certo non habemus. Hic autem sanctus et alii suprascripti: pro ueneratione Sancti Patricii. singuli de suis locis Glastonie aduenerunt. Illic duo Innocentes[349] requiescunt. qui in
35 Bethleem pro Christo martirizati fuerunt. quos Edgarus rex adquisiuit. et infra altare gloriose uirginis Marie in uetusta ecclesia deuotissime collocare fecit. Ibi Sanctus Gildas nobilis Britonum historiographus requiescit. qui

---

[347] JG: *nouem annos moram fecisse*
[348] Carley, 1985, p. 271, n. 6, points out that Giraldus Cambrensis, *Topographia Hiberniae*, and Higden's *Polichronicon* assert that Brigid was buried with Patrick and Columkilla at Down. See Tablet 3, Text 13, where relics of her clothing are listed, but the same uncertainty about her body's final resting place is expressed. A long note on Higden and Giraldus is in the lower margins of Trinity R.5.33, fols. 2v–4v, printed in Wm, pp. 189–190, n. 30. Neither Brigid nor Columkilla in JG, pp. 18–20.
[349] Wm, p. 70: *duo Innocentes a pio rege Edgaro de Bethleem illuc translati*; JG, p. 18: *Illic sunt reliquie duorum Innnocentium integre et tercii Innocentis pro magna parte*. He does not specify where they are buried.

ante altare beate virginis Marie post obitum suum sepultus fuit.[350] et ibidem sex centos. quinquagenta. et uiginti duos annos usque ad conbustionem eius in[351] eccclesie sicut iacuit et postea sicut Domino placuit: translatus fuit. Illic Sanctus Dauid Meneuensium archiepiscopus requiescit cuius reliquias quedam uenerabilis femine nomine Aelsuiza adquisiuit. et ibidem cum magna deuotione donauit.[352] Hic uetustem ecclesiam cum cimiterio dedicare disposuit. sicut antea describitur.[353] set Dominus eum prohibuit. et ei per manifestum miraculum demonstrauit: quod idem ipso eam ac cimiterium antea dedicauit. Ibi Sanctus Paulinus Northamhimbrorum archiepiscopus ad perendinandum uenit. hic muros[354] uetuste ecclesie ligneo tabulatu construere[355] fecit. et extra a summo usque deorsum in terram plumbo undique cooperire[356] fecit. Et sic illud sanctum oratorium in eadem factura usque ad conbustionem eiusdem ecclesie perdurauit. Illic Sanctus Dunstanus noster patronus.[357] et Cantuareiensis archiepiscopus requiescit. sed qualiter uenerabiles eiusdem sancti reliquie de Cantuaria usque Glastoniam translate fuerint: plenius ante descriptum est.[358] Ibi requiescunt Sanctus Aidanus[359] episcopus et Sanctus Ceolfridus abbas. et Sanctus Beda uener-

---

[350] JG, p. 72 recounts the life and adventures of Gildas and his burial *in medio uetuste ecclesie pauimento* in the year 512. After the fire of 1181, his relics were placed in a shrine in 1186 (JG, p. 178).

[351] MS: *a* erased, *in*

[352] See text 16.1 above. In ch. V, p. 16, JG calls her *quedam nobilis matrona*; in ch. VI, p. 22, the list of the collectors of relics, she is called *Aelswita*; in ch. LXIX, p. 130, on the translation of St David's relics, she is called *Elswitha*.

[353] See 3.41–53.

[354] Wm, p. 66, and JG, p. 51, record the visit of Paulinus while still bishop of Rochester in 625. The language here is closer to JG. From *muros* to *perdurauit*, the passage is the same; it is also the same on Tablet 3.57–59.

[355] JG: *construi*

[356] JG: *cooperiri*

[357] Wm, p. 70, calls Dunstan *pater magnificus*, but neither William nor John refers to Dunstan as *patronus noster*.

[358] See text 20.

[359] According to Wm, p. 69, the relics of Aidan, Ceolfrith, Benedict, Eosterwine, Hwætberht, Selfrith (Sigfrid), Bede, Hebba, Begu, Boisil and Hilda were all brought by Ticca. In Wm, p. 71, other relics are listed, but donors are not given, as they are listed in the gospel books of the abbey (*in textis euangeliorum annotantur*). In JG, p. 18, the source of the relics of each saint (except Ticca, who died at Glastonbury) is identified: Aidan, Ceolfrith, Boisil, Bede, Benedict Biscop, Hesterpini (Eosterwine), Sigfrid, Herbert, by gift of Edmund the Elder; Aidan, brother of Furseus, and Ultan, by gift of Ticca; Iltuyd, by gift of Duke Athelstan; Hilda, Hebba and Begu, by gift of Edmund the Elder; Urban, by gift of Count Aelstan of Boscumb; Anastasius, Benignus the martyr and Cesarius, by gift of King Edgar. Molanus is in William (*ossa sancti Melani episcopi et martiris*) but not mentioned anywhere in JG or in Titus A.xix. The queens Ealfleda and Batildis and the virgin Aelswiza have no donors; Mamilla, by gift of Duke Athelstan; Ursula and Daria, by gift of Abbot Henry of Blois; Crisanta, Odlie, Lucy, Walburga and Gertrude, by gift of Duke Aelfhere. On p. 122, Aidan, Celofrid, Boisil, Bede, Benedict

55 abilis presbiter et historiographus Anglorum. et Sancte Hilda quondam in Witebi abbatissa. Et corpora Sanctorum Benedicti. Estrewini,[360] Sigfridi. Herberti. Wigornensium abbatum. Et reliquie Hebbe. Begu. Borsili. Istorum uero corpora sanctorum. Sanctus Ticca de septentrionali parte. uenerabilis abbas cum .xiii. monachis suis. Danorum persecutionem fugientes:
60 secum ad Glastoniam detulerunt. et in illa sancta congregacione similiter omnibus diebus suis permanserunt. Illic[361] requiescit sanctus Idanus episcopus. et sanctus episcopus[362] Ultanus frater Sancti Fursei. de[363] quo: ualde admiranda leguntur. Ibi requiescit Sanctus Iltuith inter Walnenses multum[364] honoratus. Illic[365] autem collocata sunt ossa Sancti Urbani <pape et>
65 martiris. et ossa Sancti Anastasii martiris. ossa Sancti Cesarii martiris. ossa sancti Benigni martiris. ossa Sancti Molani[366] episcopi et martiria. Ibi etiam requiescit Sancta Ealfleda regina. et Sancta Aelsuiza uirgo tota integra in carne et osse. sicut testantur qui eam uiderunt cum cilicio et sacro uelamine suo[367] putrefactis. Illic requiescunt[368] ossa Sancte Batildis regine et ossa
70 Sancte Mamille uirginis. et[369] corpora sanctarum uirginum,[370] Ursule et Darie. Crisante et Udilie.[371] Lucei.[372] Walburge.[373] et Geretrude.[374] Omnes isti sancti prenotati: in ecclesia continentur Glastoniensi.[375] Illic insuper innumerabiles reliquie sanctorum requiescunt de dono Regum et principium pontificium. et aliorum nobilium quorum plurima nomina in antiquis

    Biscop, Hesterpine, Sigfrid, Herbert, Hilda, Hebba and Begu come in that order, as saints whose relics Glastonbury had from King Edmund.
360 MS: Here the scribe's wynn looks more like a p.
361 From here on, the language is close enough to Wm, p. 70, for comparisons to be useful. In William, the names prefaced with *Illic* or *Item; requiescit* are not repeated, but the same saints come in the same order.
362 Wm: *Ultanus episcopus frater beati*
363 Wm: *cuius gesta miranda leguntur.*
364 Wm: *multum honoratur* omitted; *famossisimus*
365 Wm: *Illic . . . ossa* omitted; *item reliquie*
366 Wm: *Melani*; St Molanus does not appear anywhere in JG, or Titus A.xix.
367 MS: *suo*; Wm: *non*. The reading *suo* would mean that the body had not decayed but the clothes had. This would be extremely uncommon. Both Wm and JG say that Ealswitha was buried with her flesh and bones still whole, but the language here is taken from Wm; JG locates the tomb *inter magnum altare et sepulcrum regis Arthuri*, and omits *non putrefactis*.
368 Wm: *eciam sunt*
369 Wm: *Insuper*
370 Wm: *uirginum* omitted.
371 Wm, JG: *Udilie, Marie Marthe, Lucie, Lucie*
372 This is a masculine ending; in Wm and JG, both Luke and Lucy are listed among the relics. As this is a list of female saints, presumably Lucy is intended.
373 Wm: *Waleburge*; *Waleburbe* T.
374 Wm: *Geretrude et Cecilie*. Here the text ceases to agree with Wm.
375 MS: The word is written out in full. The more usual form is *Glastonie*.

libris illius ecclesie scripta inveniuntur.[376] Et etiam aliorum multorum sanctorum quorum reliquie. nec cum scriptis. nec nomina scripta. nusquam reperiuntur. Ideoque de quibus sanctis sint: penitus ignoramus. Et quamuis apud nos non sit eorum plena cognicio: cognicione tamen et contemplacione diuina plenius perfruuntur.[377]

27. De rege Arthuro, et de aliis regibus. ibidem requiescentibus.[378]

In hac itaque insula. que insula Auallonie dicitur: immo in hoc tumulo sanctorum apud Glastoniam requiescit inclitus Rex Arthurus flos regum Britannie. Et Guenhauera eius Regina. qui post decessum eorum iuxta uetustam ecclesiam inter duas piramides lapideas quondam nobiliter exsculptas: honorabiliter sepulti fuerunt. et ibidem per multa annorum curricula requieuerunt. uidelicet .sex centos. et Quadraginta octo annos.[379] usque ad tempus Henrici de Soili qui post conbustionem eiusdem ecclesie: abbas fuit illius loci. predictus uero abbas a compluribus[380] sepissime admonitus: iussit inter predictas piramides fodere. si regium corpus ualerent ibidem inuenire. et antequam fodere inceperunt: cortinis totum locum circumdederunt.[381] Foderunt igitur in profundum ualde.[382] et ad extremum: ingens sarcofogum ligneum totum clausum inuenerunt et illud quam cicius potuerunt cum eorum utensilibus aperuerunt. et regium corpus intro inuenerunt. et quandam crucem de plumbo totam in una[383] parte ita descriptam. Hic iacet sepul<. .>tus[384] inclitus Rex Arthurus in insula Auallonia. Deinde tumbam regine aperuerunt. et crines capitis sui similitudinem sicut nouiter ibidem sepulta erat: circa corpus[385] suum iacuerunt. Sed cum eas[386]

---

[376] JG, pp. 20–2, lists the known collectors of relics.
[377] On p. 18, JG blames the fire for the confusion of relics: *Multorum autem aliorim sanctorum nomina et memoriam antique ecclesie incendium, ex sanctarum reliquiarum confuisione, ex toto deleuit.*
[378] Not the same as the version from Higden's *Polychronicon* in Titus A.xix, fols. 17v–18, Barber no. 3, quoted in *Chronica Monasterii de Melsa*, ed. E. Bond, RS 43, 2 vols. (London, 1866–68), II, 210–11, also adapted in Titus A.xix. John of Glastonbury, ch. 98, pp. 180–2, based on Adam of Damerham, is close in individual phrases, but not close enough for a complete collation to be worthwhile. I have recorded only significant differences. Ussher, *Antiquitates*, pp. 61–2.
[379] Date in Adam of Damerham, which, as Carley points out, would put the excavation in 1190.
[380] In Adam of Damerham, the admonitions come from King Richard.
[381] Giraldus does not mention the curtains; see Carley, p. 297, n. 388.
[382] Adam of Damerham says they dug 8 feet for the cross, and 9 feet for Arthur's grave (p. 342).
[383] JG: *altera parte*, which Townsend translates as 'the underside'.
[384] MS: original erasure; no text missing.
[385] JG: *circa ossa eiusdem*
[386] In the *Chronica Monasterii de Melsa*, which is quoting Higden's *Polychronicon*, it is *monachus unus avide cum manu attraxisset* who touches the hair (II, p. 211).

tetigerunt: totum in puluere[387] inde uenerunt. Abbas uero et conuentus cum ingenti gaudio. et honore maximo: eorum exuuias inde transtulerunt. et in mausoleo intus bebertito[388] et extra nobiliter in petra exciso. in maiori ecclesia eos ita collocauerunt. Regium uidelicet corpus per se ad caput tumbe: et reginam in orientali parte[389] imposuerunt. Et hii uersus circa epitafium subtiliter exsculpti sunt. Hic[390] iacet Arthurus: flos regum gloria regni.[391] Quem mores[392] probitas: commendent[393] laude perhenni. Arthuri iacet hic: coniunx tumulata secunda. Que meruit celos: uirtutum prole secunda.[394] Illic[395] requiescit rex Centuinus. uel[396] Kentuinus[397] in piramide saxea in cimiterio monachorum. Hic[398] de regibus Anglorum primus fuit:[399] qui insulam Glastonie liberam ab omni regali[400] seruicio uetuste[401] ecclesie concessit. sicut reges Britonum ante eum iampridem confirmauerunt. insuper et quadraginta sex. hidas terre pro anima sua fratribus[402] ibidem Deo seruientibus: in perpetuam hereditatem confirmauit. Ibi[403] requiescit rex[404]

---

[387] JG: *in nichilum*
[388] Adam of Damerham: *bipertito*
[389] JG: *reginam ad pedes*; Adam: *ad pedes, scilicet in orientali parte*
[390] Titus A.xix, fol. 22, lines 3–8, after the renovations of the chapel by John Chinnock: *Hic requiescit inclitus Rex Arthurus flos britonum. Guennora Regina de quibus tales extant versus Hic.* On the tablets, and in Titus, the verses are written as prose.
[391] Titus: *mundi*
[392] JG: *mors*, but Townsend translates 'morals'. Titus: *morum*
[393] JG: *commendat*; Titus: *commendant*
[394] Adam of Damerham: *fecunda*
[395] Titus: *Hic*. The account of Centwine is condensed, but has the same information. JG, ch. 14, p. 30, line 17, after a prophecy of Melkin and a different account of King Arthur, begins to correspond more closely. He begins: *Ibi*. Wm, p. 82, has a list of kings, bishops, and *duces* buried at Glastonbury with the locations of their tombs; it seems to be authentically William. *Pretermitto de Arturo, inclito rege Britonum, in cimiterio monachorum inter duas piramides cum sua coniuge tumulato.*
[396] Titus: *vel . . . Hic* omitted; *qui prius*
[397] MS: *Kentiuinus*, with the first i expuncted. Wm: *Kenwino in una piramide locato*; JG has only *Kentwinus*.
[398] JG, p. 30: *qui primus de regibus Anglorum libertates magnas terrasque multas contulit. Ibi requiescit Edmundus.* On p. 40, John records Centwine's specific gifts: twenty-three hides at Monkton, twenty hides in Cary, and three hides in Creech. These gifts are also listed in the account of his reign on p. 90. The total agrees with the forty-six hides mentioned here. The freedom from all royal service is recorded on p. 96, in the charter of Ine, in different phrasing: *ab omni seculari et ecclesiastico obsequio immunem statuit.* For Centwine's actual resting-place, see Carley, p. 285, n. 144.
[399] Titus: *fuit qui* omitted.
[400] Titus: *servicio regali*
[401] Titus: *uetuste . . . insuper* omitted.
[402] Titus: *fratribus . . . confirmauit* omitted; *dedit huic ecclesie.*
[403] Titus: *Hic*
[404] Titus: *rex* omitted; *Edmundus* comes after *filius Edwardi primi*. JG: *Edmundus rex*

Eadmundus filius Edwardi senioris. et[405] frater Ethelstani[406] regis. Hic[407] abbathiam Glastonie[408] Sancto Dunstano donauit. et omnes reliquias quas per[409] uniuersas terras perquirere potuit: Glastonie[410] dedit cum amplis terrarum redditibus.[411] Illic requiescit rex[412] Eadgarus filius Edmundi[413] regis. pater uidelicet[414] Sancti Edwardi martiris et[415] Sancte Eaddithe*[sic]* uirginis. Huius[416] igitur[417] regis Eadgari uenerabile[418] corpus cum per[419] plurimos annos iacuisset in terra: nichil putridi passum est corpus eius. ne[420] quedam palla in qua inuolutum fuerat. nec cetera[421] que cum eo[422] inueniebantur. ipse autem postea[423] inscrinio auro et argenteo cooperto: diuina reuelacione translatus. in Domino requiescit. Et[424] ipse omnes reliquias quas per[425] uniuersas terras perquirere potuit: cum magnis terrarum redditibus. et regalibus donis: Glastonie[426] contulit. Ibi[427] requiescit rex Eadmundus iunior cognomento[428] Irenside.[429] Et[430] ipse omnes reliquias quas per[431]

---

[405] Titus: *et ... Hic* omitted; *qui*
[406] JG: *regis Ethelstani*
[407] JG: *qui Sanctum Dunstanum ibidem abbatem constituit terrasque dedit amplissimas et libertates magnas.*
[408] Titus: *hanc*
[409] Titus: *per ... perquirere* omitted; *habere*
[410] Titus: *Glastonie dedit* omitted; *huic ecclesie*
[411] Titus: *redditibus dedit. Hic*
[412] Titus: *Edgarus rex filius predicti Edmundi*
[413] JG: *eiusdem Edmundi et pater Sancti*
[414] Titus: *uidelicet* omitted.
[415] JG: *ac*
[416] JG: *Huius ... contulit* omitted. The list of his relic donations to Glastonbury is on pp. 138–40. The account of his body's miraculous preservation and discovery by Abbot Aethelweard in 1052 is in ch. 81, p. 152, though the preservation of the pall and grave goods is not mentioned. John tells that Aethelweard, finding that the body did not fit the casket he had for it, cut it, only to have blood gush forth. For this violation he died shortly afterwards of a broken neck. The body of Edgar was put in the shrine he had provided for the head of St Apollinaris and the relics of St Vincent.
[417] Titus: *igitur regis* omitted.
[418] Titus: *uenerabile* omitted.
[419] Titus: *per plurimos annos* omitted; *diu*
[420] Titus: *ne ... fuerant* omitted.
[421] Titus: *cetera* omitted; *ea*
[422] Titus: *ipso*
[423] Titus: *postea .. cooperto* omitted.
[424] Titus: *Et ipse* omitted; *Hic rex*
[425] Titus: *per ... perquirere* omitted; *habere*
[426] Titus: *huic ecclesie*
[427] Titus: *Hic*
[428] Titus: *dictus*
[429] JG, p. 30, says that Edmund was the son of Ethelred and grandson of Edgar, and then goes on to list five bishops.
[430] Titus: *Et ipse* omitted; *qui*
[431] Titus: *per ... ualebat* omitted; *habere potuit*

multa loca perquirere ualebat: cum amplis terris et aliis pluribus bonis: dedit[432] Glastonie. isti in ueritate reges. et alii plures Britonum et Anglorum Principes: ibidem requiescunt.

28. De archiepiscopis[433]

Illic uero requiescunt corpora trium archiepiscoporum. uidelicet. Sanctus Patricius Hiberniensium archiepiscopus. Sanctus Dauid Legionum archiepiscopus. Sanctus Dunstanus Cantuarium archiepiscopus.

29. De episcopis.

Ibi requiescunt etiam nouem episcopi. silicet Sanctus Benignus. Sanctus Aidanus. Sanctus Ultanus. Sanctus Idanus. et Hedda[434] episcopus. qui in superiori cimiterio monachorum in piramide saxea quondam nobiliter
5 exculpta: adhuc requiescit.[435] Hic regiam libertatem insule Glastonie de rege Centuino ad uetustam ecclesiam impetrauit: et liberam electionem fratribus ibidem Deo seruientibus ab eodem rege perquisiuit ut habeant[436] ius eligendi. et constituendi sibi rectorem: secundum regulam Sancti Benedicti insuper et sex hidas terre cum aliis multis bonis: ad eandem
10 ecclesiam donauit. Et Brichhtwoldus episcopus et Brichtwius episcopus et Liuingus episcopus.[437] et Seifridus episcopus. et multi alii Britonum. et Anglorum episcopi requiescunt ibi. Sed[438] de hiis sumiis in ueritate securi. Ipsi uero episcopi in diebus eorum predictam ecclesiam nimis dilexerunt. et omnes reliquias quas per totas terras perquirere potuerunt: cum aliis
15 multis bonis. et sacerdotalibus ornamentis auro et labidibus preciosis desuper contextis: Glastoniam contulerunt.

---

[432] Titus: *dedit Glastonie* omitted; *huic ecclesie contulit*. Titus then goes straight to the *Duces*, omitting the conclusion of this section, and all the archbishops and bishops.
[433] Not in JG, ch. 14.
[434] Wm, p. 84, lists *sepulcra Brithuuii et Brithuoldi . . . Liuingi eciam et Selfridi*. JG, p. 30, identifies five bishops: Hedda of Winchester (674–705), Britwoldus of Wilton (bishop 995–1045), Britwius of Wells (bishop 1027–34), Liuingus of Crediton (bishop 1028–46), and Seffordus of Chichester (bishop 1125–45; died 1150). Hedda and Seffordus of Chichester do not appear in ch. 15, which lists the archbishops, bishops and abbots elected to diverse sees who were from Glastonbury.
[435] Hedda's name is the first on the second pyramid, 18 feet tall, still standing in Wm, p. 84, and JG, p. 30, but no sculpture is mentioned. In William, the first pyramid has a figure of a bishop and a royal figure in the top two panels.
[436] JG, p. 90: *habeant . . . Benedicti*. That chapter also records the gift of six hides.
[437] JG: *Liuingus episcopus* omitted MS T.
[438] These three lines have no parallel in JG. In Titus, there are five lines of general praise of all benefactors after the *duces*.

30. De ducibus.

Ibi[439] requiescit[440] Alpharus[441] dux. et Adelstanus dux. et Adelwinus[442] dux. et Aeluptus dux. Hii[443] iiii[or] duces unusquisque eorum centum libratas terre. cum aliis[444] multis bonis Glastonie[445] contulerunt.[446] De[447] abbatibus, et aliis summe religionis et magne sanctitatis uiris. ibidem requiescentibus. non certus numerus constat nobis.
[blank line]

31. De Glasteng et de fratribus suis

Legitur[448] autem[449] in antiquis Britonum gestis quod a boreali Britannie parte uenerunt in occidentem .xii. fratres et tenuerunt plurimas regiones[450] Uenedociam.[451] Demeciam. Guth.[452] Kedweli. quas proauus eorum Cuneda tenuerat. Nomina[453] eorum fratrum inferius[454] annotantur. Ludwerth.[455] Morgen.[456] Catgur. Cathmor. Merguid. Moruined. Morehel. Morcant. Boten. Morgeu. Mortineil. Glasteing. Hic[457] est ille Glasteing qui per mediterraneos anglos secus uillam que dicitur Escheborne <. .>[458] scrofam suam usque ad Wellis. et a Wellis per inuiam et aquosam uiam que Sugewege .id est. scrofe uia dicitur[459] sequens porcellos suos iuxta eccle-

---

[439] Titus A.xix, fol. 22, resumes here, having omitted the archbishops and bishops. *Hic requiescunt*
[440] JG: *eciam quiescunt*
[441] Wm, p. 84: *Alfari, Aedthelstani, Aetheluuini, Aelnoti*; Titus: *Alfarus. Ethelstanus. Adelwynus et Aelnotus*
[442] JG: *Elwinus et Elnotus duces, quorum quilibet centum*
[443] Wm: *quorum uidelicet ducum quilibet*; Titus: *Hii ... duces* omitted; *quorum unusquisque*
[444] Titus: *multis aliis*
[445] Titus: *hunc ecclesie contulit.* Titus then diverges.
[446] Wm, JG: *contulit Glastonie.* Both then go directly to the description of the two stone pyramids.
[447] This sentence has no parallel in JG or Titus.
[448] Wm, p. 52. Heading: *Quomodo multitudo popularis primitus Glastoniam inhabitauerit.* First sentence omitted. JG, ch. 2, p. 10, line 7, omitting the beginning of this section on the various names of Glastonbury here. Some of the information, in different wording, comes after Glasteing and his brothers. Ch. 2: Heading: *De Diversis Nominibus Eiusdem Insule in qua dicta Ecclesie Sita est et Quomodo Fuit Inhibitata* [sic].
[449] Wm: *autem* omitted; JG: *eciam*
[450] JG: *regiones scilicet*
[451] These are the modern regions of Gwynnedd, Dyfed, Gower, and Kidwely.
[452] Wm, JG: *Guther*
[453] JG: *Horum fratrum nomina sunt hec*
[454] Wm: *interius,* with no variants given, but his T reads *interius* (fol. 2v).
[455] Wm, JG: *Ludnerth*
[456] Wm: *Morgent,* with a t added later, T; *Morgen,* M.
[457] Wm: *hinc* T, M, but in T the n has been expuncted; JG: *Iste; est ille* omitted.
[458] MS: erasure of two letters; no text missing; Wm, JG: *Escebtiorne*
[459] JG: *nunc dicitur*

siam[460] de[461] qua nobis sermo est lactentem[462] sub malo inuenit. Unde usque ad nos emanauit quod mala[463] mali illius ealdechirchen[464] epple[465] .id est. ueteris ecclesie poma uocantur. Sus[466] quoque ealdechirche sowe[467] idcirco nominabatur.[468] Que cum cetere sues .iiii^{or}. pedes habeant mirum dictu ista
15 habuit octo. Hic igitur Glasteing postquam insulam[469] ingressus eam multimodis bonis uidit affluentem cum omni familia sua in ea uenit habitare[470] cursumque uite sue ibidem peregit. Ex cuius progenie et familia ei succedente locus ille primitis dicitur populatus. He[471] de antiquis Britonum libris sunt.

32. De diuersis nominibus eiusdem insule.

Hec itaque insula primo Ynswitrin a Britonibus dicta.[472] demum ab Anglis terram sibi subiungantibus interpretato priore uocabulo dicta est sua lingua Glastinburi.[473] uel de Glasteing de quo premissimus: etiam insula Auallonie
5 celebriter nominatur. Cuius uocabuli hec fuit origo. supradictum est quod Glasteing scrofam suam sub arbore pomifera iuxta uetustam ecclesiam inuenit. Vbi quia primum adueniens poma in partibus illis rarissima repperit insula[474] Auallonie sua lingua .id est. insulam pomorum nominauit. Aualla enim Britonice poma interpretatur Latine. uel cognominatur de quodam
10 Aualloc qui ibidem cum suis filiabus propter loci secretum fertur inhabitasse.

---

460 JG: *vetustam ecclesiam in predicta insula*
461 JG: *de qua nobis sermo est* omitted.
462 JG: *latentem* A, T, P.
463 JG: *poma*
464 Wm: *ealdecyrcenas*
465 JG: *ealdechirchensapple*
466 JG: *sus . . . octo* omitted.
467 Wm: *suge*
468 MS: *nois'/batur*
469 Wm: *insulam illam*; JG: *insulam ille*
470 JG: *habitare. Et quia ibi primum adueniens poma in partibus illis carissima repperit insulam Auallonie sua lingua, id est insulam pomorum, nominauit et cursum*
471 MS: *he* followed by a blank space; Wm: *Hec*; JG: *He . . . sunt* omitted.
472 Wm, ch. 5, p. 52. Heading: *De diuersis nominibus eiusdem insule*. JG, beginning of ch. 2, p. 10: *Hec itaque insula primo a Britonibus dicta est Ynyswytryn*; then the text differs, though it offers the same two etymologies for Avalon.
473 Wm: *Glastinbiri*
474 Wm: *insulam*

Tablet 5

33. De dignitate et sanctitate ecclesie beate Marie Glastonie ac eiusdem sancti cimiterii[475]

Est ergo Glastoniensis ecclesia[476] quas quidem nouerim[477] in Anglia antiquissima[478] quam dominus noster Ihesus Christus in honore sui[479] matris
5 et contiguum cimiterium ad sanctorum suorum sepulturam. presentaliter dedicauit. Ecclesia[480] de qua loquitur pro nimia antiquitate sua ab antiquis uetusta est dicta. et ideo cognomen sortita quia olim in Anglorum lingua ealdechirche id est antiqua ecclesia fuit appellata. In[481] ea autem et in cimiterio et in eiusdem cimiterii capella multorum sanctorum[482] corporales
10 seruantur[483] exuuie. sicut[484] prescriptum est nec a beatorum reliquiis[485] uacat illius[486] fani[487] ambitus. adeo pauimentum lapide constratum, adeo altarium[488] sub supra et infra reliquiis, confertissimis aggeruntur.[489] nec in toto illo cimiterio a profunditate .xvi. pedum usque ad eius[490] superficiem[491] a sanctorum cineribus habetur locus uacuus. Si quis e uicinio aliquod
15 edificium locandum putasset. quod obumbratione sua lucem inuideret ecclesie patuit ruine. Satisque constat homines illius prouincie nullum sanctius uel crebrius iuramentum habere: quam per ueterem ecclesiam,

---

[475] Wm, p. 66. Heading: *De sanctitate et dignitate Glastoniensis ecclesie*. The beginning is not in JG. In Titus A.xix, fol. 22, at the end of the list of kings and *duces* buried in the abbey, comes a short prayer: *Gaudeat igitur Glastonia tantis patronis munerita(?) tantis que fundatoribus et benefactoribus illustratatorum per misericordiam Domini in pace requiescant. Amen.* Then a new paragraph: *Gaudeant Glastonia ecclesia matrix omnium ecclesiarum in Anglia. quam Dominus Jhesus.* The rest is close to the text here.
[476] Wm: *ecclesia omnium*
[477] Wm: *nouerim antiquissima*
[478] Wm: *antiquissima in Anglia*, then omitted until line 9 below, *indeque cognomen sortita. In eam preter beatum Patricium et alios de quibus superius dixi, multorum*
[479] Titus: *gloriose matris sue et omnium sanctorum ibidem qui est dictum sibi cum Cimitorio presencialiter dedicauit.*
[480] Titus: *Ecclesia . . . appellata* omitted.
[481] Titus: *In quibus vero ecclesia scilicet et cimitorio atque in*
[482] Titus: *sanctorum* omitted.
[483] Titus: *exiuie seruantur*
[484] Wm, Titus: *sicut prescriptum est* omitted.
[485] Wm: *cineribus*
[486] Wm, Titus: *ullus*
[487] Titus: *fani . . . cimiterio* 5.8 omitted; *in eis locus a profunditate*
[488] Wm: *altaris latera, ipsumque altare supra*
[489] From here on the text differs from Wm p. 66 until line 14 below, *Si quis*
[490] Titus: *terre*
[491] Titus: *a sanctorum . . . monumentum obtulerunt* omitted.

nichil[492] uitantes metu sceleris[493] uindicte: quam periurare.[494] et quicunque per illam. illicite iuraret quin ei eueniret aliquod scandalem non dubitaret.
20 In[495] tanta[496] reuerentia habuerunt sancti patres nostri predictum[497] locum. quod non audebant in eo[498] loqui. uel fleuma <. . .>[499] in terram sanctam proicere. nisi in magna necessitate. uel[500] cum magna cordis compunctione. Nec audebant aliquem huius ecclesie inimicum uel aliquem enormem peccatorem secundum[501] quod intelligere poterant in predicto sacro cimit-
25 erio sepelire. propter uoces horribiles que sepe ab eis audiebantur.[502] donec effoderentur. atque de cimiterio proiecerentur. sicut[503] audiuimus de uno iam tarde factum fuisse. Multi etiam ex[504] monachis propter reuerenciam[505] huic sacro loco factam iusto Dei iudicio sepulturam inibi perdiderunt. Nullis[506] auem uenatoriam aduexit. uel quadrupedes induxit. qui: sui uel rei
30 possesse indempnis abierit: sicut[507] contigit tempore regis Edgari. Comes[508] quidam Arnulphus nomine. ancipitrem in eodem tulit qui statim de eius manu elapsus expirauit. Quidam[509] cocus abbatis Herlewini[510] equum suum in[511] cimiterium[512] induxit et continuo exalauit. Quidam uero[513] eodem modo canes suos sepe perdiderunt.[514] Tempore Ethelredi regis cum res
35 Anglie Danis infestantibus premerentur. uentum[515] est a Danis ad portam

---

492 Wm: *nichil magis uitantes*
493 Wm: *celeris*
494 Here the text in Wm diverges again; *et . . . dubitaret* is not in either Wm or JG.
495 JG: ch. 13, p. 32, line 5.
496 JG: *tanta nempe reuerentia*
497 JG: *iam dictum*
498 JG: *in dicta ecclesia aut cimiterio aliqua uana loqui*
499 JG: *fluma uel saliuam in illam terram sanctam expuere uel proiecere*
500 JG: *uel* omitted.
501 JG: *secundum . . . poterant* omitted; *notorium in dicto sacro cimiterio*
502 JG: *et fantasmata malignorum spirituum que videbantur donec.* In A, *donec effoderetur* is omitted.
503 JG: *sicut . . . fuisse* omitted.
504 JG: *huius loci monachi*
505 JG: *irreuerenciam*
506 JG: *Nullus illuc; nullus autem illuc* T.
507 JG: *sicut contigit* omitted; *Nam*
508 JG: *quidam comes nomine Arnulphus*
509 JG: *Concus quidam*
510 JG: *Hetelwini*
511 JG: *in sanctum*
512 JG: *cimiterium casu nescienter*
513 JG: *Quidam uero* omitted; *Multi eciam*
514 Here John diverges, to discuss those who underwent the ordeal of iron or water. The miracle of the Danish soldiers is not in William, but is in JG, p. 146. He first gives the death of King Aethelred, 23 April 1016, when Cnut was in England. The third sentence begins: *Unde, cum res*
515 JG: *uentum est a Danis* omitted; *uenerunt*

unam Glastonie[516] que Haghegate uocatur duobus milibus fere ab ecclesie distans. Multi[517] eorum audientes sanctitatem huius loci. ne matrem misericordie et alios[518] quorum inibi corpora pausant ad iracundiam prouocarent: recesserunt. Sed tamen[519] intrauerunt nonnulli. nec inpune. Nam uirgo fecunda arma iusticie concutiens omnes cecitate multauit. quos postea penitentes et quod iniquie gessserant publice detestantes misericorditer illuminauit. Denique[520] facta collatione crucem eleganti[521] satis opere ex auro et argento et[522] preciosis lapidibus fabricarunt et ecclesie ueteri adhuiusce[523] miraculi monumentum obtulerunt. Locus[524] siquidem ille ab antiquis tanta colebatur. deuotione ut reges regine archiepiscopi episcopi duces milites et utriusque sexus nobiles[525] cuiuscumque ordinis cuiuscumque[526] essent celsitudinis[527] se beatos fore arbitrabantur. qui locum[528] illum aliquibus possessionibus auxissent uel qui in[529] ibidem uel alibi cum aliqua portione huius[530] sancte terre sepeliri potuissent. Et[531] inter ualentes in[532] partibus transmarinis tanta[533] reuerentia habetur locus illa quod quidam eorum pro particulus[534] huius sancte terre sepe[535] mittunt et pro eorum[536] sepulturis deuotissime[537] custodiunt et sepe dicunt Anglicis in partibus illis peregrinantibus quod si dignitatem et sanctitatem istius[538] sancti[539] cimiterii scirent non tantas transmarinas[540] peregrinaciones quererent. Tres enim sunt

---

[516] JG: *Glastonie uicinam que Hawete dicitur, uno miliari et amplius ab*
[517] JG: *Verum multi*
[518] JG: *alios sanctos quorum*
[519] JG: *nonnulli subsannantes insulam intrauerunt*
[520] JG: *At illi, facta inter se*
[521] JG: *opere satis eleganti*
[522] JG: *ac lapidibus preciosis*
[523] JG: *optulerunt ob huius miraculi monimentum*. This is the end of the excerpt from John, ch. 77.
[524] Titus, fol. 22, resumes: *locus iste sanctissimus ab antiquis*
[525] Titus: *preclari*
[526] Titus: *cuiuscumque* omitted.
[527] Titus: *celsitudinis* omitted; *beatos se*
[528] Titus: *eundem locum*
[529] Titus: *in ibidem* omitted; *hic*
[530] Titus: *eius*
[531] Titus: *Et inter ualentes* omitted; *Plures enim*
[532] JG: ch. 13, p. 32, line 21: *Locus ille in partibus transmarinis tante habetur auctoritas et reuerencia quod*
[533] Titus: *tantum . . . eorum* omitted.
[534] Titus: *particillis*
[535] Titus: *sepe mittunt et* omitted: *mittere solebant*
[536] JG: *suis*
[537] Titus: *deuotissime . . . quod* omitted; *eas deuote seruantes et peregrinos dicentes: Si Anglia dignitatem*
[538] Titus: *istius . . . cimiterii* omitted; *huius sancti loci Glastonie*
[539] JG: *sancti* omitted T.
[540] Titus: *peregrinaciones quererent transmarinas*

55 cause notabiles quare terra illa sancta ad[541] Christianorum sepulturam tanta auiditate desideratur. Prima causa[542] est quia Dominus eam ad seruorum[543] suorum sepulturam[544] presentialiter dedicauit. Secunda:[545] quia omnibus hic uel alibi cum aliqua portione huius sancte terre sepultis. per sanctorum inibi[546] requiescentium preces et merita. creditur magna peccatorum remis-
60 sio. a Domino concessa. Tertia:[547] propter missas et alias oraciones que cotidie pro eis dicuntur.[548] Propter istas tres causas multi <. .> de diuersis mundi partibus usque in hodiernum diem[549] ueniunt et particulas huius sancte terre in uasculis suis humiliter petiunt et pro eorum sepulturis deuotissime custodiunt. Quidam uidelicet in bursis. quidam in cirotecis.
65 quidam in ampullis stagneis et plumbeis sicut legitur de quibusdam Saracenis fecisse in memoriam Sancti Ioseph et sociorum eius quorum corpora illis ac aliis multis testantibus in eadem terra in Domino requiescunt.

34. Quando quidam Soldanus misit pro quadam porcione huius sancti cimiterii

Contigit[550] quod quidem Reynaldus[551] nomine de Merkesburi uotum emisit ut[552] terram sanctam uisitaret. uoto completo et ipso ibidem inimicos crucis
5 Christi debellante tandem a quodam Soldano captus uinculis[553] mancipatus, et per multa tempora in eius custodia fuerat detentus. Uerum quia decoris erat et pulcher aspectu elegantisque stature ipsum de carcere educi et coram se prandere cotidie faciebat. querendo[554] ab eodem de quibus partibus esset

---

[541] Titus: *ad . . . sepulturam* omitted.
[542] Titus: *causa* omitted.
[543] Titus: *sepulturam seruorum suorum*
[544] JG: *tanta . . . sepulturam* omitted T.
[545] Titus: *Secunda est*
[546] Titus: *hic*
[547] Titus: *Tercia causa est*
[548] JG, Titus: *Propter . . . requiescunt* omitted. John adds: *Et ut euidens hiis inducam testimonium, quedam in remotis partibus orbis gesta conuenienter subiungam.*
[549] MS: The colour of the ink changes from black to brown, but the scribe does not change.
[550] Titus: *Contigit autem quod*
[551] JG: *uir nomine Rainaldus*. Titus has a condensed version of the story on fol. 22–22v: *quidam peregrinus in terra sancta a soldano captus et ab eo interrogatus, si haberet noticiam Insule Glastonie/ ubi Joseph ab Arimathia quiescit. Respondit se fore\nouit/de eadem Insula. Cui Soldanus. Si uis Glastoniam adire et unam cirotecam plenam terre illius ubi Joseph quiescit reportare te a carcere liberabo et misericordia ministrabo. Ille statim iactis sacrosanctis illus promisit. Postea a Glastonia reueniens. optulit soldano cirotecam plenam terre cimitorii parochialis Glastonie. quam ille uidens et se delusum sciens peregrino mortem minatur. Tunc peregrinus alteram cirotecam plenam terre desiderate optulit et eidem satisfecit.*
[552] JG: *in* T.
[553] JG: *vinculis est*
[554] JG: *querendo . . . ipso* omitted.

oriundus ipso cognoscente[555] se esse Anglicanum. circumstantias Anglica-
nas castra ac munitiones est statim suscitatus demum ulterius querebat si
haberet noticiam cuiusdam insule aut duas montes site ubi Ioseph ab
Arimathia nobilis decurio quiescit qui prophetam Ihesu assumpserat de
cruce: ipso se[556] dicente fuisse de dominio abbatis Glastonie ubi predicta[557]
insula situatur. statim pactum[558] inierunt quod ipsum ab omni iugo seruitu-
tis. seu[559] etiam carceris liberaret. et[560] necessaria sibi[561] ministraret. hoc[562]
adiecto quod Glastoniam adiert et licentia petita et optenta a sacrista loci.
unam cirotecam plenam terre illius ubi dictus decurio quiescit. et monachi
sepeliuntur. sibi reportaret: alioquin[563] illicentiatus nichil attemptaret tactis
sacrosanctis premissa fideliter promisit adimplere. Quo[564] Glastonie pe-
ruento a sacrista qui pro[565] tempore fuerat uidelicet Michaele de Bekerie
non[566] tamen id modicum quod petiit sed pondus equinum benigne impetrauit quo[567] facto unam cirothecam terre predicte et aliam de cimiterio
ecclesie parochialis[568] secum delaturas[569] pariter impleuit. Quo[570] reuerse:
cirotheca terre parochialis ecclesie impletam: dicto[571] Soldano optulit ut[572]
sic conuentum obseruasset. Mox dicebat[573] Soldanus se fore deceptum.
asserens hec non de terra qua optauit ipso contrarium affirmante nullam
fidem sibi[574] adhibebat ullo sensu. tandem ipso super periurio quasi
conuicto et ultimo supplicio[575] fere mancipato: aliam cirothecam de terra
prelocuta[576] repletam statim pretendebat. Quo uiso mox[577] asseruit sibi esse

---

[555] JG: *Et cognoscens ipsum Anglicum solebat ab eo inquirere de circumstanciis terre et ritibus gentis illius. Demum inter cetera scicitatus est si*
[556] JG: *se dicente fuisse* omitted; *vero affirmante illam bene nosse et se esse de*
[557] JG: *dicta*
[558] JG: *pactum inierunt* omitted; *Soldanus pepigit cum eo*
[559] JG: *seu etiam* omitted; *et*
[560] JG: *ac*
[561] JG: *sibi in uia*
[562] JG: *si Glastoniam adire uellet, et, obtenta licencia a custode loci*
[563] JG: *alioquin . . . sacrosanctis* omitted; *At ille, prestito iuramento*
[564] JG: *Eo igitur Glastoniam perueniente*
[565] JG: *pro tempore fuerat uidelicet* omitted; *tunc erat*
[566] JG: *non . . . benigno* omitted; *de eadem terra quantum uoluit*
[567] JG: *Ex qua cirotecam vnam et*
[568] JG: *parochialis extra monasterium*
[569] JG: *pariter delaturas* A, P; *delaturis* T; *delaturus* (editor's emendation).
[570] JG: *Nec multo post, reuersus in terram sanctam, adiens predictum Soldanum cirotecam*
[571] JG: *dicto Soldano* omitted; *eidem*
[572] JG: *quasi sic conuencionem*
[573] JG: *Soldanus exardescens in iram asserebat se esse deceptum, dicens hanc non esse de terra quam optauit. Rainaldo autem contrarium*
[574] JG: *sibi* omitted.
[575] JG: *fere supplicio*
[576] JG: *prelocuta* omitted; *cimiterii monachorum*
[577] JG: *mox Soldanus*

30 satisfactum. in hec uerba prorumpens. parum norunt ibidem[578] degentes quanta uirtus in ista terra consistit. quia[579] uir inter mille homines quantuscumque enormis fuerit peccator: et ibidem sepultus. penas patietur infernales. Hiis[580] predicto modo completis dicto nuntio ad propria reuerso. que dictus Soldanus dicta terra quam portauit et de noticia utriusque quam
35 habebat quid dicendo asserebat dicto[581] sacriste iureiurando seriatim referebat. Hiis auditis:[582] dictus sacrista fratribus suis et aliis premissa[583] puplicauit. Ut crescente fama sanctitatis loci ibidem degentes fierent sanctiores et alii non degentes ad uenerationem loci in posterno proproniores.

35. Quomodo Monachus quidam de Sancto Dionisio de Glastonia referebat[584]

Ad comprobandam etiam antiquitatem ecclesie de qua prefati sumus paululum digrediamur. Monachus quidam Glastonie Godefridus nomine de
5 cuius epistola et hoc et quod subiungemus capitulum assumpsimus tempore. H(enrici) Blesensis abbatis Glastonie cum in pago Parisiacensi apud Sanctum Dionisium moraretur: senior quidam ex monachis interrogauit eum quo genus Vnde domo. Respondit[585] Normannum Britannie monasterio quod[586] Glastingeia dicitur: monachum. Pape inquit an[587] adhuc stat illa perpetue
10 uirginis et misericordie matris uetusta ecclesia? Stat inquit.[588] Tamen[589] ille lepido attactu capud G(odefridi) Glastonie[590] demulcens diu silencio suspensum tenuit ac si[591] demum ora resoluit. Hec gloriosissimi martiris Dionisii ecclesia[592] illa de qua te asseris eandem priuilegi[593] dignitate[594] habent. ista in Gallia illa in Britannia uno eodem tempore exorte a summo
15 et magno pontifice consecrate. Uno tamen gradu illa supereminet. Roma

---

578 JG: *ibi*
579 JG: *quia uir* omitted; *quis vix*
580 JG: *Post hec, dicto Rainaldo ut promissum fuerat liberato et ad natale solum reuerso, Glastoniam rediens, que <dixit> Soldanus de predicta terra*
581 JG: *predicto*
582 JG: *Hiis auditis* omitted; *Que omnia*
583 JG: *premissa* omitted.
584 Wm, p. 50, with the heading; JG, end of ch. 1, p. 10, without the heading, and with different phrasing until *interrogauit*.
585 JG: *respondit se esse*
586 JG: *quo* P.
587 JG: *an* omitted.
588 JG: *inquid Godefridus. Tum*
589 Wm: *tum,* written out in full.
590 JG: *Glastonie* omitted.
591 Wm, JG: *sic*
592 JG: *ecclesia et*
593 Wm, JG: *priuilegii*
594 Wm, JG: *dignitatem*

etenim secunda uocatur.⁵⁹⁵ Et hoc propter multitudinem sanctorum inibi requiescentium. quorum primus fuit Ioseph ab Arimathia ille nobilis decurio qui et Dominum sepeliuit pro cuius sepultura Dominus locum illum elegit atque benedixit.

20 [two blank lines]

36. De fundationibus ecclesiarum in insula Auallonie⁵⁹⁶

Primam igitur⁵⁹⁷ et uetustissimam in⁵⁹⁸ Anglia ecclesiam fecerunt⁵⁹⁹ .xii. discipuli apostolorum Philippe et Jacobi in⁶⁰⁰ insula Auallonie ut⁶⁰¹ prescriptum est.⁶⁰² Secundum: fecit Sanctus Dauid Meneuenensis episcopus⁶⁰³
5 in orientali parte antiquioris ecclesie in honorem⁶⁰⁴ beate Marie.⁶⁰⁵ quando uetustam⁶⁰⁶ ecclesiam dedicare disposuit.⁶⁰⁷ ac a Domino prohibitus est: eo quod ipse eandem dedicauerat. Terciam: fecerunt .xii. uiri a boreali parte Britannie uenientes. scilicet Morgen. Catgur. Cadmor. et ceteri superius memorati. et hec similiter erat sita in orientali parte uetuste ecclesie.
10 Quartam et maiorem construxit Ina rex in honore Domini saluatoris et apostolorum Petri et Pauli⁶⁰⁸ in orientali parte aliarum. atque⁶⁰⁹ primam et uetustissimam de nouo reparauit.

---

⁵⁹⁵ Wm has a different conclusion: *Cumque ab ore uiri penderet, ille, cui prouincia suscipiendorum fratrum erat commissa, inuitos ab inuicem non reuisuros seperauit. Sed hoc hactenus.* JG: *Cumque hec colloquerentur, ille cui cura suscipiendorum hospitum erat commissa inuitos ab inuicem non se reuisuros seperauit.*
⁵⁹⁶ Wm, ch. 40, towards the middle, p. 94. Heading: *Primum priuilegium Ine*; JG, p. 94, with numerous differences; Titus A.xix, fol. 23, line 13, immediately after the relics of St David. Heading: *De fundationibus omnium ecclesiarum in insula Auallonie*
⁵⁹⁷ JG: *denique*
⁵⁹⁸ Wm, JG: *in Anglia ecclesiam* omitted.
⁵⁹⁹ JG: *fecerunt per reuelacionem Domini*
⁶⁰⁰ Wm, JG: *in insula Auallonie* omitted.
⁶⁰¹ JG: *ut prescriptum est* omitted.
⁶⁰² Wm: *est, et hec sita fuit in occidentali parte aliarum.*
⁶⁰³ JG: *archiepiscopus*
⁶⁰⁴ JG: *honore*
⁶⁰⁵ JG: *Marie, ut pretactum est*
⁶⁰⁶ JG: *ueterem*
⁶⁰⁷ From here JG differs in wording, noting that the second church was called St Mary Minor, and mentioning Glasteing as builder of the third church.
⁶⁰⁸ JG goes directly from here to the chapel, as part of the same chapter.
⁶⁰⁹ Wm: *atque . . . reparauit* omitted. Ends with a reference to Ine's kinsman Mules, in whose honour he gave the church, and a long verse passage, inscribed in the church. That section comes at the end of JG, ch. 47, pp. 92–4, but the early part of the chapter records various donations of hides of land to the abbey, not earlier buildings.

37. De capella argentea quam ibidem fecit Ina cum suis uasis[610]

Fecit[611] etiam idem rex construere quamdam capellam ex auro et argento. cum ornamentis et uasis similiter aureis et argenteis. ac infra predictam[612] uetustam ecclesiam collocauit. Ad capellam illam itaque construendam:
5 duo milia et sexcenta et quadraginta libras argenti donauit. Et altare: ex ducentis et sexaginta quatuor libris auri erat. Calix cum patena: de .x. libris auri. Incensarum[613] .de .viij. libris. et .xx. mankis auri. Candelabra: ex .xii. libris et dimidia argenti. Coopertoria[614] librorum euangelii: de .xx. libris et .lx. mankis auri. Uasa aquaria et alia uasa altaris: ex .xvii. libris auri. Pelues:
10 de .uiij. libris auri. Uas ad aquam benedictam: ex .xx. libris argenti. Ymago[615] Domini et beate Marie et .xii. apostolorum: ex centum et .lxxv. libris argenti. et .xxviij. libris auri. Palla altaris et ornamenta sacerdotalia: undique auro et lapidibus preciosis subtiliter contexta. Hunc ergo thesaurum ob amorem sancte[616] Dei genetricis et uirginis Marie: monasterio Glastonie.
15 dictus rex contulit deuotissime. Insuper scripto regio terras. possessiones. et libertates eiusdem ecclesie confirmauit.[617]

38. De duabus piramidibus[618]

Illud quod clam pene omnibus est libenter predicarem. si ueritatem exculpere possem quid ille piramides sibi uelint que aliquantis pedibus eb ecclesia ueteusta posite cimiterium monachorum pretexunt. Procerior
5 sane[619] et propinquior ecclesie habet quinque tabulatus et altitidinem[620] .xxvi. pedum. Hec pre nimia uetustate et si ruinam minetur: habet tamen antiquitatis[621] nonnulla spectacula que plane possunt legi licet non plene possunt intelligi. In superiori enim[622] tabulatu est ymago pontificali scemate facta. In secundo ymago regiam pretendens pompam[623] et littere .her. sexi.

---

[610] Wm, pp. 96–98; Titus A.xix, fol. 23, lines 23ff. The heading is the same.
[611] JG, p. 96: *Infra quam eciam fecit construi capellam argenteam ex duobus milibus* . . . The information is the same, but much of the wording differs. Only major differences in information are noted.
[612] Wm: *predictam uetustam ecclesiam* omitted; *maiorem*
[613] Wm: *incensarium*; JG: *thuribulum*
[614] JG: *ornatus textuum euangelii*
[615] JG: *imagines*. Does this suggest that the image or images did not survive, or could not be identified, by John's time?
[616] Titus: *sancte Marie*
[617] Wm, JG: *confirmauit in hec uerba*. Ch. 42 in Wm, and ch. 49, p. 97, in John contain the text of the privilege of Ine. Titus stops here.
[618] Wm, p. 84, with heading; JG, p. 30, right after the list of kings, bishops and *duces* buried at Glastonbury. No heading. Begins: *Sunt eciam ibi due piramides que, aliquantis*
[619] JG: *sane* omitted.
[620] JG: *altitudine* T.
[621] JG: *nonnulla antiquitatis*
[622] JG: *enim* omitted.
[623] JG: *effigiem et hee litere*

10   et blysier.[624] In tercio. nichilominus nomina. Wencrest. Bantonmp. wineweng.[625] In quarto: .Hate. wulfred.[626] et Eanfled. In quinto:[627] qui et inferior est ymago et hec scriptura. Logwor.[628] Weslicas. et Bregden. Swelwes.[629] Hwingendes. Bern.[630] Altera uero piramis habet .xviii. pedes et iiii^{or} tabulatus. in quibus hec leguntur: Hedde episcopus et Bregored. et
15   Beorward. Quid hec significent non temere diffinio. sed ex suspicione colligo eorum inferius[631] in sarcofagis[632] lapideis et ligneis contineri ossa. quorum superius[633] leguntur nomina. Certe Logwor.[634] is pro[635] certo asseritur esse de cuius nomine Logweresbeorh[636] dicebatur qui nunc Monsacutus dicitur. Bregden a quo BrentaKnolle.[637] qui nunc Brentemers[638] dicitur.
20   Beorward[639] nichilominus abbas post Hemgiselum de quibus et de ceteris qui occurrere poterunt ex hinc liberiori campo exultabat oracio.[640]

Tablet 6

39. Nomina sanctorum in ecclesia Glastoniensi requiescetium sub breuitate collecta[641]

Hec sunt nomina sanctorum in Glastonia quiescentium breuiter collecta. Ibi requiescunt .xii. discipuli Sancti Philippe apostoli quorum primus et custos
5   fuit Ioseph ab Arimathia qui Dominum sepeliuit. Multi ex paganis per eos ad fidem Christi conuersi ac baptizati ibidem requiescunt. quorum propter

---

[624] Wm: *Blisyer*; JG: *Blisier*
[625] MS: from here on, all the 'w's except the initial letter of wulfred are wynns, notably different from the more rounded p. Wm: *Winethegn*
[626] JG: *Wlfred*
[627] JG: *quinto tabulatu*
[628] Wm: *Logwor*; JG: *Logior*
[629] Wm: *Syelwes*
[630] JG: *Berci*; *Bera* T.
[631] Wm, JG: *interius*
[632] Wm, JG: *sarcofagis lapideis et ligneis* omitted; *cauatis lapidibus*
[633] Wm, JG: *exterius*
[634] JG: *Logior, siue Logwor*.
[635] JG: *pro certo* omitted; *esse*
[636] JG: *Logweresburgh*
[637] JG: *Brentknol*
[638] Wm: *Brentamirse*; JG: *Brentmareis*
[639] Wm: *Beorwald*; JG: *Beorward abbas fuit huius loci*.
[640] William goes on to mention the series of abbots; John mentions and praises the bishops, dukes, abbots and other magnates who are nameless, but buried there.
[641] Like the similar list on Tablet 4, this seems to be loosely based on Wm, ch. 22, p. 70, *De diuersis reliquiis Glastonie repositis*. But this list seems to be compiled from material elsewhere on the tablets. The complete list of Patrick's companions, for instance, is found only in the Charter of St Patrick in the texts of Wm and JG; see Tablet 2, above, for the twelve disciples, Phaganus and Deruvianus, and Patrick.

eorum multitudinem non est numerus. De Sanctis Phagano et Deruuiano utrum ibi requiescunt uel inde repatriauerunt non inuenimus scriptum. Sed multi ex eorum discipulis ibidem requiescunt. qui per .cc.lxvii. annos
10 quidam post alios usque ad aduentum Sancti Patricii in prefata insula. sicut anachorite habitauerunt. Illic requiescunt .xii. sancti quos Sanctus Patricius sic nominatos ibidem inuenit.[642] Brumban. Hyregaan. Brenwal. Wencreth. Bamtonmeweng. Adelwlred. Loyor. Wellias. Breden. Swelwes. Hinloernius et alius Hin. Ibidem requiescunt Sanctus Patricius Hiberniensium
15 apostolus in Glastonia abbas primus. Sanctus Benignus eiusdem Sancti Patricii contuuernalis et discipulus. Sanctus Indractus cum sociis suis. Sanctus Gildas Britonum historiographyus. Sanctus Dauid Meneuensium Archiepiscopus.[643] Sanctus Dunstanus Cantuariensis archiepiscopus. Sanctus Aidanus episcopus cuius animam Sanctus Cuthbertus in celum deferri
20 uidit ab angelis. Sanctus Idus [sic] episcopus. Sanctus Ultanus episcopus frater Sancti Fursei. Sanctus Eadgarus rex. Sanctus Appollinaris martyr. Sanctus Vincentius martyr. Sanctus Ceolfridus. et Sanctus Ticca de septentrionali parte abbas. Sanctus Beda uenerabilis presbiter. corpora Sanctorum Benedicti. Esterwini. Sigfridi. Herberti. Wiornensium abbatum. Ossa
25 Hebbe. Begu. Borsili. horum corpora: uenerabilis abbas Ticca Glastoniam asportauit. Sanctus Guthlacus anachorita. Sanctus Columkilla de Hibernia. Sanctus Iltuith de Wallia. Sancta Wenta uirgo. Ossa Sancti Urbani <pape> et martiris. ossa sancti Anastasii martiris. ossa sancti Cesarii martitis. ossa sancti Benigni martiris. ossa Molani episcopi. Sancta Hilda uirgo et in
30 Witebi abbatissa. Sancta Ealfleda regina. Sancta Ealsuitha uirgo tota in carne et ossa integra. ossa Sancte Batildis Regine. ossa Sancte Mamille uirginis. Corpora sanctarum uirginum Ursule. et Darie. Crisante. Utilie. Lucei. Yalberge.[644] Gertrude. Omnes isti sancti prenotati in ecclesia continentur Glastoniensi. Sunt[645] uero preter istos sancti innumerabiles. quorum

---

[642] See above, Tablet 2, text 11.14–16.
[643] Wm, p. 70, puts Ticca's relics from Northumbria, Paulinus, and the Innocents before Dunstan. The order in which the following saints come varies considerably from that here, and omits saints mentioned here. Aidan is not mentioned, nor the list of Northumbrian saints from Ceolfrid to Borsil, nor is Edgar, nor Guthlac the anchorite, nor Vincent and Appollonius, nor Hilda nor Columkilla. Most of these are mentioned elsewhere in Wm; see notes to Tablet 4. But Wenta, virgin is not in Wm, which, however, includes some saints not given here: the martyr Besilius and the saints Mary, Martha and Cecilia. All of these, as well as numerous others, are in JG, p. 19. Compare Tablet 4, where many of these do appear.
[644] MS: The scribe's exemplar may have an initial wynn; the name is ordinarily *Walburga*.
[645] Though a commonplace, this sentence is very like the first sentence of JG, ch. 6, p. 20, De multorum sanctorum Particularibus reliquiis ibidem Reconditis *Sunt uero, preter superius enumeratos, sancti innumerabiles quorum particulares hic habentur reliquie quorum pleraque nomina apud nos scripta uidentur et plurimorum nomina scripta non habemus set scripts sunt in libro uite.*

35 particulariter ibi habentur reliquie. quorum plerique nomina in antiquis libris predicte ecclesie scripta uidentur.[646] Et plurimorum nomina: scripto expresa non habentur: sed sunt scripta in libro uite.

40. De capella Sanctorum Michaelis et Ioseph et sanctorum in cimiterio requiescentium.

Scientes[647] igitur sancti patres nostri[648] dignitatem et sanctitatem huius[649] sancti cimiterii quandam[650] capellam in eius medio construxerunt. quam in
5 honore Sancti Michaelis[651] et sanctorum inibi[652] requiescentium dedicari[653] fecerunt. sub cuius altare ossa[654] mortuorum ac sanctorum reliquias licet[655] incognitas in magna <. .> multitudine cumulauerunt. Et missam de[656] cimiterio in eo cotidie celebrari constituerunt.[657] Capella siquidem illa. anno Domini .M.CCC.lxxxii. pre uetustate pene consumpta. per preceptum Do-
10 mini Iohannis Chinnock abbatis in predictorum sanctorum honore. de nouo est reparata uidelicet in honore Sancti Michaelis animarum principis. Et in honore sanctorum in predictis cimiterio et capella requiescentium. Quorum[658] primus fuit Ioseph ab Arimathia ille nobilis decurio qui et Dominum sepeliuit. Ob cuius memoriam predictus abbas fieri fecit in eadem capella
15 tres ymagines quomodo Ioseph cum aduitorio Sancti Nichodemi Dominum de cruce deposuit atque sepeliuit. Et secundum illud quod ex traditione patrum didicimus. facta est ymago media secundum longitudinem stature corporis Christi. Qui det omnibus hic et ubique. In ipso quiescentibus. et omnibus pro eis orantibus uitam et requiem sempiternam. Amen.

---

[646] Wm: *quorum quedam nomina in antiquis ecclesie libris annotantur.*
[647] This paragraph is printed in Carley, 'A Grave Event', p. 142, n. 10, with modernized punctuation. It is also found in Titus A.xix, fols. 21v–22, as part of the history of the abbey; other bits of this section are on Tablet 3. Titus: *Igitur scientes*
[648] Titus: *nostri dignitatem et* omitted.
[649] Titus: *predicti*
[650] Titus: *quandam capellam* omitted.
[651] Titus: *Michaelis animarum principis*
[652] Titus: *ibidem*
[653] Titus: *dedicare*
[654] Titus: *ossa mortuorum ac* omitted.
[655] Titus: *licet . . . multitudine* omitted.
[656] Titus: *de cimiterio* omitted.
[657] Titus: *de . . . Quorum*, line 13 below, omitted.
[658] Titus: *Quorum quidem sanctorum omnium orimus extitit Sanctus Joseph ab Arimathia ob cuius memoriam dominus Johannes Chynnoke ipsam capellam renouauit.* Titus stops here; the epitaph of King Arthur follows.

41. Indulgentia morum pontificum legatorum archiepiscoporum episcoporum Glastoniensi concesse[659]

Sancti Phaganus et Deruuianus impetarunt ab Eleutherio <papa> .x. annos.
Sanctus Patricius impetrauit a Celestino <papa> .xii. annos.
5 Idem Sanctus Patricius dedit Centum dies.
Alexander <papa> quartus Unum annum et Quadraginta dies.
Innocentius <papa> quartus. Viginti dies.
Nicholaus legatus Anglie et Thosculanensis episcopus .xxx. dies
Item idem. Viginti dies.
10 Willemus legatus Anglie et Eliensis episcopus. Sexaginta dies.
Octobonis legatus Anglie. Quadraginta dies.
Sanctus Dunstanus Cantuariensis Archiepiscopus. Centum dies.
Lanfrancus Cantuariensis archiepiscopus. Centum dies.
Radolphus Cantuariensis Archiepiscopus. Quindecim dies.
13 Theobaldus Cantuariensis Archiepiscopus. Quindecim dies.
Sanctus Thomas Cantuariensis Archiepiscopus. Centum dies.
Ricardus Cantuariensis Archbiepiscopus. Triginta dies.
Iohannes Cantuariensis Archiepiscopus. Quindecim dies.
Walterus Eboracensis Archiepiscopus. Tredecim dies.
20 Dauid Casellensis Archiepiscopus. Decem dies.
Henricus Dublinensis Archiepiscopus. Triginta dies.
Iohannes Dublinensis Archiepiscopus. Triginta dies.
Bernard Ragusine Archiepiscopus. Septuaginta dies.
Item idem. Quadraginta dies.
25 Wilelmus Ragensis Archiepiscopus. Viginti dies.
Iohannes Mucisensis Archiepiscopus. Quadraginta dies.
Henricus Tarentinus Archiepiscopus. Quadraginta dies.
Alexander Couentrensis et Lichfeldensis Episcopus. Viginti dies.
Ricardus Dunelmensis Episcopus. Viginti dies.
30 Eustachius Eliensis Episcopus. Quindecim dies.
Willemus Exoniensis Episcopus. Quindecim dies.
Alius Willemus Exoniensis Episcopus. Quadraginta dies.
Item ibidem. Viginti dies.
Petrus Exoniensis Episcopus. Quadraginta dies.

[659] MS: The indulgence list is in two columns; I have numbered the second column consecutively with the first. Most of the entries have full stops between the name of the bishop and the indulgence, and another full stop at the end of the entry. Sometimes it is difficult to tell whether there was a full stop or not. I have regularized the scribe's usual practice, and put full stops after names, around all roman numerals, and at the ends of all lines. The words for numbers almost always have initial capital letters; I have normalized to capitalize the initial letters of all numbers written as words; *dies* is always written in the lower case. The numbers written in Roman numerals are in general not capitalized. For the identification of bishops, see Part 2, 4. Glossary.

35 Item idem. Quadraginta dies.
    Item idem. Quadraginta dies.
    Item idem. Quadraginta dies.
    Item idem. Quadraginta dies.
    Item idem. Viginti dies.
40 Item idem. Viginti dies.
    Thomas Exoniensis Episcopus. Quadraginta dies.
    Item idem. Quindecim dies.
    Egidius Herefordensis Episcopus. Viginti dies.
    Willelmus Herefordensis Episcopus. Quadraginta dies.
45 Item idem. Viginti dies.
    Ricardus Herefordensis Episcopus. Quadraginta dies.
    Iohannes Norwicensis Episcopus. Viginti dies.
    Laurentius Roffensis Episcopus. Quindecim dies.
    Brithwoldus Saresburiensis Episcopus. Centum dies.
50 Willelmus Saresburiensis Episcopus. Tresdecim dies
    Nicholaus Saresburiensis Episcopus. Quindecim dies.
    Henricus Wigorniensis Episcopus. Viginti dies.
    Walterus Wygorneiensis Episcopus. Quindecim dies.
    Item idem. Viginti dies.
55 Item idem. Decem dies.
    Ricardus Wyntoniensis Episcopus. Viginti dies.
    Willelmus Wyntoniensis Episcopus. Viginti quinque dies.
    Item idem. Viginti dies.
    Iohannes Wyntoniensis Episcopus. Viginti dies.
60 Alius Iohannes Wyntoniensis Episcopus. Quadraginta dies.
    Item idem: Viginti dies.
    Elyas Landavensis. Episcopus. Quindecim dies.
    Item idem. Viginti dies.
    Iohannes primus Landavensis Episcopus. Quindecim dies.
65 Alius Iohannes Landauensis Episcopus. Quadraginta dies.
    Willelmus primus Landeuensis Episcopus. Triginta dies.
    Willelmus secundus Landauensis Episcopus. Viginti dies.
    Willelmus quartus Landeuensis Episcopus. Viginti dies.
    Willelmus quintus Landeuensis Episcopus. Viginti dies.

    [column 2]
70 Item idem:[660] Viginti dies.
    Geruasius Meneuensis Episcopus: Quadraginta dies.
    Dauid Meneuensis Episcopus: Quadraginta dies.

---

[660] MS: The punctuation after the name of the bishop changes from a full stop to a punctus flexus for column 2.

Iohannes Corkagensis Episcopus: Quadraginta dies.
Item idem: Viginti dies.
75 Gilbertus Euachdunensis Episcopus: Quadraginta dies.
Item idem: Quadraginta dies.
Walterus Ossoriensis Episcopus: Tresdecim dies.
Michael Ossoriensis Episcopus: Quadraginta dies.
Item idem: Viginti dies.
80 Robertus Waterfordensis Episcopus: Decem dies.
Stephanus Waterfordensis Episcopus: Decem dies.
Item idem: Decem dies.
Item idem: Viginti dies.
Item idem: Viginti dies.
85 Item idem: Quadraginta dies.
Walterus Waterfordensis Episcopus: Viginti dies.
Item idem: Viginti dies.
Item idem: Tresdecim dies.
Maurus Ameliensis Episcopus: Quadraginta dies.
90 Iocelinus Ardnacensis Episcopus: Quindecim dies.
Pancras\s/ius Botontinus Episcopus: Quadraginta dies.
Alanus Clonensis[661] Episcopus: Decem dies.
Romanus Croensis Episcopus: Quadraginta dies.
Lambertus Aquinensis Episcopus: Quadraginta dies.
95 Matheus Veglenensis[662] Episcopus: Quadraginta dies.
Gilbertus Dunkeldensis Episcopus: Viginti dies.
Item idem. Tresdecim dies.
Radulphus Kildarensis Episcopus: Tresdecim dies.
Augustinus Laodicensis Episcopus: Quadraginta dies.
100 Robertus Laornensis Episcopus: Decem dies.
Perronus Larinensis Episcopus: Quadraginta dies.
Thomas Lichlinensis Episcopus: Quadraginta dies.
Item idem. Quindecim dies.
Robertus Limiricensis Episcopus: Quadraginta dies.
105 Item idem: Quindecim dies.
Item idem: Tresdecim dies.
Thomas Lismorensis Episcopus: Quadraginta dies.
Item idem: Tresdecim dies.
Donatus Limnicensis Episcopus: Quadraginta dies.
110 Hugo Midensis Episcopus: Viginti dies.

[661] MS: *Elonensis*, but no such bishopric exists. Cloyne, in Ireland, had two bishops named Alan.
[662] MS: *Neglenensis*, with a face drawn in the initial N, but there is no such bishopric. Veglen had a bishop Matthew.

Item idem. Decem dies.
Willelmus Monoplitanis Episcopus: Quadraginta dies.
Ciprianus Bouensis⁶⁶³ Episcopus: Quadraginta dies.
Brithwius Welnensis Episcopus: Centum dies.
Sauericus Bathoniensis et Wellensis Episcopus .C. dies Insuper omnes dies relaxionis penitentie Glastoniensis ecclesie auctoritate pontificali confirmauit.
Rogerus Bathoniensis Episcopus: Triginta nouem dies.
Willelmus primus Bathoniensis et Wellensis Episcopus: Viginti dies.
Item idem. Viginti dies.
Item idem. Viginti dies.
Item idem. Decem dies.
Willelmus secundus Bathoniensis et Wellensis Episcopus: Viginti dies.
Willelmus tertius Bathoniensis et Wellensis Episcopus: Viginti dies.
Robertus Bathoniensis et Wellensis Episcopus: Viginti dies.
Item idem. Quindecim dies.
Willelmus Bathoniensis et Wellensis Episcopus: Viginti dies.
Walterus Bathonensis et Wellensis Episcopus: Quadraginta dies.
Item idem: Quadraginta dies.
Iohannes Bathoniensis et Wellensis Episcopus: Quadraginta dies dedit et omnes indulgentias a quibuscumque Pontificalis huc concessas diocesana auctoritate ratificauit. Ad hec anni triginta unus et dies quinquaginta quatuor. capellam Sancti Michaelis in vicino monte sitam et huic loco annexam pia deuotione uisitantibus: a diuerso pontificibus specialiter conceduntur.

Summa totius indulgentie Glastoniensis ecclesie et montane capelle: sexaginta quatuor anni ac centum nonaginta et septem dies.⁶⁶⁴

---

[663] MS: *Nouensis*, but there is no such bishopric. Bova, in Italy, had a bishop Cyprian.
[664] This addition is correct, if even the extra days for leap years have been counted every fourth year.

VI

'ARTHUR REDIVIVUS': POLITICS AND PATRIOTISM IN REFORMATION SCOTLAND

David Allan

It has in recent years become ever clearer that the Arthurian corpus occupied a particularly prominent position in the developing historiographical controversy between Scotland and England. A major achievement of modern scholarship has been to draw attention to the hotly-contested status of Arthurian materials, and particularly of the *Prophetiae Merlini*, in the period following the outbreak of the Wars of Independence in 1285. We now see plainly that Arthur's growing identification with English dominion in the British Isles, together with Merlin's portentous vision of its future re-establishment, contributed seminally to the construction of an ideology legitimizing the imperialism of the southern kingdom.[1] Nowhere was the vital association of Arthurianism with the forcible re-unification of Britain by an expansionist Plantagenet dynasty rendered more visible than in Edward I's intelligently symbolic convening of latter-day Round Tables during his triumphant progresses through the brow-beaten Celtic fringe: at Nevyn in Caernarvonshire in 1284 and again at Falkirk in 1302, for example, *Malleus Scotorum* underlined the potent Merlinic credentials of

---

I have benefitted in the preparation of this essay from the advice and assistance of a number of scholars, most notably Dr John Withrington.

[1] See most recently, for example, J. P. Carley and J. Crick, 'Constructing Albion's Past: An Annotated Edition of *De Origine Gigantum*', *Arthurian Literature* XIII (1995), 41–114; a good overview is W. Ullman, 'On the Influence of Geoffrey of Monmouth in English History', in his *The Church and the Law in the Earlier Middle Ages: Selected Essays* (London, 1975), pp. 257–76. Geoffrey's towering presence in English historiography is best summarized by E. D. Kennedy in 'XII: Chronicles and Other Historical Writing', *A Manual of the Writings in Middle English*, ed. A. E. Hartung (New Haven, 1989), 8, and in the prefaces to the *Historia Regum Britannie of Geoffrey of Monmouth*, 5 vols., ed. N. Wright (Cambridge, 1985–91).

his recent military conquests through the living evocation of an historical Arthurian community.[2]

Such public demonstrations of Edward's claim to the Scottish throne were pursued vigorously in a war which saw hammer and pen wielded with equal fervour and ferocity. England's right to dominion over Scotland was asserted in 1301 in a letter to Pope Boniface VIII, in which Arthur's supposed subjugation of the Scots was cited as evidence that fealty was due: according to Geoffrey of Monmouth, it was argued, the realm was held by Auguselus only in his capacity as a vassal of Arthur.[3] Not surprisingly, such claims had met with an indignant Scottish response: Baldred Bisset, one of Scotland's commissioners in Rome, rejected Edward's tenuous case on the specific grounds that Arthur was a notorious illegitimate who had disinherited the worthy Mordred.[4] With the fall of Llewelyn ap Gruffyd in 1282 and the supposed ceding of Arthur's crown to Edward at Caernarvon, England had little more to fear from its troublesome neighbour to the west. The struggle against Scotland, however, would last for centuries to come, and, in this always acrimonious conflict, Arthur would continue to play a significant part.[5]

Nevertheless, insufficient attention has perhaps hitherto been accorded to a later and no less perplexing phase in Anglo-Scottish relations, the sixteenth and early seventeenth centuries. This, after all, was the period during which Scotland began to witness the emergence of indigenous support for political union with England, at the same time as falling under the influence of Jean Calvin's particularly disruptive strain of Protestant

[2] R. S. Loomis, 'Edward I – Arthurian Enthusiast', *Speculum* 28 (1953), 114–27.

[3] E. K. Chambers, *Arthur of Britain* (London, 1927; repr. 1966), p. 128. See also A. Gransden, *Historical Writing in England, i, c.* 550–*c.* 1307 (New York, 1982), pp. 441–3.

[4] For Bisset's *Processus Baldredi contra figmenta regis Angliae*, see F. Alexander, 'Late Medieval Attitudes to the Figure of King Arthur: A Reassessment', *Anglia* 93 (1975), 19. That copies of the text of the *Processus* were circulating in Scotland in the manuscripts of Walter Bower's *Scotichronicon* of the mid-fifteenth century no doubt helped maintain a sense of injured Scottish pride. It was doubtless with similar fervour and a desire to maintain the status quo that copies of Edward I's correspondence on the subject were included by John Hardynge in London, British Library, Lansdowne 204, a presentation copy of his own *Chronicle* that was seemingly given to Henry VI in 1457. The transformation of Mordred from treacherous villain to national hero was first remarked upon by R. H. Fletcher, *The Arthurian Material in the Chronicles, Especially Those of Great Britain and France* (Boston, 1906), p. 241.

[5] Edward's supposed disinterment of the tombs of Arthur and Guinevere at Glastonbury on 19 April 1278 was, of course, the most potent means whereby both to lay to rest the myth of the returning hero and to cast the king himself as 'legitimate successor to the Arthurian imperium' [J. C. Parson, 'The Second Exhumation of King Arthur's Remains', *Arthurian Literature* XII (1993), 176]. For a discussion of the role played by Arthurian prophecy in English imperialism, see J. R. S. Phillips, 'Edward II and the Prophets', in *England in the Fourteenth Century*, ed. W. M. Ormrod (Woodbridge, 1986), pp. 189–201.

theology. Both of these developments were radical departures in Scottish public life. And they lent a new dimension to contemporary political discourse, throughout this period making the instantiation of the Merlinic historic vision – through a much closer relationship with Protestant England – seem first a desirable possibility, then a realistic probability, and finally, in 1603, a problematical reality. This paper is an attempt by a historian of Scotland's political thought and intellectual culture to assess some of the uses to which Arthur and Merlin were being put by Scotsmen addressing national politics during what one scholar has appositely described as 'the long sixteenth century'.[6] For it is my chief contention in what follows that the period between the early 1540s and approximately 1615 saw a substantial re-appraisal of the Arthurian tradition by influential Scottish writers, many of them closely associated with the wider development of pro-Reformation and unionist political argument. Although hitherto largely unexplored by modern critics, their contributions to the re-evaluation of Arthurian literature and scholarship were substantially to moderate what had often been Scottish suspicion of Arthur and hostility towards Merlin.[7] In the process, I shall argue that they also helped prepare the ground ideologically for the self-confident Jacobean re-assertion of British imperialism during the early years of the seventeenth century.

I

The principal significance of the humanist historiography introduced into Scotland in the sixty years prior to the Reformation lay in its conscious rejection of precisely the kinds of myth and legend which Geoffrey of Monmouth had once so shamelessly purveyed. Distrust of the legend of Arthur certainly seems at first sight to have increased with the gradual, though eventually triumphant, emergence of the new scholarship in Scotland during the early decades of the sixteenth century.[8] With obvious relish,

---

[6] M. Lynch, *Scotland: A New History* (London, 1991), p. 169.
[7] For recent discussions of Scottish attitudes to Arthur, see Alexander, 'Late Medieval Scottish Attitudes'; S. Kelly, 'The Arthurian Material in the *Scotichronicon* of Walter Bower', *Anglia* 97 (1979), 431–8; R. J. Goldstein, *The Matter of Scotland. Historical Narrative in Medieval Scotland* (Lincoln, NE, 1993), esp. pp. 148–9; J. Withrington, 'The Arthurian Epitaph in Malory's *Morte Darthur*', *Arthurian Literature* VII (1987), 103–44. For the acrimonious Anglo-Scottish diplomatic background to Hardynge's *Chronicle*, see E. D. Kennedy, 'John Hardynge and the Holy Grail', *Arthurian Literature* VIII (1988), 185–206.
[8] The emergence of humanism in Scotland has received some attention, as in J. Durkan, 'The Beginnings of Humanism in Scotland', *Innes Review* 4 (1953), 5–24; J. MacQueen, 'Some Aspects of the Early Renaissance in Scotland', *Forum for Modern Language*

Hector Boece, author of the *Scotorum Historiae* (1527), portrayed the king of Britain as the product of the 'necromancy of Merlyne', as 'gottin in adultery' and as merely 'in gloir of marciall dedis, na less wailyeand than uther princes of Britan'.[9] Worse, Boece rejected the notion that Arthur had even conquered Scotland. Instead, flatly contradicting 'Galfride, writer of the History of Britonis', he claimed that Arthur had died in battle on the River Humber, condignly despatched by King Lothus for an act of base treachery towards his former Scottish allies (380). John Mair, too, the Parisian divine whose *Historia Maioris Britanniae, tam Angliae quam Scotiae* (1521), with its plangent call for reconciliation between the warring kingdoms, has properly been regarded as the foundation of critical documentary scholarship in Scotland, as well as of intelligently-argued unionism, seems to have been scarcely more attracted to the dubious Arthurian mythology retailed by Geoffrey and his English copyists.[10] Drawing heavily upon the intellectually-fashionable theory of natural law to hammer home the irrefutable logic of unionism, the Sorbonnist, a celebrated master of the latest neo-scholastic analytical techniques, could bring himself to utter not a single kind word in relation to the hoary Galfridian tradition. For the judicious Mair, as Arthur Williamson has argued, ' "Merlin's knotty sayings" were so patently ambiguous as to mean nearly anything – as the use of them made by Caxton and the English chroniclers made only too evident.'[11]

Yet a slightly later Scottish exponent of unionist propaganda, the mysterious James Henrisoun, already offers a clear though intriguing contrast with John Mair and all that had gone before (102). Henrisoun was an Edinburgh burgess who enjoyed lucrative commercial links with the Netherlands and particularly with the port of Middleburg. Like so many other significant contributors to the Scottish Reformation, he had been affected deeply by his Continental travels and had early been converted to the Protestant cause. By 1547, as Scotland's anxious Catholic government struggled to resist the rising tide of religious reformism which had followed James V's untimely demise in 1542, Henrisoun was in exile. Resident in London in the employ of the duke of Somerset, Protector to the infant Edward VI of England, he appears to have been charged with the production

---

Studies III (1967), 201–22; also *Humanism in Renaissance Scotland*, ed. J. MacQueen (Edinburgh, 1990).

[9] *The Chronicles of Scotland Compiled by Hector Boece, Translated into Scots by John Bellenden, 1531*, STS, 2 vols. (Edinburgh, 1938), I, 360, 376.

[10] John Mair, *A History of Greater Britain as well England as Scotland*, ed. and trans. A. Constable (Edinburgh, 1892).

[11] A. H. Williamson, *Scottish National Consciousness in the Age of James VI: the Apocalypse, the Union, and the Shaping of Scotland's Public Culture* (Edinburgh, 1979), p. 101.

of polemical literature designed to reconcile his fellow Scots to the difficult idea of a union of Protestant co-religion between the two kingdoms.[12] In this capacity, Henrisoun was precociously to register a profound shift in contemporary political consciousness, becoming probably the first Scotsman to refer, and with singular comfort, to a political entity called 'Great Britain'.[13] Certainly his *The Godly and Golden Booke for concorde of England and Scotland* (1548), which recalled the irresistible logic of Mair, employs the persuasive rhetoric of natural law in arguing for the advantages of a Protestant, Edwardian union of Scotland and England: 'By conjunctyon of matrymony', Henrisoun glibly enthused, 'malice is extyncte, amyte is embraced, and indisolvable aliance and consanguinite is procured!'[14]

But of more particular interest to Arthurian scholars will be Henrisoun's slightly earlier *An Exhortacion to the Scottes, to conforme themselfes to the honorable, Expedient, & godly Union betwene the two Realmes of Englande & Scotlande* (1547), published in London.[15] In *An Exhortacion*, Henrisoun sets out comprehensively to demolish the ideological underpinnings of Scottish independence. This had long rested on dubious national foundation-myths whose principal feature was, of course, a denial of the English claim to enjoy an ancient and unbroken dominion over the whole island.[16] Now departing from Mair, who had simply incorporated the traditional Galfridian story into his *Historia*, Henrisoun contemptuously cast aside the legend of Britain's original settlement by the daughters of King Diocletian, king of Syria (213).[17] Derision was also heaped upon other conventional claims of historic national autonomy, with the argumentative Henrisoun displaying again a formidable aptitude for tortuous scholastic logic. He

---

[12] Henrisoun has had limited coverage, though the exception is M. H. Merriman, 'James Henrisoun and "Great Britain": British Union and the Scottish Commonweal', in *Scotland and England, 1286–1815*, ed. R. A. Mason (Edinburgh, 1987), pp. 85–112. On the anglophile party in Scotland see also Merriman, 'The Assured Scots: Scottish Collaborators with England during the Rough Wooing', *Scottish Historical Review* XLVII (1968), 10–34. The associated pamphlet barrage is referred to in his 'War and Propaganda during the "Rough Wooing" ', *Scottish Tradition* 9/10 (1979/80), 20–30.

[13] The classic discussion of the origins of the terminology of 'Great Britain' remains S. T. Bindoff, 'The Stuarts and their Style', *English Historical Review* 9 (1945), 192–216.

[14] James Henryson, *The Godly and Golden Booke for Concorde of England and Scotland*, reprinted in *Calendar of Scottish Papers*, 3 vols. (Edinburgh, 1898), I, pp. 141–5.

[15] Again displaying the uncertain spelling of his name, this appeared as James Harryson, *An Exhortation to the Scottes to conforme themselfes to the honorable, Expedient, & godly Union betweene the two Realmes of Englande and Scotland* (London, 1547) but is fortunately accessible in *The Complaynt of Scotlande*, ed. J. A. H. Murray, EETS, e.s. 17 (London, 1872), pp. 207–36.

[16] On the ideological background to Henrisoun, see R. A. Mason, 'Scotching the Brut: Politics, History and National Myth in Sixteenth-Century Britain', in his ed. *Scotland and England*, pp. 60–84.

[17] Cf. Mair, *History of Greater Britain*, pp. 2–3.

agreed, disarmingly enough, with the traditional Scottish chronicles, which claimed that '[the] Scottes wer then in Britayn (as our writers alledge)'. But he then fell mercilessly on his unsuspecting victims: 'then wer thei subiectes to Constantine, because the stories be evident, that he had al Britayn in possession' (218).

In *An Exhortacion*, however, Henrisoun also confronts the second central tenet of late medieval Scottish historiography. This was the assertion that no historical ruler of Scotland had ever done homage or acknowledged his subordination to the kings of southern Britain – and least of all to any prince named Arthur. This argument, revolutionary for a Scottish polemicist, involved Henrisoun's unquestioning acceptance of the fundamental historicity of Arthur's *imperium*. But it also encouraged him to go somewhat further. It led him to concede, without equivocation, the clearly inferior feudal position in which the Galfridian legend had always insisted that King Lothus, father of Gawain and ruler of southern Scotland, had stood in relation to the peerless Arthur. There simply can be no doubt, says Henrisoun, about the 'sundry homages and recongicious of subieccion, made to Arthur, and other kynges of the Britaynes' (225).

Henrisoun's inventive and highly tendentious references to the Arthurian tradition in fact took their place alongside other pro-unionist propaganda emanating both from his fellow Scottish polemicists like John Eldar and from their English collaborators such as William Patten.[18] In each case, the impetus for closer relations with England in the 1540s appears to have stemmed from a potent confluence of growing Protestant devotion and instinctive opposition to any continuation, under the infant Mary's guardians and advisors (who included the infamous Cardinal David Beaton), of Scotland's 'Auld Alliance' with Catholic France: as Eldar puts it in his provocative *A Proposal For Uniting Scotland with England* (1544), addressed to Henry VIII, the cause of his writing is simply Scotland's still, in the years since 1542, 'being reuled as it was in [James V's] tyme, be the advyse of the Cardinall, associatt with proud papisticall buschops' (7).[19]

---

[18] John Eldar had been responsible for *A Proposal For Uniting Scotland with England, Addressed to King Henry VIII* (1544), reprinted in *Miscellany of the Bannatyne Club*, I (Edinburgh, 1827), pp. 1–18. William Patten wrote *The Expedicion into Scotland, of the Most Woorthely Fortunate Prince, Edward, Duke of Somerset* (1548), reprinted in [Sir] J[ohn] G[raham] Dalyell, *Fragments of Scotish History* (Edinburgh, 1798), Sigs. Li(r)–Zii(r).

[19] As A. M. Stewart notes, the 'ideological warfare' to which these polemicists were contributing was 'particularly divisive and complex in Scotland because of the mixing of politics and religion', *The Complaynt of Scotland (c.1550)*, ed. A. M. Stewart, STS, 4th series, 11 (Edinburgh, 1979), p. xxxiv. For a modern account of Scottish politics in the 1540s and 1550s, encompassing both Mary's minority and her personal rule, see Lynch, *Scotland*, pp. 202–7.

Outspoken views of this kind, not least because they were being articulated with the open support and encouragement of ambitious English governments, naturally attracted the most vociferous Scottish opposition. This included the well-known text *The Complaynt of Scotland* (c. 1548), attributed to Robert Wedderburn, a St Andrews graduate and minister at Dundee, in which the uncritical and damaging endorsement of Arthurian materials by anglophile controversialists like Henrisoun and Eldar duly attracted special attention.

In Chapter X of *The Complaynt*, for example, it is pertinent that the author 'declaris', as he puts it, 'quhou the inglismen gifis vane credens to the prophesies of merlyne' (64). *The Complaynt* identifies no individual opponent. But it seems clear that the infamous 'oratours of Ingland' must have included Henrisoun among Wedderburn's Scottish contemporaries, as well as a train of medieval English chroniclers labouring in the style of Geoffrey. Their error, insists Wedderburn, had been to give 'ferme credit to diverse prophane propheseis of merlyne and til uther ald corrupit vaticinaris'. Moreover, those prophecies 'hes affermit in there rusty ryme that scotland and ingland sal be undir ane prince' (65). The proponents of union had interpreted these untrustworthy prognostications so partially, so mischievously, and so blatantly 'to there aven affectione', that Wedderburn regarded them as a worthless guide to contemporary national politics. Even worse, Merlin's new Scottish mouthpieces had overlooked a rather more important portent in Higden's *Polychronicon*: England and Scotland will indeed be united 'undir ane prince', he concludes, twisting the argument against the neo-Arthurians, because the English will in due course themselves suffer 'conquest be the scottis' (67).

Wedderburn's anguished plea, probably the work of an anti-unionist himself not unsympathetic to the Protestant cause, neatly underlines that a vigorously anglophilic literature had been generated by his fellow countrymen, provoked by the policies of the young Queen's French Catholic guardians. This literature may well have been influenced – we can reasonably conclude that the London-based Henrisoun was so guided – by the growing currency in mid-sixteenth-century England of political prophecy not merely as a way of describing but as a method for influencing the conduct of public affairs.[20] Whatever its relationship to English literary trends, by the end of the 1540s such material was exhibiting in Scotland an

---

[20] Our understanding of the significance of prophetic writings in Tudor England has been greatly aided by the recent work of Sharon Jansen, whose observation that 'by the sixteenth century, political prophecies are not simply a way of understanding the present. They have become a way of shaping the present', may well be applicable to the Scottish context also: *Political Protest and Prophecy Under Henry VIII* (Woodbridge, 1991), p. 18.

eagerness not only to accept the authenticity of Arthur's ancient British dominion but to assert the essential veracity of the associated Merlinic prophecies themselves. This unprecedented turn of events, as Wedderburn's acute discomfiture shows, was worrying enough. Yet there are further indications amid the literature of the even more turbulent 1550s that the increasingly confident use of Arthurian materials and motifs actually measured the growing political weight and cultural authority of these hitherto marginalized radical forces within the country.[21] One largely unnoticed work illustrates this momentous development with particular power. It has habitually been dismissed by students of Scottish literature for its rather laboured style and its anachronistic commitment to the dated *genre* of allegorical romance.[22] Yet John Rolland of Dalkeith's *The Sevin Seages; Translatit out of prois in Scottis meter*, published in Edinburgh in 1578 but composed, according to references in the colophon, in or around the fateful and revolutionary year of 1560, contains significant further employment of Arthurian materials by an author who was almost certainly sympathetic to the Reformation and who was also probably prepared as a consequence to entertain the very serious possibility of closer relations with England.[23]

II

Rolland's *The Sevin Seages* is not the earliest Scottish redaction of this ubiquitous frame: the Asloan Manuscript, dated *c.* 1515, provides a rather different text, recently edited by Catharine van Buuren, though one which still makes an interesting comparison with Rolland's efforts.[24] His derived from the Latin prose *Historia Septem Sapientum Romae* (the earliest extant manuscript of which is contained in an Innsbruck codex dated 1342). This was probably mediated through a lost London reprint of 1550 (attributed to

---

[21] The emergence of British unionism in early Reformation Scotland remains very largely a closed book, though there have been two attempts to prise it open: A. H. Williamson, 'Scotland, Antichrist and the Invention of Great Britain', in *New Perspectives on the Politics and Culture of Early Modern Scotland*, ed. J. Dwyer, R. A. Mason, and A. Murdoch (Edinburgh, 1982), pp. 34–58; and Mason's own 'The Scottish Reformation and the Origins of Anglo-British Imperialism', in his ed. *Scots and Britons: Scottish Political Thought and the Union of 1603* (Cambridge, 1994), pp. 161–86. I am greatly indebted to both discussions in what follows.

[22] E.g. 'He was the last of his school. He versified a romance and composed an allegory long after these fashions were outworn', J. M. Smith, *The French Background of Middle Scots Literature* (Edinburgh, 1934), p. 28.

[23] Iohne Rolland, *The Sevin Seages, Translatit out of prois in Scottis meter* ... (Edinburgh, 1578), republished as John Rolland of Dalkeith, *The Seven Sages in Scottish Metre*, ed. D. Laing, Bannatyne Club (Edinburgh, 1837).

[24] *The Buke of the Sevyne Sagis: A Middle Scots Version of the Seven Sages of Rome, Edited from the Asloan Manuscript (NLS ACC. 4233), c.1515*, ed. C. van Buuren (Leiden, 1982).

Copland) and can be traced to its original, Wynkyn de Worde's translation of c. 1520.[25] These specifically English provenances may well repay detailed research, for they perhaps again hint at the existence of a matrix of anglophile connections – literary, political, commercial – by means of which more favourable attitudes towards Arthuriana were being injected into mid-sixteenth-century Scottish intellectual culture. The principal significance of this text, however, lies in Rolland's skilful treatment of the traditional Merlinic tale of *Sapientes* and in his decision to add a collection of pointed moral essays to each of the familiar stories. These enable him to offer a striking commentary on Scottish public affairs at the very moment of the country's permanent political and religious re-orientation.

Rolland firstly places *Sapientes* in sequence as 'The Fourt Taill of the Emprice'. It thus immediately secures a greater prominence than it is able to achieve as the seventh tale both in Asloan and in the major 'Southern Version' available within the Auchinleck manuscript (107).[26] Rolland's basic framing of the tale also has other thought-provoking features, of which Robert Wedderburn might well have been justifiably suspicious and Henrisoun, perhaps, equally admiring. As elsewhere in his *Sevin Seages*, for example, the wiles and deceits of the 'Emprice' – or of 'our Quene' as he suddenly and unguardedly refers to her in the *moralitas* – brook large in *Sapientes* (122). In Scotland in 1560, with the Protestant Lords of the Congregation and John Knox's reformist clergy leading both a civil rebellion and a campaign of moral vilification against Mary Queen of Scots, such an emphasis on feminine untrustworthiness and malignancy was particularly pointed. Further enhanced by Rolland's insistent harping upon her being 'Full of dissait, with fenyeit fals plesance', indeed a veritable 'mirrour of mischance', it had a clear subversive resonance. And, in the light of the disturbed political conditions in Scotland at the time of its composition, Rolland's highly sympathetic treatment of the Merlinic substance of *Sapientes* is of even greater interest.

The circumstances described at the opening of this allegorical tale directly recall for us the tenor of John Eldar's earlier objections to contemporary Scottish governance, overseen and overborne, in the jaundiced view of the Edwardian 'oratours of Ingland', by Francophilic courtiers, papist

---

[25] The provenance of Rolland's text is in part the subject of G. Buchner, *Die Historia Septem Sapientum nach der Innsbrucker Handschrift v.J. 1342. Nebst einer Untersuchung uber die Quelle der Sevin Sages der Johne Rolland von Dalkeith* (Leipzig, 1889). See also *The Seven Sages of Rome*, ed. K. Campbell (Boston, Mass., 1907). On Scotland's southern literary connections in general see G. Kratzmann, *Anglo-Scottish Literary Relations 1430–1550* (Cambridge, 1980).

[26] Cf. *The Buke*, ed. van Buuren; also *The Seven Sages of Rome (Southern Version); Edited from the MSS*, ed. K. Brunner, EETS, o.s. 191 (London, 1932).

advisors and self-serving sycophants.[27] Rolland's empress spins a lurid tale of a royal court in the thrall of the seven 'Maisters', by whose 'sorcerie, Inchantment and cunning' the emperor – conventionally Herod but in Rolland's text usefully and ambiguously un-named – is beguiled and, literally, blinded (110). Like the administration of the dowager Mary of Guise-Lorraine in Edinburgh between 1554 and 1560, which had surrounded the young Queen and was believed by its Protestant opponents to have overcome the better instincts and prudent judgment of a lawful sovereign, 'All the Impire almaist thay maid clere daft'. The masters' prize for so successfully ensnaring the emperor and his subjects is, moreover, wealth and riches. For their advice and dubious counsel, they extract 'ane Ducat' or, that filthiest of lucre to the Scottish anglophile and religious reformer, 'ane French Croun' (111).[28] That the adolescent and already-widowed Queen of Scots had herself allegedly compromised her own birthright and her soul for 'a French Croune' – having been married-off by the Guises to the short-lived and sickly François II of France – lends an acutely sardonic edge to Rolland's text at this pivotal point.

Integral to a strongly politicized adaptation of the sages' story is also the rehabilitation of Merlin's credibility and reputation as a seer. Requested by the emperor to seek a cure for his apparently inexplicable affliction, in Rolland's narration the masters scour the realm before at last encountering a 'young barne', unmistakeably Merlin (114). His illegitimacy, baldly attested in other versions of the legend, is passed over in significant silence by a strangely diplomatic Rolland: when

> ... thir sevin Inquyrit the Name,
> he said Merling, quhairof I thing na schame (114).[29]

Further reverential treatment of the Arthurian prophet follows. The seven duplicitous sages are forced openly, if somewhat implausibly, to acknowledge his pre-eminent virtue: addressing Merlin directly, they 'persave weill, ye have wisdome and lair' (114). Yet, reflecting Rolland's likely subscription to a unionist re-reading of the *Prophetiae*, Merlin comprehensively defeats their conspiracy. This he achieves through a display of his unsurpassed perceptiveness and acute political wisdom. He reveals to a grateful emperor, just as in a conventional Scottish *speculum principis* exemplar, how

---

[27] A rich literature grew out of the contemporary criticism of Scottish governance under Mary: its outstanding historical expression is Robert Lindsay of Pitscottie's *History of Scotland from 1436 to 1565*, ed. R. Freebairn (Edinburgh, 1728).
[28] Cf. *The Buke*, ed. van Buuren, p. 304, in which no French coinage appears.
[29] Cf. *Seven Sages*, ed. Brunner, p. 109, where other children 'cleped him sschrewe faderles'.

>   ... baith yow and your Impire
>   Lang time bygone hes reulit at thair desire (117).³⁰

Furthermore, Rolland's text peculiarly reflects in its treatment of Merlin the distinctive nature of the recent dissensions among the Scottish people. These had been voiced as recently as 1559 in the celebrated, brazen appeal of the Protestant clergy *To the Nobility, Burghs, and Community of this Realm of Scotland*, a rallying-cry which would in due course bring about the humiliation of the unfortunate Queen of Scots specifically at the hands of her own leading subjects. Merlin, sounding much like Knox and the vociferous Calvinist preachers who sought both to rouse the Scottish lords to arms and to show the Queen of Scots the error of her ways, eloquently brings to the emperor's notice what Mary too had been forced to hear: the 'complaintis of your Barrounis & Lordis'. And, through his carefully-worded counsel, Rolland's Merlin actually ensures that, as the sixteenth-century Scottish theory of kingship above all would require, 'Justice suld ring into your land' (117).³¹

Rolland's use of Merlinic materials is, then, in suggestive conformity with an emerging Protestant and unionist vision of Scotland's past and future, one in which Merlin's hackneyed prophecies began to acquire a new and very particular resonance. In the associated *moralitas*, indeed, Merlin's contentious status as a seer and as a source of political wisdom is straightforwardly affirmed. Though still 'in youth and tender age', Rolland comments admiringly of the most credible prophet of English imperialism:

>   God of his grace had gevin him mair knawledge
>   In wit, Science, hid with subtilitie.... (121)

In a text and a tale which probably enjoyed some significant popularity in late sixteenth- and early seventeenth-century Scotland, and which was certainly re-printed again in 1592, 1620 and 1631, the favourable treatment of the problematical Merlin can only be regarded as a telling indication of the recent transformation of national politics achieved by those who had sought his rehabilitation in Scotland.³²

---

30 The tradition of 'mirror for princes' literature in late medieval Scotland forms the subject of R. J. Lyall, 'Politics and Poetry in Fifteenth and Sixteenth-Century Scotland', *Scottish Literary Journal* 3 (1976), 5–29.
31 On the central notion of *iustitia* in contemporary Scottish political thought see R. A. Mason, 'Kingship and Commonweal: Political Thought and Ideology in Reformation Scotland' (unpublished Ph.D. dissertation, Edinburgh, 1983).
32 On re-publications, see H. G. Aldis, *List of Books Printed in Scotland Before 1700* (Edinburgh, 1904). The *DNB*, however, suggests additional re-printings of Rolland in 1599 and 1606. Although the estimation of wider public popularity of texts in sixteenth-

III

Henrisoun and Rolland may in their different ways provide tantalizing evidence that an increasingly creative and sympathetic adoption of Arthurian motifs characterized writers who were active within the emerging anglophile, Protestant, and reformist party in Scotland in the two decades leading to the eventual outbreak of the Reformation in 1560. But it is also likely that the profound antipathy towards Merlin in particular, which had distinguished so much of earlier Scottish historiography in the grand medieval tradition of Fordun/Bower, continued even beyond John Mair and late into the sixteenth century. With the success of the Reformation, and the final deposition of Mary Queen of Scots, in 1567, this might seem surprising. Indeed, with the accession of her Protestant son, James VI, who before the end of the century would also become heir-apparent to Queen Elizabeth's throne in England – potentially therefore capable of being presented to both peoples as a plausible *Arthur redivivus* – the Scottish treatment of Arthur himself does seem to have begun to reflect the growing hegemony in public discourse of a reformist, if never (as the case of Wedderburn shows) wholly anglophile, tendency. The status of Merlin, however, remained essentially problematical. This was especially so in the early years of James' Scottish reign, before Elizabeth's childlessness and a Stewart solution to the consequent problem of the English succession could properly be foreseen. The survival of such difficulties into the Jacobean age is transparently revealed in the most influential and controversial historical tract to appear in sixteenth-century Scotland, George Buchanan's *Rerum Scoticarum Historia* (1582).[33]

Buchanan, erstwhile tutor to the young James VI and a humanist scholar of formidable international repute, was indelibly marked as a supporter of the revolutions of 1560 and 1567: his justificatory *De jure regni apud Scotos dialogus* (1579) stands as the notorious high water-mark of sixteenth-century Scottish Protestant radicalism, with its bare-faced enunciation of

---

century Scotland is neither an exact nor a meaningful science, 45 copies of *The Sevin Seages* were on the stock of the deceased Edinburgh bookseller, Robert Smyth, when his testament was proved in February 1604: *Miscellany of the Bannatyne Club*, II (Edinburgh, 1836), p. 234. This certainly suggests that someone with a close knowledge of the contemporary book-buying public had judged this text worthy of significant commercial investment. The standard commentary on the anglicization of Scottish reading tastes, which notes *en passant* the currency of unionist literature at least in the 1540s, is M. A. Bald, 'Vernacular Books Imported into Scotland: 1500 to 1625', *Scottish Historical Review* 23 (1926), 254–67.

[33] On Buchanan's later status and influence as the virtual embodiment of a celebrated Scottish Renaissance, see D. Allan, *Virtue, Learning and the Scottish Enlightenment: Ideas of Scholarship in Early Modern History* (Edinburgh, 1993), esp. ch. 1. Modern biographical treatment is available in I. D. Macfarlane, *Buchanan* (Cambridge, 1981).

the principle of legitimate resistance to an ungodly Catholic prince (or, more to the point, princess). Buchanan, then, was intellectually incautious by nature, and no easy respecter of reputations. And the *Historia* does treat in revealing detail the origins and career of Arthur, thus opening up for Buchanan the opportunity also to assess the real significance of Merlin. But Buchanan, concerned above all to establish the historicity of an ancient Scottish monarchy which was not only independent but properly constitutional, relied heavily upon the narrative framework afforded by Hector Boece's *Historiam Scotorum*. This seems deeply to have coloured his approach.

In keeping with this source, Arthur's illegitimacy is brought forcefully to the reader's attention by Buchanan. The adultery of Uter and Igerne is recounted in a tone of obvious presbyterian distaste. It is clear enough that Buchanan wishes to emphasize the point that 'from this adulterous intercourse sprung Arthur his son'.[34] Indeed, Arthur remains throughout 'the fruit of this stolen interview', even though his personal qualities attract Buchanan's grudging admiration:

> In the dawn of manhood [he] displayed such admirable symmetry of person, such superiority of mind, and gave so many indications of his future greatness, that the eyes and affections of his parents and of the people, already marked him out as a successor to the throne (237).

Yet Buchanan's careful casting of Arthur, however favourable to his individual virtues, allows no possibility of his having enjoyed legitimate sovereignty over Scotland. Arthur's relations with King Lothus, if generally amicable, remain fundamentally voluntary on both sides. Lothus declines to challenge Arthur's claim to the English throne. And subsequently, Buchanan suggests, Lothus elects freely to renew a traditional alliance between the Scots and the Britons (238). This arrangement, of course, conveniently enables the Scots to share the glory of Arthur's well-attested victories but in no way obliges Buchanan to acknowledge strict southern overlordship in the north of the island.

Such merely ambivalent sketching of character does not extend to Buchanan's coruscating dismissal of the shadowy Merlin. Uter's defeat of the 'modesty' of Igerne, the paternal taint of which Buchanan repeatedly reminds Arthur's potential admirers, is itself attributed bluntly to 'the art' of the manipulative sorcerer. It is the work of 'the audacious and wicked Merlin' (236–7). Buchanan suggests, too, that Merlin sought his own ignominy, choosing 'rather to be notorious for a vile action, than remain

---

[34] *The History of Scotland, Translated from the Latin of George Buchanan*, ed. J. Aikman, 6 vols. (Edinburgh, 1827–9), II, 236.

uncelebrated'. With regard to his prophetic talents, moreover, Buchanan judges Merlin simply 'an egregious impostor, and cunning pretender, rather than a prophet' (233). Indeed,

> His vaticinations are widely spread, but they are obscure, and contain nothing certain, on which, before the event happens, any rational anticipation can be founded, or which, after it has happened, can be explained as a true prediction (234).

What is more, Buchanan alleges – in a manner reminiscent of that other notably anglophobic Protestant, Robert Wedderburn – that those contemporaries who believed that England would shortly unite with Scotland were guilty of gullibility in the face of Merlin's patently absurd utterances: the prophecies, he claims, because they can clearly be 'twisted, and accommodated to a great number of different events', are now being 'interpolated, and augmented by new additions'. This is simply, Buchanan concludes definitively, an example of the 'folly of credulous men'.

IV

George Buchanan's ambivalence towards Arthur and frank hostility to Merlin was not, however, to set the tone for the weight of subsequent Scottish public discourse: in this one respect at least, Scotland's greatest humanist scholar and political theorist was not to prove especially influential. More typical of the greater Scottish reverence for Arthuriana was his polemical opponent, John Lesley, bishop of Ross, a Catholic partisan of the deposed Queen of Scots, whose *De origine, moribus, et rebus gestis Scotorum* (1578), written from his Continental exile, is all the more striking for the favourable terms in which it alludes to Arthur's qualities. For example, James IV of Scotland is described by Lesley as having wished sincerely to emulate the greatest of British princes:

> He was of sik corage, that quhom evir he hard maist commendet in vertuous and valyeant actes, he intendet and kaist, him ay to follow, bet heiring of not ane in ancient antiquitie amang all his predeccesours, to quhom he wald be sa conforme as to King Arthur; remembreng of King Arthuris Knychts, and thair forme deseyring to follow quha war knychtes of the round table, that tyme he wald be called a knycht of King Arthuris brocht up in the wodis.[35]

Such sentiments, appearing in the decades before the Union of the Crowns

---

[35] John Lesley, *Historie of Scotland*, ed. E. G. Cody and W. Murison, trans. J. Dalrymple, STS, 2 vols. (Edinburgh, 1890–5), II, 128.

but after James VI's elevation to his native throne, emphasize that Arthurian materials were increasingly embraced by the generality of Scottish scholars. Moreover, one becomes aware in the period surrounding James's actual assumption of the English crown just how much of a substantiation of ancient Galfridian prophecy the momentous events of 1603, in the hands of skilful propagandists and sympathetic commentators, could be made to appear.[36] One is also struck, in retrospect, by just how prescient for the political future had been the daring works of Henrisoun and Rolland, preparing the ground for a veritable barrage of Arthuriana which coloured and helped set the tone of the uncertain new world of Jacobean Britain.

An eagerness to cite Arthurian authorities was, for example, increasingly to characterize the emerging Scottish political leaders who would dominate the affairs of the united Stuart kingdoms. Emerging out of a Gaelic tradition in which it had played 'a minor but significant' part from the fifteenth century onwards, the Arthurian genealogy purveyed by that most British (and Protestant) of seventeenth and eighteenth-century Highland dynasties, the Campbells, earls and later dukes of Argyll, is eloquent testimony to the political symbolism of this compelling motif in Jacobean Scotland.[37] Nor were the Campbells alone in optimistically donning the mantle of Arthur. It is known that James VI himself considered seriously the adoption of the name 'Arthur'; and we learn elsewhere that he frantically pursued other Arthurian parallels at the time of his English coronation.[38] In the words of the observant Venetian State Secretary, Giovanni Carlo Scaramelli, who described the comportment of the new King in April 1603, James seemed to be:

> disposed to abandon the titles of England and Scotland, and to call himself King of Great Britain, and like that famous and ancient King Arthur to embrace under one name the whole circuit of one thousand seven hundred

---

[36] The debate and propaganda generated by the Union of the Crowns is analysed in B. Galloway, *The Union of England and Scotland, 1603–1608* (Edinburgh, 1986).

[37] W. Gillies, 'Arthur in Gaelic Tradition – Part One: Romances and Learned Lore', *Cambridge Medieval Gaelic Studies* 3 (1982), 41–75. On the Campbell genealogies, see his 'The Invention of Tradition, Highland-Style', in *The Renaissance in Scotland: Studies in Literature, Religion, History and Culture*, ed. A. A. Macdonald, M. Lynch and I. B. Cowan (Leiden, 1994), pp. 144–56; also W. D. H. Sellar, 'The Earliest Campbells – Norman, Briton or Gael', *Scottish Studies* 17 (1979), 109–25. For their political import, see e.g. E. J. Cowan, 'The Political Ideas of a Covenanting Leader: Archibald Campbell, Marquis of Argyll, 1607–1661', in *Scots and Britons*, ed. Mason, p. 256.

[38] On James's name-games, see Lynch, *Scotland*, p. 238; on the coronation, see K. M. Brown, 'The Vanishing Emperor: British Kingship and its Decline, 1603–1707', in *Scots and Britons*, ed. Mason, esp. p. 64.

miles, which includes the United Kingdom now possessed by his Majesty, in that one island.[39]

In any case, whether as Solomon, as Constantine, as Brutus, as David, as Augustus or as Arthur, the self-styled King of Great Britain certainly enjoyed an almost unparalleled versatility of image upon which the developing ideology of Stuart kingship could build.[40] And there are clear indications that the *Prophetiae Merlini* in particular were finding a renewed relevance as his loyal Scottish subjects tried to come to terms with the historical and political implications of a Jacobean Britain.

A special significance appears to have attached in Scotland after 1603 to the strict veracity of Merlin's prophecies and their later elaborations: as Rupert Taylor suggests, the Union of the Crowns 'seemed for a time to have fulfilled the Scottish prophecies'.[41] The *Whole Prophesie of Scotland*, for example, was published in Edinburgh, in the very year of James' departure for Whitehall Palace, by 'Robert Waldegrave, Printer to the Kings most Excellent Majestie'.[42] This publication seems to have attached a starkly contemporary significance to its ambiguous contents, Merlin's authenticity and literal accuracy being asserted uncompromisingly:

> Merling saies in his booke who will reade right,
> Althoght his sayings be uncouth, they shalbe true found (3).

Indeed, here the prophecy of the Lion appears to be the key to its striking political pertinence: 'Then shall the Lyon be best in the broad North', proudly proclaims the text. Republished in Edinburgh in 1615 by Andrew Hart (also publisher to the loyal Stuart poets William Drummond of Hawthornden and Sir William Alexander), these prophecies, placing Merlin in the elevated company of the Scotsman Thomas of Ercildoune and other unimpeachable seers, were evidently thought to offer a Scottish audience a compelling and authoritative framework within which to interpret their own changed political circumstances.[43]

---

[39] *Calendar of State Papers and Manuscripts: Venetian*, 10 vols., ed. H. F. Brown (London, 1900), X, 5: 17 April 1603.

[40] See D. Allan, 'Prudence and Patronage: The Politics of Culture in Seventeenth-Century Scotland', *History of European Ideas* 18 (1994), 467–80.

[41] R. H. Taylor, *Political Prophecy in England* (New York, 1911), p. 78.

[42] *Whole Prophesie of Scotland* (Edinburgh, 1603), reprinted in *Collection of Ancient Scottish Prophecies, in Alliterative Verse*, Bannatyne Club, 44 (Edinburgh, 1833), pp. 3–9.

[43] On *The Whole Prophesie* and its usage under James VI and I, see *The Romance and Prophecies of Thomas of Ercildoune*, ed. J. A. H. Murray, EETS, o.s. 61 (London, 1875), pp. xxx–xlii.

As fundamental political developments in Britain rendered these cultural traditions suddenly less seditious, Scotland's leading *litterateurs* were not slow to follow the example of the hired printers and propagandists, smoothly incorporating valorizing references to the Merlinic prophecies into their poetic and dramatic works.[44] Like Campion and Jonson in England, Scottish men of letters of the early seventeenth century sought in didactic literature to impress upon contemporaries that a canon of ancient predictions, of which Merlin's were by far the best-known, had been perfectly consummated in 1603. Drummond's panegyrical *The River of Forth Feasting* (1617), for example, written on the occasion of the king's single subsequent visit to his Scottish capital, harped upon the prophetic fulfilment that had been James's capturing of an imperial British crown:

> This is that King who should make right each Wrong,
> Of whom the *Bards* and mystick *Sibylis* sung,
> The Man long promis'd, by whose glorious Reign,
> This Isle should yet her ancient Name regain . . .[45]

Sir William Alexander, who as tutor had already taught the two young men who most clearly embodied the new Arthurian symbolism (Archibald Campbell, 7th earl of Argyll, and Prince Henry, son of James VI), made similar remarks in his Senecan masterpiece *Monarchicke Tragedies* (1607).[46] Other scholars, including both scientists and historians, took up the refrain. James Maxwell, astrologer and mathematician in Edinburgh, re-visited the difficult territory of Merlin's questionable gifts, publishing the *Admirable and Notable Prophecies* (1615) in which the seer's reputation was stoutly defended:

> I doe thinke that he was not a diabolicall but onely a natural magician, well seen in the admirable secrets of nature and especiallie in astronomy . . .[47]

Patrick Gordon of Ruthven, too, in his *Famous History* (1615), went so far as to re-work the story of Robert the Bruce – a most problematical king of Scots for the unionist man of letters – by having Thomas of Ercildoune, Merlin's Scottish *alter ego*, appear as the king's wise and far-seeing

---

[44] Particularly interesting on this subject is R. F. Brinkley, *Arthurian Legend in the Seventeenth Century* (Baltimore, 1932), esp. pp. 1–25.
[45] William Drummond, *Works* (Edinburgh, 1711), pp. 37–8.
[46] Quoted in Brinkley, *Arthurian Legend*, p. 9.
[47] Quoted in A. H. Williamson, 'Number and National Consciousness: the Edinburgh Mathematicians and Scottish Political Culture at the Union of the Crowns', in *Scots and Britons*, ed. Mason, p. 201.

counsellor.[48] And the less scrupulous patriotic historians of the Jacobean age even began to attempt to naturalize Merlin as a Scotsman, the shadowy originator of the *Prophetiae* suddenly re-emerging among the ranks of those select individuals whose nationality it was possible to overlook in the shameless search for clinching evidence of age-old Scottish wisdom and virtue. The jurist and unionist scholar Sir Thomas Craig of Riccarton, in his great *De unione regnorum Britanniae tractatus* (1605), and even the professor of humanities at Pisa and Bologna, Thomas Dempster of Muresk, in the monumental *Historia ecclesiastica gentis Scotorum* (1627), each attempted to convince an unpersuaded wider public, through co-option of the now-sanitized Merlin, of Scotland's own ancient line of sages and seers.[49]

Arthur and Merlin had, then, effectively completed a seventy-year metamorphosis in Scotland: from being the preoccupation of a radical and dangerous periphery under Mary of Guise, they had become naturalized and accepted as the common currency of the greater part of the Jacobean political and cultural establishment. Indeed, when presented and perceived in Scotland through the prism of such a patriated Arthurian interpretation, the Union of the Crowns itself was capable of appearing, in the eyes at least of its wishful supporters, nothing less than the expected consummation of the most creditable ancient predictions. A final example will perhaps suffice in illustration of the successful entrenchment of Arthuriana in Scotland's early modern cultural politics, strongly indicating, as it does, the secure relationship which had been established between the tradition of sub-Merlinic political prophecy and the victorious forces of unionist Protestantism. Dr Alexander Pennecuik, Whig unionist and enthusiastic collector of antique Scots poetry during the reign of George I, may have looked back

---

[48] Patrick Gordon, *The Famous History of Robert the Bruce* (Dort, 1615). So sensitive was Gordon's subject, despite his recourse to Ercildoune, that he covered his own position by stating categorically that it was not his purpose to 'wrong the *Union*'. In fact, Gordon has Ercildoune, 'an aged Sire', predict to the Bruce the later unionist achievements of James VI:
>There oe'r the Globe of Sea and Earth he stands,
>Which to the *North* joins *South's* fair Diadem,
>And *Boreas* spacious Empire all commands,
>And all where *Titan* cools his fiery Team   (47)

Emphasizing Gordon's unqualified success in avoiding the accusation of sedition for using such a traditional icon of Scottish patriotic nationalism as the Bruce, the work was actually re-published in Edinburgh in 1718 as part of the unionist literary backlash following the 1715 Jacobite rebellion, and again in Glasgow in 1753 in the wake of the '45. It is from the latter edition that I take my quotation.

[49] See Sir Thomas Craig, *De Unione Regnorum Britanniae Tractatus*, ed. and transl. C. Sanford Terry, Scottish History Society, 60 (Edinburgh, 1909), p. 379; also *Thomae Dempsteri Historia ecclesiastica gentis Scotorum sive, De scriptoribus scotis*, 2 vols., ed. D. Irving, Bannatyne Club, 21 (Edinburgh, 1829), II, 448.

on the formative events of 1603 from the commanding heights of self-confident Augustan Scotland. But he too emphatically belonged to that peculiar world of Arthurian myth-history first constructed in Scotland, more than a century earlier, by authors like Henrisoun, Rolland and the Jacobean propagandists. Pennecuik appears even still to have accepted wholesale the prophetic interpretation of the Union of the Crowns, with all its evocatively Merlinic associations. For, in his *A Geographical, Historical Description of the Shire of Tweeddale* (1715), he offered this touchingly personalized account of the Peeblesshire village of Drumelzier:

> There is one thing remarkable here, which is, the burn, called *Pausayl*, [which] runs by the east side of this church-yard into *Tweed*, at the side of which burn, a little below the church-yard, the famous prophet *Merlin* is said to be buried. The particular place of his Grave, at the Foot of a Thorn tree, was shown me many years ago, by the old and Reverend Minister of the place, Mr *Richard Brown*: and here was the old prophecy fulfilled, delivered in Scots rhyme to this purpose;
>
> > When *Tweed* and *Pausayl* meet at *Merlin's* grave,
> > *Scotland* and *England* shall one *Monarch* have;
>
> for the same day that our King James the Sixth was crowned king of *England*, the river *Tweed*, by an extraordinary flood, so far overflowed the banks, that it met and joined with *Pausayl* at the said Grave; which was never before observed to fall out, nor since that time.[50]

V

The sceptical Scottish historians of the eighteenth-century Enlightenment would later mock their predecessors – by implication, Henrisoun, Rolland and Pennecuik alike – for their uncritical acceptance of what seemed to the condescending *literati* of Edinburgh an entirely fabricated myth-history. Lord Hailes, for example, would in 1773 dismiss his forbears' response to such matters as one of 'superstitious credulity'.[51] Another, the bombastic John Pinkerton, whose single-minded denigration of the Celtic races even then possessed an unsavoury odour, suggested in his *An Enquiry into the History of Scotland* (1789) that Arthur himself was merely a garbled remembrance of the Roman leader Aurelius Ambrosianus on the part of the

---

[50] *Works of Alexander Pennecuik Esq. of New-Hall, M.D.* (Leith, 1815), p. 253. Punctuation original. I am grateful to Dr Iain Brown of the National Library of Scotland in Edinburgh for assistance in identifying Pennecuik's work.

[51] Lord Hailes, *Remarks Concerning the History of Scotland* (Edinburgh, 1773), ch. III.

feckless Welsh.[52] Yet for a time at least, during the sixteenth and seventeenth centuries, there were Scotsmen who were prepared to accommodate Arthurian ideas and motifs into their thoughts. This was, I have argued, because Arthur and Merlin gave them a new and relevant way of thinking about their own complex political realities, particularly with regard to changing relations with England.

The potent fusion of unionism and Protestantism in Scotland at the time of the 'Edwardian Moment' in the 1540s, and thereafter the expansion of literary and intellectual opposition to the regimes of the odious Marys – Guise and the Queen of Scots – provided a powerful force for the transmission of the Galfridian Arthur and Merlin into Scotland, and for their transformation into acceptable political symbols. By the time of the Union of the Crowns, that metamorphosis was, notwithstanding the singular George Buchanan, already largely complete. The achievement of Henrisoun and Rolland was in assisting James VI's later printers, propagandists and men of letters so successfully to fashion a public image for the first King of Great Britain in which his Arthurian credentials were to play no insignificant part. Questions, of course, remain, and it has not been the purpose of the present paper more than to indicate where a number of these may lie. How substantial the Arthurian contribution actually was to the establishment and early survival of that increasingly problematical political entity, the united Anglo-Scottish state, is, for example, profoundly difficult to estimate. In retrospect, however, one aspect of the cultural significance of the Scottish Reformation and of the Union of the Crowns seems reasonably clear. The *Prophetiae Merlini* and the legend of Arthur acquired a position in Scotland which only the rise of advanced documentary scholarship and methodological scepticism in the eighteenth century would finally begin to subvert.

---

[52] John Pinkerton, *An Enquiry into the History of Scotland*, 2 vols. (London, 1789), II, 67. His more sinister views on the respective merits of the competing races in the British Isles had earlier been advertized in the *Dissertation on the Origin and Progress of the Scythians or Goths* (London, 1787).

NOTE

VII

'GENTYL' AUDIENCES AND 'GRETE BOOKES':
CHIVALRIC MANUALS AND THE *MORTE DARTHUR*

Karen Cherewatuk

Even a casual reading of the *Morte Darthur* reveals that Malory is not a detached critic of but rather a loyal adherent to chivalry. There is, for example, the tone of 'moral earnestness' he adopts in articulating the oath of the Round Table.[1] The same 'moral earnestness' appears in the oft-cited passage on 'vertuouse love'. There Malory posits for the knight a traditionally Christian hierarchy of responsibilities: 'Therefore, lyke as May moneth flowryth and floryshyth in every mannes gardyne, so in lyke wyse lat every man of worshyp florysh hys herte in thys worlde ... But firste reserve the honoure to God, and secundely thy quarell muste com of thy lady' (1119.21–29). Because this passage appears in Vinaver's edition before Guinevere's and Launcelot's tryst in Mellyagaunce's bed, its meaning is confused. In the Winchester manuscript, this definition of love comes after the 'Great Tournament' and immediately following Arthur's speech to Gareth on 'worshyp' and 'jantilnes', thereby indicating a theme running throughout the *Morte Darthur*.[2] In this context, the author's advice to the 'man of worshyp' is straightforward, the kind of statement one expects from chivalric moralists like Ramon Lull or Christine de Pizan: serve God and then (and only then) thy lady. In his 'Tristram' Malory shows little concern for moral complexities but rather revels in another side of chivalry, the

---

I am grateful to the trustees of the British Library, the Pierpont Morgan Library, and the Faculty of Advocates for permission to cite their manuscripts.

[1] See *The Works of Sir Thomas Malory*, ed. E. Vinaver, rev. P. J. C. Field, 3 vols. (Oxford, 1990), pp. 120, 15–27. Henceforth, references to this text will be cited parenthetically. The phrase 'moral earnestness' is Derek Brewer's. See his 'Malory: The Traditional Writer and the Archaic Mind', *Arthurian Literature I*, ed. R. W. Barber (Cambridge, 1981), 94–120 (p. 102).

[2] See *The Winchester Malory, a Facsimile Edition*, ed. N. R. Ker (Oxford, 1976), fol. 435r. I am grateful to Kevin T. Grimm for pointing out to me Vinaver's editorial practice.

competitive world of masculine action. After Palomydes unhorses the hero, Malory reveals an insider's sympathy for Tristram: 'Here men may undirstonde that bene men of worshyp that man was never fourmed that all tymes myght attayne, but somtyme he was put to the worse by malefortune' (484.18–20).

Such intrusions into the text reveal not only the author's varied ideas about chivalry but also the audience for whom he wrote. In the 'Tristram' Malory cites hunting terms to evoke what he sees as inevitable and immutable class differences:

> Wherefore, as me semyth, all *jantyllmen* that beryth *olde armys* ought of ryght to honoure sir Trystrams for the goodly tearmys that *jantylmen* have and use and shall do unto the Day of Dome, that thereby in a maner all *men of worshyp* may discever a *jantylman* frome a *yoman* and a *yoman* frome a *vylayne*. For he that *jantyll* is woll drawe hym to *jantyll tacchis* and to folow the *noble customys of jantylmen*. (375.22–29, emphasis mine)

Malory leaves no doubt that he places himself and his readers among the 'jantylmen' rather than the 'yoman' or the 'vylayne'. His concern with lineage and old arms recalls the claims made by Sir John Paston and his uncles, William and Clement, that they were gentlemen descended since the Norman Conquest. Like Malory, the Pastons' argument relies on notions of 'worshipfull gentlemen' and ancient heraldic arms.[3] Even Malory's leave-taking of his audience, the final words in the *Morte Darthur*, are addressed to 'you all jentylmen and jentylwymmen that redeth this book', with the request to 'praye for my soule' (1260.20–22). These passages, and many passing references, suggest that Malory wrote for a limited audience

---

[3] The original documents by which the Pastons succeeded in advancing this mostly fictive claim have been lost, but a copy of a certificate made in the name of Edward IV survives. I cite it from the *Paston Letters and Papers of the Fifteenth Century*, ed. N. Davis, 2 vols. (Oxford, 1971–76), no. 897, 2.551.25–552.55 (emphasis mine): 'Also they shewed a great multitude of *old deeds*, without date and with date, wherein their ancestors were alwaies sett first in witnes and before all other gentlemen. Also they shewed how that their ancestors had in *old time* and of late time married with *worshipfull gentlemen*, ... and made open by evident proofe how they and their ancestors came lineally descended of *right noble and worshipful blood* and of great lords sometime liveing in this our realme of Ingland. And also they made open proofe how they were nere of kin and blood to many of *the worshipfullest* of the country. . . . They shewed a lineall discent how their first ancetor Wulstan came out of France, ... and how Wulstan had issue Wulstan, which *bare armes gould flowret azure*, and how he had issue Raffe and Robert, which Raffe senior *bare armes* as his father and Robert the younger *bare silver flowret azure*. And Robert had issue Edmund and Walter, which Edmund the elder *bare as his father*, and his brother, because he married Glanviles daughter, a *cheife indented golde, the field silver flowret azure*; . . . and how Sir John Paston was heire to all those, for they dyed sans issue. And this was shewed by writing of *olde hand* and by *olde testaments and evidences*.'

of peers, most likely members of his immediate social circle – chivalric insiders, who could appreciate the 'jantyl tacchis' of the *Morte Darthur*.

Taken cumulatively, these authorial intrusions may indicate the early readership of the *Morte Darthur*. Malory's holograph manuscript probably circulated in households like his own, not among the nobility, but among members of the educated gentry. David Starkey reminds us that in England, unlike France, the nobility was 'a tiny status group', admired and imitated by the 'much larger group of gentlemen'. The gentry essentially were composed of the greater landowners, merchants, or members of certain professions (like law) who could support a 'gentle' lifestyle through their wealth.[4] The upward movement of members of the gentry explains why Malory places so much emphasis on 'worshypful' behaviour and 'jantyl' action. In his fictive world most members of the Round Table are in fact noble, related to Arthur or Launcelot by blood, yet as the tales of the fair unknown indicate, even nobles like Gareth must prove themselves worthy. Malory thus was committed to a chivalric system, which although conservative, allowed certain members of the gentry to rise on the social scale and perhaps even allowed him to enter the circle of the King.[5] One need only

---

4 Starkey, 'The Age of the Household: Politics, Society and the Arts, c. 1350–c. 1550', in *The Later Middle Ages*, ed. S. Medcalf (New York, 1981), pp. 225–90, especially pp. 226–7. See also Andrew Lynch, 'Good Name and Narrative in Malory', *Nottingham Medieval Studies* 34 (1990), 141–51, especially p. 146.

5 In 'Malory's *Le Morte Darthur* and Court Culture under Edward IV', *Arthurian Literature XII* (Cambridge, 1993), 133–55, R. Barber argues that Sir Thomas Malory of Newbold Revel, whom Barber accepts as author, probably 'moved for several years, among the lower levels of the court' (p. 134). Barber's argument is necessarily speculative, but he draws strong parallels between Malory's attitude toward and the details of his tournaments in the *Morte Darthur* and the actual practice of the sport during Edward's reign, as well as between Malory's oath of the Round Table and books known to have circulated at court (pp. 146–51). Barber clarifies: 'I am not arguing that he was actually a member of Edward's household, but that he was one of the throng of minor gentry who came and went around the court, pursuing the king's favour or that of the great magnates who were often to be found there' (p. 135). See also Barber's 'Chivalry and the *Morte Darthur*' in *Companion to Malory*, ed. E. Archibald and A. S. G. Edwards (Cambridge, 1996), pp. 30–2.

One such great magnate with whom scholars have identified the author of the *Morte Darthur* is Anthony Wydeville, Lord Scales, second Earl Rivers, Edward's brother-in-law and Caxton's most important patron. Supporting the authorship of Malory of Newbold Revel, Hilton Kelliher argues in 'The Earliest History of the Malory Manuscript', in *Aspects of Malory*, ed. T. Takamiya and D. Brewer (Cambridge, 1981), pp. 143–58, that it was probably Wydeville who supplied Caxton with his copy text and the Winchester Malory. Arguing for authorship by the Cambridgeshire Malory, Thomas of Papworth St Agnes, R. Griffith has suggested that it was Wydeville who lent Malory the French romances necessary for the composition of the *Morte Darthur*. See his 'The Authorship Question Reconsidered', in *Aspects of Malory*, pp. 159–78, especially pp. 170–2 and 'Arthur's Author: the Mystery of Sir Thomas Malory', *Ventures in Research*

consider the meteoric rise of the Paston family during the fifteenth century and the subsequent careers of the brothers John II (or Sir John, who was knighted) and John III at court.

In her work on the miscellanies that contain Middle English romances, Felicity Riddy has shown that these manuscripts were not luxury books, commissioned by the nobility, but for the most part plain copies, prepared for and circulated among families of the gentry.[6] In this essay I will place Malory's *Morte Darthur* in the context of the manuscripts which include the teaching texts of knighthood, the chivalric manuals. These are familiar to Malorians from Beverly Kennedy's *Knighthood in the Morte Darthur*.[7] Yet Kennedy does not discuss the provenance and patronage of the chivalric manuals. Examined from the vantage of one particular group of manuscripts, the so-called 'great books', issues of patronage may help put flesh and blood on the nebulous group of readers Malory refers to as 'jentylmen and jentylwymmen'.

The phrase 'grete booke' appears in the correspondence of one of the volume's patrons, Sir John Paston (who is also known as John II). In a letter of 1468, William Ebesham, the book's main scribe, requests payment for work he had already completed: 'My moost woorshupfull and moost speciall maistir, with all my seruyce moost lowly I recommaunde [me] vnto your gode maistirship, beschyng you moost tendirly to see me sumwhat rewardid for my labour in the *grete booke*.'[8] Ebesham's term 'grete booke' obviously refers to the long volume he has copied out at Paston's request. In his will of 1481/82, Sir Richard Roos uses the term to bequeath to his niece his '*grete booke* called Saint Grall'.[9] Since Roos' volume contains not only the *Queste* but also an *Estoire* and a *Mort*, we see that the term 'great book' applied to a volume not only long but also composite in nature.

---

1 (1972), 7–43. Whether one accepts the candidacy of Thomas of Newbold Revel or Papworth St Agnes, the patronage of Wydeville would surely indicate that Malory had some contact with court culture.

6 *Sir Thomas Malory* (Leiden, 1987), chs. 1 and 3, especially pp. 14–30 and 73.

7 *Knighthood in the Morte Darthur* (Cambridge, 1985).

8 *Paston Letters*, no. 751, 2.387.1–3, emphasis mine. The impoverished scribe concludes this letter with the sad request: 'And in especiall I beseche you to send me for almes oon of your olde gownes, which will countirvale much of the premysses, I wote wele. And I shall be yours while I lyve and at your comaundement. I haue grete mystir of it, God knowis, whom I beseche preserue you from all adversite. I am sumwhat acquayntid with it' (2.387.32–7). References to the *Paston Letters and Papers* henceforth will be noted parenthetically in my text.

9 See Carol Meale's discussion of Roos' volume, now London, British Library Royal 14.E.III in 'Manuscripts, Readers and Patrons in Fifteenth-Century England: Sir Thomas Malory and Arthurian Romance', *Arthurian Literature IV* (Cambridge, 1985), 93–126; the quotation (with my emphasis) is from p. 103.

Malory thus uses the term when he invents a provenance for his 'Tale of the Sankgreal':

> So whan sir Bors had tolde hym of the hyghe aventures of the Sankgreall such as had befalle hym and his three felowes, . . . than sir Launcelot told the adventures of the Sangreall that he had sene. And all thys was made in *grete bookes* and put up in almeryes at Salysbury. (1036.16–22, emphasis mine)

Perhaps when Malory wrote out the words 'grete bookes', he actually had his eye on the volume from which he had translated the 'Sankgreal', which was very likely a composite manuscript like Roos'. In this essay I depart somewhat from fifteenth-century usage of 'great book'. I use the term in the limited sense first suggested by Curt Bühler when he referred to the kind of miscellany that Ebesham had assembled for Paston: a single-volume anthology containing several chivalric manuals and treatises of knightly ritual. The volumes Bühler was describing were, like Roos' romance manuscript, in fact long and composite, but they specifically functioned as knightly encyclopedia or anthologies.[10] It is in this context of the great books or chivalric anthology that I would like to explore the readership of the *Morte Darthur*.

Sir John Paston's great book, now London, British Library, Lansdowne 285, is just that, a vast compendium of chivalric treatises.[11] It contains the 'maner and coronation of the kynges and queenes in Engelonde'; 'how knyghtis of the bath shulde be made'; various 'chalenges and actes of armes' – both ordinances of war and challenges to jousts and tournaments; an English translation of the fifth-century military manual by Vegetius, the *De re militari*; and the 'Book of Governance of kings and princes' which is Lydgate and Burgh's translation of the pseudo-Aristotelian *Secreta secretorum*. According to the scribe's bill (*Paston Letters* no. 755, 2.391–92), intended for the volume but now bound separately was Stephen Scrope's

---

[10] C. F. Bühler, 'Sir John Paston's *Grete Booke*, a Fifteenth-Century "Best Seller" ', *Modern Language Notes* 56 (1941), 345–51. Bühler argues for the 'mass production' of chivalric anthologies which contain a core of three texts: Vegetius' *De re militari*, Christine de Pisan's *Epistle of Othea*, and the pseudo-Aristotelian *Secreta secretorum*. He concludes: 'The books were obviously written for the landed gentry and the success which this "edition" appears to have enjoyed seems to entitle it to the distinction of being "a fifteenth-century best-seller" ' (p. 351). Bühler's argument for 'mass production' and 'best seller' status was in part based on the faulty assumption that Lansdowne 285 and Paston's great book were two different volumes when in fact they are the same. G. A. Lester corrects Bühler's error in *Sir John Paston's 'Grete Boke', a Descriptive Catalogue with an Introduction of British Library MS Lansdowne 285* (Cambridge, 1984), *passim*, especially pp. 47–8. Nonetheless, Bühler's notion of a chivalric anthology with core texts is central to my argument.

[11] For a complete list of the contents of the manuscript, see Lester, pp. 9–12.

translation of Christine de Pizan's *Epistle of Othea*.[12] Ebesham's outline of the volume and the actual contents of Lansdowne 285 suggest that Paston intended his book to encompass various aspects of chivalry: chivalric rituals and combats ('the maner of coronation'; 'how knyghtis... shulde be made'; and the various challenges); a practical treatise on warfare (Vegetius); a *speculum principis* (the *Secreta secretorum*); and an ethical or religious manual of chivalry (Christine's *Othea*). In his own inventory of his library, Paston summarizes the idea of the great book quite succinctly as 'my boke of knyghthod' (*Paston Letters*, no. 316, 1.518.38). Paston's library held not only this didactic book of chivalry, but also manuscripts containing chivalric romances (the 'Deth off Arthur', 'the Greene Knyght', 'off Guy', 1.517.4, 14, and 17) and a book of heraldry ('a boke wyth armys portrayed in paper', 1.518.37). This library list suggests a range of interests for the late fifteenth-century gentle-reader, from instruction in knighthood to chivalric romances. In this context it is noteworthy that Paston's great book was assembled in the same year that Malory completed the *Morte Darthur*, 1468–59.

An earlier and far more elegant great book – vellum instead of paper, with beautiful initials and full page illuminations rather than plain ink throughout – belonged to Sir John Astley. It is now New York, Pierpont Morgan Library 775. Although not noble by birth, Astley had earned a reputation for his knightly exploits in the lists. This no doubt aided him in acquiring the titles of Knight of the Body to Edward IV and Knight of the Garter, both in 1461.[13] 1461 was also the year that John Paston had been sent to the court by his father in order to gain noble allies to aid in the family's property disputes. John II succeeded in part because, after initial opposition to the Pastons, Anthony Wydeville, Lord Scales, Edward IV's brother-in-law, became their protector.[14] When Wydeville prepared for his famous joust against the Bastard of Burgundy, Sir John Astley served as his coach. We do not know whether Sir John Paston witnessed Wydeville's triumph over the Bastard at Smithfield in June of 1467, but we do know

---

[12] As I explain below, the translation of Christine's *Othea* is borrowed directly from Astley's great book. It is perhaps worth noting here that Scrope, the translator, had at one time been a suitor for the hand of Sir John II's aunt, Elizabeth. See *Paston Letters*, nos. 18, 84, and 446 (1.30, 1.155, and 2.31–2) and Starkey, 'The Age of the Household', pp. 232–3.

[13] Lester, '*Grete Boke*', p. 94.

[14] For Wydeville's support of Sir John Paston and the family, see his letters of 1469 supporting the Paston's claim on Caister Castle, nos. 904 and 905, 2.571–2, and from the same period, Margaret's letter to John II reporting her own conversation with Lord Scales. Her acerbic words indicate her impatience with her courtly son: 'Ye arn beholdying to my lord of his good report of you in this contre, for he reported better of you than I trow ye deserue' (no. 201, 1.339.39–40).

that he accompanied Wydeville and watched him joust following the wedding of Margaret of York to Charles, duke of Burgundy in July of 1468 (no. 330, 1.539.25–33). If not all intimate friends, Astley, Wydeville, and Paston certainly travelled in the same court circle.

This network of relationships is reflected in Astley's and Paston's great books. A comparison of the two manuscripts shows that Astley had made his volume available to Paston, who had his scribe copy the bulk of it – down to paragraphing and meaningless blank spaces in texts.[15] Following Bühler's line of argument, G. A. Lester posits that the core of the great books already existed together, that 'a miscellaneous collection of texts mainly to do with knighthood had grown up around certain longer works – Vegetius, *The Book of Governance, Othea* – in the 1450s'.[16] It is likely that Astley had his bookmaker arrange the collection and augment it to his taste, by including, for example, the two pieces documenting Astley's own deeds in arms.[17] The dependence of Paston's book on Astley's suggests an interesting social practice: a gentleman seeks to improve himself by imitating a knight of the highest renown – not only mimicking him in chivalric conduct but also in reading material. Paston was indebted, however, not only to Astley for lending the book but to Wydeville for political support. Paston's respect for both men is evident from the table of contents: his great book recounts not only Astley's deeds in arms but also Wydeville's. In fact two pieces Paston had added recount Wydeville's combat against the Bastard of Burgundy.[18] The further inclusion of documents on Burgundian tourneys and *pas d'armes* indicates Sir John's continued interest in knightly display,[19] an interest he breathlessly reveals in writing about Margaret of York's wedding: 'And as for the Dwkys coort, as of lordys, ladys, and gentylwomen, knytys, sqwyirs, and gentyllmen, I herd neuer of non lyk to it saue Kyng Artourys cort' (no. 330, 1.539.34–36). Paston's book thus demonstrates the topicality, admiration for, and currency of knightly combat. Its bulk nonetheless consists of the three chivalric texts borrowed from Astley's book: the Vegetius, the *Book of Governance*, the *Othea*. Richard Barber summarizes the whole book with these categories: 'ceremonial;

---

[15] For a detailed comparison of the two books, see Lester, '*Grete Boke*', pp. 31–4.

[16] Lester, '*Grete Boke*', p. 47 and Bühler, 'Sir John Paston's *Grete Booke*', p. 351.

[17] These are the challenges Astley accepted from Philippe de Boyle and Piers de Masse (or Massy). See Pierpont Morgan 775, fols. 275r–79r.

[18] These are documents relating first to a proposed feat between Wydeville and the Grand Bastard and second to the actual combat between them held at Smithfield. See Lansdowne 285, fols. 18r–22v and 29v–43r, listed in Lester, '*Grete Boke*', as L11 and L15 on p. 10 and discussed on p. 45.

[19] These are documents on a Burgundian tournament, a *pas d'armes*, and the *Pas du Perron Fée*. See Lansdowne 285, fols. 44r–46r, 52r–56v, and 60r–82v and in Lester, '*Grete Boke*', L18, L22, and L23 on pp. 10–11.

joust; war; and statecraft'.[20] To this list I would add the category of knightly ethics in the form of the *Othea* intended for the volume.

The survival of the Paston family correspondence allows us to tease out the relationship between book patrons and chivalric practice at Edward IV's court. Such a glimpse into fifteenth-century book production is rare. One might think that books like Astley's and Paston's were limited to readers at the king's court, were it not for a similar and completely unrelated great book compiled in Scotland – this one made by Sir Gilbert of the Haye (also known as Sir Gilbert Hay). In the same decade that Astley's scribe was at work, 1450–60, Haye was translating from French and copying a series of prose translations for William Sinclair, earl of Orkney and Chancellor of Scotland.[21] Haye's book, now Edinburgh, National Library of Scotland, Acquisitions 9253, contains a different set of texts from the two English great books. Its contents include the 'Buke of the Law of Armys', Haye's translation of the *Tree of Battles* of Honoré Bouvet [also Bonet], which is a summary of the legal issues of war; the 'Order of Knighthood', Haye's translation of Ramon Lull's *Book of the Ordre of Chyvalry*; and the 'Governance of Princes', his translation of the *Secreta secretorum*. Haye rendered these texts as free paraphrases rather than as close translations; Haye's occasional additions reflect his interest in knighthood as 'a social, moral, and spiritual force to the common good'.[22] In sharp contrast to the English compilers, Haye included no documents on jousts, tournaments, or coronations. Nonetheless, Haye folds into his translation of Lull a full description of the knighting ceremony which expands on Lull's symbolism.[23] The

---

[20] Barber, 'Malory's Le *Morte Darthur* and Court Culture', p. 12.

[21] Haye's great book is the first extended volume in Scots prose. It has been recently edited under the title *The Prose Works of Sir Gilbert Hay*, ed. J. A. Glenn, 3 vols., Scottish Text Society, 4th series, 21 (Edinburgh, 1993). The date 1456 comes from Haye's prologue, National Library of Scotland, Acc. 9253, 1v. The manuscript later came into the possession of Sir Walter Scott and was housed in his library at Abbotsford; it is now owned by the Faculty of Advocates and is deposited at the National Library of Scotland.

In addition to translating chivalric manuals into Scots, Haye is also known as a poet. Riddy, *Sir Thomas Malory*, p. 29, notes that in his decasyllabic 'Buik of Alexander', composed in the same decade as the *Morte Darthur*, Haye faces a task like Malory's: to fashion from diverse sources, mostly French, a coherent life of one of the nine worthies.

[22] J. Cartwright, 'Hay, Sir Gilbert', in *The Dictionary of the Middle Ages*, ed. J. R. Strayer (New York, 1985), pp. 115–16. For information on Gilbert Hay, see Glenn, *Prose Works*, VI, 1.

[23] See Glenn, *Prose Works*, III, pp. 31–3. Although we do not know the precise French version of Lull's manual from which Haye translated, in the modern edition of *Le Livre de l'ordre de chevalerie* missing from the ceremony are the knight's bath and the accolade. See *Le Livre de l'ordre de chevalerie*, ed. V. Minervini (Bari, 1972), ch. 5. In Astley's and Paston's great books, the knighting ceremony comes as a separate entry: 'How Knyghties of the bath shulde be made' in Pierpont Morgan 775, fols. 195v–98v and in Lansdowne 285, fols. 7v–9r.

extremely plain volume, paper with myriads of pointing hands, was appropriate for its patron, a man of war. One gets the clear sense that Haye's volume might well have been carried into battle by the Chancellor Earl.

Despite the differing selection of texts in Haye's and the London great books, a similar pattern emerges: each volume contains one practical manual of warfare (in Haye, the 'Buke of Law of Armys'; in Astley and Paston, Vegetius); one treatise on knightly ethics (in Haye, Lull's 'Ordre of Chivalry'; in Astley and Paston, Christine's *Othea*); and one selection on princely behavior and statecraft (in all three books, a version of the *Secreta secretorum*). These volumes, then, reflect knightly ideals as practised in the different arenas of the battlefield, the court, and (for Astley and Paston's books) the lists. Each volume addresses a knightly audience, for the specific purpose of instruction or edification. Most important, the great books show that in the decades prior to and contemporaneous with Malory's completion of the *Morte Darthur* in 1468–69, chivalry was not a unified ideal but an aggregate of varying rituals, ideals, and standards set by gentlemen.

The pattern of the great books – a selection of a treatise on warfare, on chivalric ethics, on princely behaviour, and sometimes on knightly ceremonial – persists even in two royal manuscripts. Since these volumes contain works besides chivalric documents, they are not by my definition great books. They are, nonetheless, worth noting. The first, London, British Library Royal 15 E VI, is a French production of the mid-fifteenth century. John Talbot gave this volume to Margaret of Anjou on her wedding to Henry VI in 1455. Margaret's sumptuous book, illustrated by artists who are followers of the Bedford master, contains mostly poems and romances, all in French.[24] Included toward the end of the volume, however, is Bouvet's *Tree of Battles*; *The Book of Politics*, a translation of Giles of Rome's *De regimine principum*;[25] Christine de Pisan's *Fayttes of Armes*, her compilation of Vegetius and Bouvet (and hence a very practical treatise on warfare,

---

[24] For a description of the volume's contents, see M. Kekewich, 'Edward IV, William Caxton, and Literary Patronage in Yorkist England', *Modern Language Review* 66 (1971), 481–7, especially pp. 485–6. For a discussion of the volume's illuminations, see J. J. G. Alexander, 'Painting and Manuscript Illumination for Royal Patrons in the Later Middle Ages', in *English Court and Culture in the Later Middle Ages*, ed. V. J. Scattergood and J. W. Sherborne (London, 1983), pp. 141–62, Cp. 151.

[25] The *De regimine principum* is a *speculum principis* the Augustinian friar Giles of Rome composed in the 1270s for the young Philip the Fair of France. According to Nicholas Orme, 'The Education of the Courtier', in *English Court and Culture*, 'This treatise, as well as providing one of the most complete accounts of the duties of kings, contained a section of twenty-one chapters on the education of aristocratic boys and girls. It was well-known in late-medieval England in Latin; several members of the aristocracy are known to have possessed French translations, and a single copy even survives in an English version, made in about 1400' (p. 66). It thus covers the same topics as the versions of the *secreta secretorum* but does so more fully.

the first part giving actual battle plans and the second the laws of Christian warfare); and a document on the Order of the Garter. Margaret's book thus contains two treatises on warfare, a *speculum principis*, and a treatise on knightly ceremonial.

The second book, London, British Library Royal 14 E II, is an equally lavish work, executed between 1473–83 by Flemish artisans for Edward IV.[26] Edward's book contains five moral works, among them Lull's *Order of Chivalry* and Christine de Pisan's *Othea*. If, as is likely, Margaret's book was among the Lancastrian possessions of which Edward took possession on ascending the throne in 1461 and if we consider these two royal manuscripts together, the king would have had in his library nearly all of the texts contained in Astley's, Paston's, and Haye's great books.[27] While Edward IV does not have the reputation of a great reader, his brother-in-law, Anthony Wydeville does. A good many Malorians have speculated that it was Wydeville who made copies of the *Morte Darthur* available to Caxton.[28] Might Wydeville also have made available from the royal library to the printer Lull's *Ordre of Chivalry*, translated and published by Caxton in 1484, as well as Christine's *Fayttes of Armes*, translated and published by Caxton in 1489?[29] As tempting as this speculation is, this need not be the case. The great books demonstrate that these chivalric manuals were in circulation as Malory wrote. They were probably available to Malory and to Caxton, as they were to Astley, Paston, and Haye.

Malory was writing a series of romances, not a chivalric encyclopedia. Nonetheless, as I have argued elsewhere, there is a metaphoric relationship between the structure of the *Morte Darthur* and the plan of the great books.[30] Like a great book, the *Morte Darthur* presents in one volume a syncretic vision of knighthood. The 'Tale of King Arthur', which centres on the establishment of the king's rule, illustrates both idealistic and practical lessons for the young monarch, like those Aristotle teaches Alexander in the *Secreta secretorum*. Malory's 'Arthur and Lucius', with its emphasis on

---

[26] For a description of the volume's contents, see Kekewich, 'Edward IV', p. 484.
[27] Missing from Edward IV's library would be the *Secreta secretorum*, the *De regimine principum* taking its place as the treatise on princely behaviour and statecraft.
[28] These critics follow Hilton Kelliher; see my discussion of Kelliher in n. 5. Pursuing Kelliher's argument, P. J. C. Field has recently speculated that Wydeville's library might have provided Malory with his sources. See Field's the *Life and Times of Sir Thomas Malory* (Cambridge, 1993), pp. 144–5.
[29] Wydeville was beheaded in 1485, and Caxton published Christine's *Fayttes* in 1489. Although he was not alive when Caxton brought out the book, Wydeville earlier could have introduced Caxton to the work.
[30] K. Cherewatuk, 'Sir Thomas Malory's "Grete Boke" ', in *Malory and the New Historicism*, ed. T. D. Hanks, forthcoming.

martial chivalry, illustrates both the tactics of Vegetius and the law of arms of Bouvet. Chivalric manuals rarely discuss romantic love, except for Christine's *Othea* in which the goddess advises young knights to keep the middle way, that is, to love moderately. Moderate love, winning worship, and lawful marriage, concerns dear to Christine, are treated humorously in Malory's two tales of coming of age, 'Launcelot' and 'Gareth'. Most fully represented in Astley and Paston's great books are practical treatises of chivalric combat. Before Malory, the tale of Tristram had always been a love story. In Malory's hands, 'Tristram' becomes a catalogue of chivalric exercise, illustrating *jousts à plaisance*, with rebated weapons; *jousts à outrance*, with sharp points; *pas d'armes*, the most stylized form of jousting; duels; and *mêlees* or tournaments. In the 'Sankgreal', contra his source, Malory equates Christian virtue and knightly deeds, as does Lull's hermit in the *Book of the Order* and Christine's goddess in the *Othea*. The final movement of the *Morte Darthur*, comprising 'Launcelot and Guinevere' and the 'Morte'-proper, draws together the diverse meanings of chivalry to create a cumulative explanation for the fall of the Round Table. The legacy of the great books may be seen in Malory's complex, single-volume presentation of chivalry.

What I wish to stress here is the similarity between the audiences of the great books and of the *Morte Darthur*. In terms of production, the great books range from the simple but fair paper copies of Paston and Haye, to the de luxe volume of Astley, to lavish royal manuscripts. In terms of patronage, Astley's and Haye's volumes were commissioned by knights (respectively, by Astley himself and the Chancellor Earl). Paston, a squire aspiring to the knighthood, probably ordered his copy for a very practical reason: to learn its chivalric lessons and to imitate his superiors. The knights involved in the production of the great books thus range across a spectrum. Whether the compiler be, like Haye, a knight working outside of the Scottish court; or whether the patrons be, like Astley, a renowned knight of the Garter, or, like Paston, a member of the gentry struggling to get a toe-hold at court – the great books reflect a shared chivalric culture. It is worth noting that it was knights who in the mid-fifteenth century first caused these chivalric manuals to be brought together. For the great books, patrons, audience, and, in the case of Haye, even the scribe and translator prided themselves on being knights and gentlemen.

Lacking Malory's holograph, we turn to the Winchester Malory. Of all the texts considered in this essay, it most resembles Paston's book. It was an expensive production because of its length, not because of lavish labour on the part of scribes or illuminators. The Winchester Malory is a great book in the original sense of Paston's scribe. As Malory wrote, he probably had in mind an audience very much like the Paston family, householders most eager to learn about and practise knighthood and to have their own non-noble social status validated. Such readers were probably the intimate companions of Sir Thomas Malory.

In his prologue to the *Morte Darthur*, Caxton blurs our sense of Malory's original audience by his rhetorical excess when he claims that 'dyvers gentylmen of thys royame of Englond' clamoured for stories of Arthur (*Works* cxliii.5). Here Caxton is fashioning his own audience, creating a wide readership for Malory's work by evoking an image of gentle readers whose tastes should be imitated.[31] Yet in the prologue to the *Morte*, Caxton refers to one particular 'noble jentylman' who required him to print Arthurian tales (cxliv.1), and this member of the nobility is probably Anthony Wydeville. Some have speculated that Wydeville originally desired the *Morte Darthur* for the education of his young charge, the Prince of Wales, for whom moral readings were required.[32] If so, Malory's text would have travelled the same path as the great books: from the hand of a knight, to a gentle audience, and up to a noble one. That path was the very one Malory and his fellow 'jentylmen and jentylwymmen' hoped to follow.

---

[31] See E. Kirk, ' "Clerkes, Poets and Historiographs": The *Morte Darthur* and Caxton's 'Poetics' of Fiction', in *Studies in Malory*, ed. J. W. Spisak (Kalamazoo, MI, 1985), pp. 275–95, and Russel Rutter, 'William Caxton and Literary Patronage', *Studies in Philology* 84 (1987), 440–70.

[32] According to Edward IV's ordinance for the education of Edward, Prince of Wales, issued in 1473, at mealtime the prince was to be entertained with 'noble storyes as behoveth to a prynce to understand'. By this document, the care of the prince was committed to the queen's brother, Anthony Wydeville. See N. Orme, 'The Education of Edward V', *Bulletin of the Institute of Historical Research* 57, 136 (1984), 119–30; the quotation from the rolls is from p. 127.

Contents of previous volumes

I (1981)

Constance Bullock-Davies	Chrétien de Troyes and England
Richard Barber	The *Vera Historia de Morte Arthuri* and its Place in Arthurian Tradition
Michael Lapidge	An Edition of the *Vera Historia de Morte Arthuri*
Derek Brewer	Malory and the Archaic Mind
Karl Heinz Göller	From Logres to Carbonek: the Arthuriad of Charles Williams

II (1982)

Neil Wright	Geoffrey of Monmouth and Gildas
Beate Schmolke-Hasselmann	The Round Table: Ideal, Fiction, Reality
Fanni Bogdanow	The Tradition of the Troubadours and the Treatment of the Love Theme in Chrétien de Troyes' *Chevalier au Lion*
Toshiyuki Takamiya and Andrew Armour	Kairo-kō: A Dirge
Mary Wildman	Twentieth-Century Arthurian Literature: an Annotated Bibliography

III (1983)

Claude Luttrell	The Prologue of Crestien's *Li Contes del Graal*
Derek Brewer	The Presentation of the Character of Lancelot: Chrétien to Malory
M. F. Thomas	The Briar and the Vine: Tristan Goes North
Irene Joynt	Vengeance and Love in 'The Book of Sir Launcelot and Queen Guinevere'

IV (1984)

David N. Dumville	An Early Text of Geoffrey of Monmouth's *Historia Regum Britanniae* and the Circulation of Some Latin Histories in Twelfth-Century Normandy
Richard Barber	Was Mordred Buried at Glastonbury? An Arthurian Tradition at Glastonbury in the Middle Ages
Rosemary Morris	Uther and Igerne: A Study in Uncourtly Love
Carol Meale	Manuscripts, Readers and Patrons in Fifteenth-Century England: Sir Thomas Malory and Arthurian Romance
Tony Hunt	Ernest Chausson's 'Le Roi Arthus'

V (1985)

Martin Puhvel	Art and the Supernatural in *Sir Gawain and the Green Knight*
Lister M. Matheson	The Arthurian Stories of Lambeth Palace Library MS 84
Angelika Schneider	A Mesh of Chords: Language and Style in the Arthurian Poems of Charles Williams

VI (1986)

David N. Dumville	The Historical Value of the *Historia Brittonum*
Neil Wright	Geoffrey of Monmouth and Bede
Rosemary Morris	The *Gesta Regum Britanniae* of William of Rennes: An Arthurian Epic?
Merritt R. Blakeslee	*Mouvance* and Revisionism in the Transmission of Thomas of Britain's *Tristan*: The Episode of the Intertwining Trees

VII (1987)

Linda M. Gowans	New Perspectives on the Didot Perceval
Elizabeth Andersen	Heinrich von dem Türlin's *Diu Crône* and the *Prose Lancelot*: an Intertextual Study
Geraldine Barnes	Arthurian Chivalry in Old Norse
John Withrington	The Arthurian Epitaph in Malory's *Morte Darthur*
Joanne Lukitsh	Julia Margaret Cameron's Photographic Illustrations to Alfred Tennyson's *Idylls of the King*

VIII (1988)

Elizabeth Archibald	Arthur and Mordred: Variations on an Incest Theme
Jan Janssens	Un 'Fin' Amant' et l'ironie romanesque: Lancelot et la chanson de change
D. D. R. Owen introduction and transl.	Guillaume le Clerc: The Romance of Fergus
Edward Donald Kennedy	John Hardyng and the Holy Grail

IX (1989)

Oliver Goulden	*Erec et Enide*: The Structure of the Central Section
W. R. J. Barron and Françoise Le Saux	Two Aspects of Laȝamon's Narrative Art
Claude Luttrell	The Arthurian Hunt with a White Bratchet

Christine Poulson	Arthurian Legend in Fine and Applied Art of the Nineteenth and Early Twentieth Centuries: A Catalogue of Artists

X (1990)

A. H. W. Smith	Gildas the Poet
Armel Diverres	The Grail and the Third Crusade: Thoughts on *Le Conte del Graal* by Chrétien de Troyes
Christine Poulson	Arthurian Legend in Fine and Applied Art of the Nineteenth and Early Twentieth Centuries: A Subject Index

XI (1992)

Janet Grayson	In Quest of Jessie Weston
Richard Wright	Index to *Arthurian Literature*, volumes I–X

XII (1993)

Martin B. Shichtman and Laurie A. Finke	Profiting from the Past: History as Symbolic Capital in the *Historia Regum Britanniae*
N. M. Davis	Gawain's Rationalist Pentangle
Helen Phillips	*The Awntyrs off Arthure*: Structure and Meaning. A Reassessment
Felicity Riddy	John Hardyng's Chronicle and the Wars of the Roses
Bonnie Wheeler	Romance and Parataxis and Malory: the Case of Sir Gawain's Reputation
Richard Barber	Malory's *Le Morte Darthur* and Court Culture under Edward IV

XIII (1995)

Claude Luttrell	The Heart's Mirror in *Cligés*
Lesley Johnson	Return to Albion
James P. Carley and Julia Crick	Constructing Albion's Past: an Annotated Edition of *De Origine Gigantum*
Corinne J. Saunders	Women Displaced: Rape and Romance in Chaucer's *Wife of Bath's Tale*

XIV (1996)

Barbara N. Sargent-Baur	Alexander and the *Conte du Graal*
Fanni Bogdanow	Robert de Boron's Vision of Arthurian History
Louise D. Stephens	Gerbert and Manessier: The Case for a Connection
Lisa Jefferson	Tournaments, Heraldry and the Knights of the Round Table: A Fifteenth-Century Armorial with Two Accompanying Texts